THE MAKING OF HORROR MOVIES

THE MAKING OF HORROR MOVIES

KEY FIGURES WHO ESTABLISHED THE GENRE

JENNIFER SELWAY

WHITE OWL

AN IMPRINT OF PEN & SWORD BOOKS LTD.
YORKSHIRE – PHILADELPHIA

First published in Great Britain in 2021 by
PEN AND SWORD WHITE OWL
An imprint of
Pen & Sword Books Ltd
Yorkshire - Philadelphia

ISBN 978 1 52677 470 5

A CIP catalogue record for this book is available from the British Library.

Typeset in Times New Roman 11.5/14 by
SJmagic DESIGN SERVICES, India.
Printed and bound by CPI Group (UK) Ltd, Croydon CR0 4YY

Pen & Sword Books Ltd incorporates the Imprints of Pen & Sword Books
Archaeology, Atlas, Aviation, Battleground, Discovery, Family History, History,
Maritime, Military, Naval, Politics, Railways, Select, Transport, True Crime,
Fiction, Frontline Books, Leo Cooper, Praetorian Press, Seaforth Publishing,
Wharncliffe and White Owl.

For a complete list of Pen & Sword titles please contact
PEN & SWORD BOOKS LIMITED
47 Church Street, Barnsley, South Yorkshire, S70 2AS, England
E-mail: enquiries@pen-and-sword.co.uk
Website: www.pen-and-sword.co.uk

Or

PEN AND SWORD BOOKS
1950 Lawrence Rd, Havertown, PA 19083, USA
E-mail: Uspen-and-sword@casematepublishers.com
Website: www.penandswordbooks.com

Contents

Introduction

In 1985, an edition of *Wogan*, the BBC's hugely popular early evening chat show, opened with the sight of an eerily lit, upright coffin. The lid swung open like a door and out stepped Terry Wogan, wrapped in a black cloak, ready with his introduction for the first guest, 'a man who's had more stakes through his heart than I've had hot dinners'. It was Christopher Lee.

Though he must have been wincing at this corny tribute (and it looked as though Wogan was too), Christopher Lee, ever the gentleman, proved to be a game and courteous guest.

With his dark good looks and aristocratic bearing, Lee's place in cinema history as a king of horror is assured. Though by 1985 he had been in self-imposed exile for the best part of a decade, trying to escape the tyranny of the typecast ... by going to Hollywood.

Those who made their names in horror films usually had a love/hate relationship with the genre. In 1932, the British Board of Film Censors introduced the H certificate in the wake of the release of James Whale's *Frankenstein* starring British-born Boris Karloff, and Tod Browning's *Dracula*, both made in 1931. H stood for Horrific, reflecting the censor's uncertainty as to how it should best categorise films that were deliberately intended to frighten or disturb.

And once the idea of the 'horror film' took hold in the public imagination, it was the shock value which sold the picture; the creepiness, the tension, the supernatural, the danger, the threat of violence – and the reliably bankable horror movie stars.

While the audience wants to be a little frightened, many who read Mary Shelley's *Frankenstein* or see one of the many screen versions for the first time are surprised that the monster evokes pity more than terror. Nobody watches the original *King Kong* (1933) without weeping for the giant ape in his last noble stand, batting away aircraft from the pinnacle of the Empire State Building, with Fay Wray safe in his tender grasp.

Lon Chaney, known as the 'man of a thousand faces' who starred in *The Hunchback of Notre Dame* (1923) and *The Phantom of the Opera* (1925), could also make audiences melt. In an interview for *Movie Magazine* in 1925 he said: 'I wanted to remind people that the lowest types of humanity may have within them the capacity for supreme self-sacrifice. The dwarfed, misshapen beggar of the streets may have the noblest ideals.'

Pathos is a crucial factor but the horror label meant that these films were brazenly promoted as a challenge to the audience. How scared will you be? How much can you take? The posters and trailers upped the ante at every opportunity. 'If you have a weak heart' began the trailer for the 1935 film *The Bride of Frankenstein*, 'better leave now ... because [shots of excitable villagers rampaging through the forest] ... Frankenstein returns ... in search of a mate!' Enter Elsa Lanchester in that role.

The poster for the 1957 Hammer film *The Abominable Snowman* starring Peter Cushing laid it on the line, screaming: 'We dare you to see it alone!'

With this sort of publicity becoming the norm, horror films – with a few exceptions – were not seen as serious cinema, though many positively revelled in their low-budget schlock value. Some of Vincent Price's finest work in the 1960s was in the Edgar Allen Poe-inspired B-movies directed by Roger Corman, who was known as the 'Pope of Pop Cinema'.

Corman's production company, American International Pictures (AIP), was described in *The New York Times Magazine* as having the same status in the American film industry as 'the man hired to sweep behind the elephants in the circus parade'. Yet – while the horror genre is often mocked – the films, their stars and often their producers are remembered, whereas thousands of once highly regarded movies and actors are now forgotten. In 1933, the year that *King Kong* was released, the Academy Award went to *Cavalcade*. But almost a century later everyone still knows about the giant ape. Dracula has appeared on screen at least 350 times, and counting: each iteration welcomed with curiosity and interest.

Peter Cushing, like his great friend Christopher Lee, also flinched somewhat at the term 'horror'. He preferred the word 'fantasy', as he explained gently in a filmed interview with the BBC in 1973. 'Horror to me is a film like *The Godfather*,' he said (which had recently been released), 'or anything to do with war, which is real and can happen and unfortunately will no doubt happen again some time.'

The word 'fantasy' conjures up something entirely different. Fantasy speaks of dreams and nightmares, of folk legends and fairy tales. In the 1920s, with Europe reeling from the horrors of the First World War and Germany culturally isolated in defeat, this delirious sensibility fed into German Expressionist cinema with its wild distortions of reality. Max Schreck, perhaps the first true horror star, appeared in the 1922 silent vampire classic *Nosferatu*, directed by F. W. Murnau. In 1997 the film critic Roger Ebert said of *Nosferatu*: 'Here is the story of Dracula before it was buried alive in clichés, jokes, TV skits, cartoons and more than thirty other films. The film is in awe of its material. It seems to really believe in vampires.'

We like to think that horror films draw on deep-seated fears and desires, and on archetypal figures. It does to some extent. But whereas *Nosferatu* has an air of brooding authenticity because it is so solemn, it is simply a rip-off of Bram Stoker's high Victorian novel *Dracula*. Just as the werewolf was more or less invented by Curt Siodmak, scriptwriter for the 1941 film *The Wolf Man* which propelled Lon Chaney Jr (son of Lon Chaney) to stardom.

As Peter Cushing politely suggested, the makers of classic horror films knew that their playful excursions into gothic fantasy were nothing compared with the horror of war, of which some had direct experience. As a small child, Ingrid Pitt, born in Warsaw, was imprisoned with her family in Stutthof concentration camp. F. W. Murnau was in the German Air Force during the First World War. Bela Lugosi, who played Dracula in the 1931 film and who was born in 1882, served as an infantryman in the Austro-Hungarian Army during the First World War. He received a medal after being wounded while serving on the Russian front. Christopher Lee joined the RAF for the Second World War and also worked for British intelligence.

During the Second World War, there was even an unofficial moratorium on the making of horror films in Britain because they were not seen as conducive to maintaining the public's morale. The first to break the ban was the 1945 film *Dead of Night*, an effective horror anthology directed by Alberto Cavalcanti and made at Ealing Studios.

In the post-war world, horror took on very different forms at the cinema. The atom bomb and the malign effects of radiation, combined with the irresponsibility of mad scientists, provided the source material for any number of Hollywood films from *Godzilla* to *Attack of the 50 Foot Woman* to *I Was a Teenage Werewolf*. Psychological terror was exploited by the master, Alfred Hitchcock, in the 1960s. Who hasn't stepped into the shower remembering Janet Leigh's fate in *Psycho*?

Today Hammer and horror go together like love and marriage. But it wasn't always so. Hammer Film Studios had been producing moderately successful films since the mid-1930s, including the Dick Barton films. Its initial experiment in the horror genre was the 1955 adaptation of Nigel Kneale's *The Quatermass Xperiment*. After that came *The Curse of Frankenstein* in 1957, its first gothic horror and a huge box-office success. *Dracula* followed quickly (the first of many Dracula films), making a star of Christopher Lee.

Many Hammer films were made in glorious gory Technicolor but their unique selling point was the implicit sexual content. Dracula was not merely a rather camp dinner guest, he was also strangely attractive, his fatal kiss both desirable and terrifying. Women who starred in Hammer films were invariably beautiful, predatory and not averse to a little lesbian dalliance. And all this barely repressed erotic content would be played out against a background of what was clearly the Home Counties. In the newly swinging 1960s and well into the 1970s it was a recipe for success.

I talked to Jimmy Carreras, grandson of James Carreras who founded Hammer. Jimmy, who now lives in Australia, worked on five Hammer films in the early days and helped his father Michael Carreras after he took over the company:

> My grandfather was an extrovert, charming and a gifted entrepreneur, it was a business to him, a business he was good at – he loved the 'glamour' of the film industry and did not hesitate to reap the rewards. My father, unsurprisingly, was by contrast an introvert, much more involved with the 'art' of cinema. Their relationship was difficult, complicated, perhaps they should never have worked together – but they did.
>
> They had some very good people working regularly as a team, not only the obvious Peter Cushing and Christopher Lee, but the directors, writers, art directors, composers, musical directors and technicians who made the

production format unique. Also having their own studio at Bray gave the productions a consistently high quality and 'feel'. The 'style' was in its day what made 'Hammer' the brand a household name in horror, but today I think the quality of the productions is better appreciated.

Every now and then stories appear about resurrecting Hammer films, but Jimmy Carreras is doubtful about the chances of this happening. 'There have been several attempts to revive the brand, none successfully,' he says. 'I think now it is probably too late. It's a nostalgic brand, I don't think today's horror films would sit well under the Hammer banner.'

But though Hammer may not live again, horror is a many-headed serpent and, like all screen monsters, it is never really destroyed. The horror genre goes in and out of fashion but we always know that one day … it will return.

Horror films encompass everything from the dreamy staginess of F. W. Murnau's Expressionist fantasies to American teen slasher movies, from sci-fi to high Victoriana, from body horror to folk horror, from films that reflect our fear of 'the other' to films that find the true terror within ourselves. Some are beautiful, some are violent and crude, some are serious and some are dottily camp. This selection is based on those movers and shakers who remain household names because they set the bar high and made horror the perverse pleasure which gives us a happy dose of escapism along with the grimly enjoyable knowledge of what we are escaping from.

Chapter One

Tod Browning – 'Go bite yourself!'

'We didn't lie to you folks,' says the master of ceremonies at a circus sideshow. 'We told you we had living, breathing monstrosities…'.

Tod Browning's 1932 film *Freaks* is one of the strangest movies ever made. It was also a box-office disaster that appalled audiences and was banned in Britain for thirty years. In the late 1960s it achieved a kind of cult status on the late night, independent cinema circuit, finding a place in the counterculture's embrace of all things weird. Now, with its theme of physical deformity, it would be a tricky film to programme even after the most careful and sensitive contextualisation. The title itself condemns it.

In the film, Cleopatra (played by Olga Baclanova) is a trapeze artist. The circus 'midget' Hans (Harry Earles) has a crush on her ('She's the most beautiful big woman I ever saw') even though he has a fiancée (played by Daisy Earles) who is also of restricted growth. When she finds out that Hans is in line to inherit a fortune she agrees to marry him, even though she is having an affair with the circus strongman Hercules (Henry Victor).

She begins to poison Hans on their wedding day and when the other sideshow performers (the 'freaks') discover that she is laughing at them, they plot their revenge. These were real circus performers – women without arms, conjoined twins, a bearded lady, an intersex character, a man without legs. As a result, Hercules is castrated and Cleo has her feet amputated and is left permanently tarred and featured – half woman, half chicken.

Even on its release, *Freaks* did Tod Browning no good at all. One woman who attended a preview threatened to sue MGM on the grounds that she had suffered a miscarriage.

After it flopped at the box office he went from being one of Hollywood's highest paid directors to something of an embarrassment.

Yet his lifelong obsession with the grotesque, the morbid and the macabre undoubtedly struck a chord with audiences who had seen a generation of young men return from the battlefields of the First World War without limbs or faces or minds; who knew what it was like to become – through disability – an outsider in an unforgiving world.

Charles Albert 'Tod' Browning was born in Louisville, Kentucky on 12 July 1880 – the second son of Charles and his wife Lydia (who was over 6 foot tall). Among the family, his uncle Pete (born 1861) was a famous baseball player nicknamed the 'Louisville Slugger'.

Pete suffered from mastoiditis, which left him almost completely deaf and in chronic pain. He self-medicated with alcohol, was a noted eccentric and philanderer and died from 'asthenia' at the age of 44. This was a catch-all term employed by doctors, which meant a weakening of the body and was usually a euphemism for tertiary syphilis.

Avery, Tod's elder brother – who became a successful coal merchant – was also somewhat eccentric. He was germ-phobic and wore a long dark overcoat whatever the weather. A 'sister', Virginia, was actually a cousin but raised by Tod's parents.

In keeping with the family's slightly odd behaviour, Charles senior ended his days (he died of a stroke in 1922) endlessly shelling peanuts and papering the walls of the bathroom with identical red and green two-cent postage stamps that had been steamed from letters.

As a child, Tod began staging shows in an old shed in the family home which he described as 'performances to astound'. The *Louisville Herald-Post* attended and described Browning as 'a precocious youngster, a Barnum perhaps in the making'.

At the time, Louisville was a boom town and between 1888 and 1892 staged a Satellites of Mercury carnival financed by local businesses. The first Kentucky Derby had been run in 1875, attracting huge crowds then and in subsequent years. It was a city accustomed to hucksters and chancers and showmen. The young Browning was drawn to this rackety life and 'ran away to the circus' in 1898 with the Manhattan Fair and Carnival Company, acting as a barker for a 'Wild Man of Borneo' act.

The 'wild man' who could equally be an 'Aztec' or an 'Australian' would be available for scrutiny in a pit. Characters who would bite the heads off snakes or rats were a staple of circuses at the time. Browning also promoted himself as 'Bosco the Snake Eater' and worked at various times as a handcuff escape artist, a contortionist, a ringmaster, a jockey and he put on blackface for a vaudeville act known as 'Lizard and Coon'.

There was no end to his abilities, and he also had himself buried alive as the 'Hypnotic Living Corpse'. *Reel Life* magazine reported on this act in 1914:

> He would fall into a trance. Then he would be lowered several feet under the ground and the earth thrown over him. A wooden shaft permitted the wonder-struck crowd, one by one, to gaze down upon his inert form in the bottom of the pit – and incidentally supplied him with air.

Sometimes he would be buried for as long as forty-eight hours. He worked with magicians, including the famous Leon Herrmann, performing the dangerous bullet-catch illusion, and with a Mongolian magician who produced goldfish bowls out of thin air.

During this period, he married Amy Louise Stevens, the 23-year-old daughter of a pawnbroker. The couple lived with her parents as Browning's income was negligible. He often borrowed from his mother-in-law and failed to pay back the loans. The couple divorced in 1910.

Browning then spent a period living in cheap, squalid boarding houses, moving from town to town. Times were hard for many. In one house, he opened the door of the bathroom he shared with the other lodgers, including a near-destitute woman with two small children. The woman was there in the bathroom. She had already killed one of her children, who was lying dead on the floor. She was holding the other child, who had blood pouring out of its throat into the bathtub. Browning closed the door quietly and phoned the police.

There are many routes into the movie business and, in its early years, Hollywood would draw in emigrés, aristocrats, ingénues, intellectuals and showmen. And as David J. Skal and Elias Savada write in their biography of Browning: 'Much like Tod Browning himself, the motion picture had worked its way up from carnival roots.'

Browning's introduction to the new cinema industry came from his meeting with the film director D. W. Griffith, who was also from Kentucky. Both of them had attended the same school in Louisville though at different times.

In 1913, Griffith asked Browning to appear with a comedian, Charles Murray, in a couple of Biograph Company comedies called *Scenting a Terrible Crime* and *A Fallen Hero*. Browning moved to Los Angeles and worked for the Komic subsidiary of the Reliance-Majestic Studios under Griffith (who had now left Biograph). He appeared in around fifty one-reel comedies and had top billing in *Nell's Eugenic Wedding* (1914) scripted by Anita Loos (who would later write the 1953 film *Gentlemen Prefer Blondes*). In it a man eats a bar of soap, vomits everywhere … and that's about it. The taste for the bizarre in Hollywood's early days never ceases to amaze.

Browning was living in a bohemian apartment house called the Reiter Arms at the intersection of Sunset and Hollywood Boulevards. There were a lot of card games and alcohol-fuelled parties. He also developed a taste for flashy automobiles.

In 1915, Tod Browning appeared as an extra in D. W. Griffith's silent epic *Intolerance,* which was released the following year, and directed his own first short film called *The Lucky Transfer*, in which a female reporter uncovers a jewel theft. He followed it up with *The Living Death* (1915), in which an over-protective father deliberately misdiagnoses his prospective son-in-law's poison ivy as leprosy to prevent him marrying his daughter. The theme of obsessive parental relationships is repeated in *The Burned Hand* (1915), in which a man kidnaps his own daughter following an acrimonious divorce.

In June of that year Browning, almost certainly steaming drunk, drove full tilt into a railway flatbed car loaded with iron rails. One of his passengers was killed and another badly injured. Browning fractured his right leg in three places, suffered serious internal injuries and lost all his teeth. For the rest of his life he wore false teeth, which caused him considerable discomfort.

He was out of action for the best part of a year, returning to work to make *Jim Bludso*, a feature-length steamboat drama filmed on location on the Rio Vista in San Francisco and released in 1917. He married a vaudeville actress, Alice Lillian Houghton, and took a new job with Metro Pictures for whom he made nine feature films.

By 1919 he was with Universal Studios where he directed *The Wicked Darling* starring Priscilla Dean. Dean was one of the top stars of the day and one whose career stalled with the arrival of the talkies. Significantly for Browning, the film marked the first time he worked with the actor Lon Chaney.

The Virgin of Stamboul (1920) was a big sand 'n' sheikhs production which cost half a million dollars to make and starred Wallace Beery. Across the US, cinema foyers were turned into harem tents to promote the film.

The Bioscope, a British magazine said: 'The film cannot be regarded very seriously as a picture of Oriental life and chapter but it makes fine entertainment.'

By the early 1920s, Browning's drinking was again causing problems. Universal Studios laid him off because he had gained a reputation for being unreliable. At a New Year's Eve party at the St Francis Hotel in San Francisco (the same hotel where, in 1921, Fatty Arbuckle was said to have raped an actress who subsequently died of her injuries), Browning yanked out his upper and lower dentures and threw them at his assistant, shouting, 'Go bite yourself!'

At the time, he was having an affair with the 16-year-old Chinese-American actress Anna May Wong, who would be a sensation in *The Thief of Baghdad* (1924) with Douglas Fairbanks.

So, all in all, it's hardly surprising that, in 1923, Browning's wife Alice walked out on him.

In an interview, he later admitted that his career was at a low point. He said he had, 'a reputation for being contrary and temperamental and uncertain. The rumour got around that I had a nasty disposition – and let me tell you it was true.'

Of his wife's departure, he said: 'It was vaguely annoying after she'd gone that my clothes weren't in shape, the house disorderly and meals irregular.' But despite his flippancy he was desperate to win her back, which eventually he did.

Apart from keeping house, Alice was also a canny operator and was instrumental in persuading studio boss Irving Thalberg to take Browning on at MGM. In 1925, Browning directed *The Unholy Three*, a silent murder thriller about a criminal gang comprised of a midget jewel thief (Harry Earles who would star in *Freaks*) masquerading as a baby in a pram, a cross-dressing ventriloquist (played by Lon Chaney) who pretends to be a little old lady, and a strong man (Victor McLaglen).

MGM had misgivings about this oddball story but Thalberg proved his bosses wrong and the film was a box-office sensation. *The New Yorker* magazine described it as 'a ghoulish combination of cruelty and hard laughter, irony and action'.

MGM ran a tight ship. It produced a new picture every week and twelve to fourteen-hour days were the norm. Browning was a hard taskmaster, unwilling to break for lunch. He had become something of a dandy too, favouring loud-patterned suits, two-tone shoes and a waxed moustache, which did something to disguise his dental problems.

He directed Lon Chaney in *The Blackbird* (1926). Chaney plays a Limehouse crook who pretends to be his fictitious crippled twin. Then in *The Road to Mandalay* (1926), shot over thirty days at breakneck speed, Chaney plays a father who desperately tries to prevent the marriage of his daughter to his criminal partner.

John Gilbert, hated by Louis B. Mayer as it happens, was cast in *The Show* (1927). The two men had had a brawl in the bathroom at Gilbert's wedding to Greta Garbo, though Garbo herself never showed up. In *The Show*, Gilbert is an illusionist in a carnival freak show playing John the Baptist, who has his head severed every night by Salome (played by Renée Adorée). A rival plans to have him decapitated for real.

Said the *New York Herald Tribune*: 'Tod Browning revels in murkiness. His cinematic mind is a creeping torture chamber, a place of darkness, deviousness and death.'

Browning did nothing to disprove this assessment in his next film *Alonzo the Armless* (1927), which would later be titled *The Unknown*. An armless circus knife thrower and sharpshooter Alonzo (Lon Chaney) is, in reality, a fugitive. His double thumb would give him away to the police so he has his arms bound. His glamorous partner in his act, Nanon (Joan Crawford), cannot bear being pawed by men but she feels comfortable around Alonzo. Eventually, to win her love, Alonzo has his arms amputated, but by now Nanon has got over her aversion and fallen into the arms of the circus strongman.

Mordaunt Hall in *The New York Times* on 13 June, 1927 reviewed it:

> It is gruesome and at times shocking, and the principal character deteriorates from a more or less sympathetic individual to an arch-fiend... . The role of Alonzo, who poses as the Armless Wonder with a Spanish circus, is one that ought to have satisfied Mr. Chaney's penchant for freakish characterisations, for here he not only has to go about for hours with his arms strapped to his body, but when he rests behind bolted doors, one perceives that he has on

his left hand a double thumb. Mr. Chaney really gives a marvellous idea of the Armless Wonder, for to act in this film he has learned to use his feet as hands when eating, drinking and smoking. He even scratches his head with his toe when meditating.

Chaney and Browning worked together again in *London After Midnight* (1927), a version of the vampire myth which Browning would return to in his most celebrated film, *Dracula*. This film has been lost: the last known copy destroyed in a fire at MGM Studios in 1967.

By now there were signs of a 'moral panic' over Browning's films with Chaney – the disturbing sexual symbolism, the themes of amputation and disfigurement, the general air of morbidity. In October 1928, Robert Williams was charged with the murder of 21-year-old housemaid Julia Mangan in Hyde Park. Her throat had been cut and he was similarly injured but survived.

Williams had seen *London After Midnight* and felt he was possessed by a vision of Lon Chaney. He said:

> I felt as though my head was going to burst and that steam was coming out of both sides. All sorts of things came to my mind. I thought a man had me in a corner and was pulling faces at me. He threatened and shouted at me that he had me where he wanted me.

Williams was reprieved from hanging on medical grounds.

Of course, the public loved to be revolted and the Chaney/Browning partnership was guaranteed to deliver the goods. In a 1928 interview Browning said: 'Chaney would amble into my office and say "What's it gonna be boss?" I'll say that this time a leg comes off, or an arm, or a nose, or whatever it may be.'

But Browning knew there was a line that could not be crossed:

> The thing you have to be most careful of in a mystery story, is not to let it verge on the comic. If a thing gets too gruesome and too horrible, it gets beyond the limits of the average imagination and the audience laughs. It may sound incongruous, but mystery must be made plausible.

West of Zanzibar (1928) brings together all the elements of the perfect Browning/Chaney collaboration. Chaney plays a cuckolded magician who is crippled in a fall from a balcony on the day his wife leaves him. There's voodoo, an abandoned daughter and a revenge plot.

Browning made ten films with Chaney. But after so long there were signs that the public was tiring of the deadly duo. 'It would be a good idea if Browning let someone else play his malignant cripple for a change,' wrote Donald Beaton in *Film Spectator*.

The 13th Chair (1929) was Browning's first talkie. A murder mystery, it cast Bela Lugosi as a mere police inspector, though in it he already seems to be auditioning for *Dracula*.

Universal Studios wanted to do *Dracula* and they wanted Lon Chaney in the title role. To Browning's great sadness, Chaney died suddenly of throat cancer on 26 August 1931. Browning was a pallbearer at his funeral.

Browning took on the task of directing *Dracula* (1931) with Lugosi, who had already played the part on stage many times, in the lead. It is not Browning's greatest film, though it is his most famous. It is a clonking, stagey work with cinematographer Karl Freund's work lending atmosphere. Browning was under tremendous financial pressure from his bosses at Universal, and a Spanish language version was being shot at night on the same set. It represents, say Skal and Savada, 'a film of silences, a stubborn clinging to the silent era that nourished him [Browning].' The only music is the overture from *Swan Lake* for the opening credits and a few snatches of Wagner during the film.

It was a tremendous success and immediately propelled Universal into production of *Frankenstein*, which would be directed by James Whale.

Browning made *Iron Man* (1931) for Universal with Jean Harlow and Lew Ayres before starting on *Freaks* for MGM.

Olga Baclanova, who plays the trapeze artist Cleopatra, recalled meeting the cast:

> First I meet the midget and he adores me because we speak German and he's from Germany. Then he shows me the girl that's like an orangutan; then a man who has a head but no legs, no nothing, just a head and a body like an egg. Then he shows me a boy who walks on his hands because he was born without feet. He shows me little by little and I could

not look. I wanted to cry when I saw them. They have such nice faces, but it is so terrible ... . Now, after we start the picture, I like them all so much.

Not everyone felt the same. During production, MGM sent cast and crew to separate cafeterias and there were reports that F. Scott Fitzgerald, while employed (briefly and unsuccessfully) as a scriptwriter for MGM, had been so appalled when sitting next to the conjoined twins at lunch that he threw up.

Browning jauntily told an LA reporter that the professional jealousy among the cast was amazing: 'Not one of them had a good word for the other,' he said.

After *Freaks* bombed, Browning was sidelined. He had wanted to make a film version of *They Shoot Horses Don't They?* about the notorious dance marathons held during the Depression years. It would be filmed in 1970 by Sydney Pollack starring Jane Fonda. But MGM was losing faith in Browning's appeal.

Browning certainly went to dance marathons, as playwright Budd Schulberg writes in his autobiography *Moving Pictures*:

> The marathon dance was in vogue then and we went a few times to the Santa Monica pier to watch the young zombies drag themselves around the floor in a slow-motion dance macabre. Even more appalling than the victims on the dance floor were the regulars, affluent sadists in the front row seats every night, cheering on their favourites who kept fainting and occasionally throwing up from exhaustion. One of the most dedicated of the regulars was Tod Browning, who never missed a night and who got that same manic gleam in his eyes as when he was directing *Freaks*.

To make matters worse, Browning's champion at MGM, Irving Thalberg, died in 1936. Browning's final film, *Miracles for Sale* (1939), was a murder mystery about a magician who exposes a fake medium. Robert Young and Florence Rice starred.

Soon after, Browning announced his retirement. 'When I quit a thing, I quit. I wouldn't walk across the street now to see a movie,' he said. He and Alice (who died in 1944) retired to Malibu.

He developed throat cancer (just like Chaney) in the 1950s and had his larynx removed so he was unable to talk – poignant for a man who had made his fortune in the silent era. Nobody from the old days stayed in contact with him, and he died in 1962.

In his last years, he moved in with Dr Harold Snow and his wife who took care of him. Dr Snow was a vet who had also cared for the Brownings' dogs.

He left one last strange request. Lucky was a house painter and a man Browning liked to share a drink with. Browning stipulated that Lucky should sit up all night with Browning's body at the undertakers in Santa Monica and drink a case of Coors beer in his memory.

Chapter Two

Bela Lugosi – 'Dracula is Hamlet to me.'

There are two poles on planet horror – Dracula and Frankenstein's monster. Even small children know who they are and love to portray them; swishing an imaginary vampire cape, baring imaginary fangs or mimicking the stumbling gait of Frankenstein's creature. These characters are a common reference point for all, so familiar that they are oddly cosy.

Yet they are relatively recent creations, and both were sparked into life at the same time in the same place. In the summer of 1816, Lord Byron rented the Villa Diodati in the village of Cologny near Lake Geneva and stayed there with his physician and friend John Polidori. His other guests included the poet Percy Bysshe Shelley, who was with his future wife Mary Godwin, and Mary's stepsister Claire Clairmont who bore Byron a child.

It was a terrible summer, a hellish house party in many respects and the weather kept them all indoors, taking turns to tell stories. Mary, later Mary Shelley, and barely out of her teens, devised what would be published as *Frankenstein or The Modern Prometheus*. Polidori, inspired by a story of Byron's, wrote *The Vampyre*.

In this book, a sinister British aristocrat, Lord Ruthven, is revealed to be a vampire and leaves destruction in his wake.

Polidori – who killed himself at the age of 25 in 1821 by drinking prussic acid – transformed the vampire from a creature in European folklore into the form that is recognised today – a fiend in the guise of an aristocratic bounder who preys among high society. The popularity of Gothic romantic horror simmered nicely throughout the nineteenth century and was taken on by the Irish author and theatre manager Bram Stoker, whose great novel *Dracula* was published in 1897.

Yet it is the film industry, even when it was new and only just beginning to flex its extraordinary muscle, which has kept these two stories alive for more than a century. Not only alive, but perpetually re-invented. There have been hundreds of Dracula and Frankenstein films and TV versions. Many of them have been awful but some have been remarkable. It's an indication of the potency of these stories that they are continually revisited. Not only that, but the names of the two actors who originally played them have lived on, while many other stars of the 1930s have long been forgotten.

With the perfect vision of hindsight, it seems obvious that the Hungarian actor Bela Lugosi – a middle-aged, frustrated classical actor with a poor command of English – must have known what a significant role Dracula would be and how foolish he was to subsequently turn down the role of Frankenstein's monster.

But nothing is ever a dead cert in Hollywood. The script department for the 1931 *Dracula* film was concerned that the public didn't 'get' vampires and would need to have all the lore explained to them.

Bela Ferenc Dezso Blasko was born on 20 October 1882 in the town of Lugoj in Hungary, which is now in western Romania. Film publicists would make much of the fact that this town is a mere 400 kilometres from Bran Castle, sometimes called Dracula's castle. Bran Castle is the only castle in all of Transylvania that resembles Bram Stoker's description of the vampire's lair. It also has an association with Vlad the Impaler. The fifteenth-century ruler of Wallachia, famed for his cruelty to enemies and anyone who displeased him, was sometimes referred to at the time as Dracula. *Dracul* means dragon or devil in Romanian.

Bela, pronounced Bay-la, was the youngest of four children. Their father István was a baker and their mother, Paula de Vojnich, was Serbian. István's business prospered and in 1883 he was in a position to set up a savings bank, the Lugoj Volksbank. It was a comfortable middle-class household. The elder son would become an engineer, the second entered the civil service and Bela's older sister Vilma married a lawyer.

Prone to exaggeration throughout his life, Bela claimed that he got on so badly with his father that he ran away to work in a mine and didn't return home until his father died. But Blasko senior died when Bela was 12, which makes the claim unlikely. The more prosaic truth is that Bela – not gifted academically – was apprenticed to a locksmith. And then, at the age of 18, he became an actor, changing his name to Lugossy, which was taken from his hometown. The 'ossy' ending indicated an aristocratic lineage.

Later Bela would say: 'In Hungary acting is a profession. In America, it is a decision.'

Acting was also a respected profession. At the end of the nineteenth century, Hungary had a vigorous theatrical tradition. Small troupes of players toured the country. Between 1903 and 1904, he was connected to the Franz Joseph Theatre in Temesvar and he appeared in a production of *Trilby*, a popular adaptation of George du Maurier's novel about the mysterious Svengali. Bela did not take the lead but there are hints of his ability to convey menace, for a critic noted that as Svengali's evil henchman Lugosi was 'absolutely spell-binding'.

In 1910, he was based in Szeged playing Vronsky in *Anna Karenina*, Cassio in *Othello*, Laertes in *Hamlet* and Lucentio in *The Taming of the Shrew*. He also appeared as Romeo and was described as a 'beautifully fiery, passionately loving and dying Romeo'. The reviewer went on to note that 'women … praise his manly beauty even beyond his acting talent'. By 1911 he had arrived in Budapest as a member of the National Theatre of Hungary and had settled on the name of Lugosi.

Though as an actor he could have claimed a deferment, he joined the Army when war broke out in 1914 and rose to the rank of lieutenant in the 43rd Royal Hungarian Infantry, serving in the trenches and fighting the Russians. He was badly wounded at Rohatin (now in Ukraine) and then again in the Carpathian Mountains. After his recovery, he left the armed forces in 1916. Although he would exaggerate many aspects of his life, he rarely spoke about his wartime experiences, though he kept a gold rouble with a hole drilled through it which must have come from a Russian soldier.

He returned to the National Theatre and in Debrecen (Hungary's second city after Budapest) he played Jesus Christ in an Easter performance of *The Passion*.

There was nothing very holy about Lugosi's lifestyle at the time. 'There were long chains of love affairs,' he said. 'This is not bragging. This was the life of a young and lusty actor in the provinces.'

He fell in love with Ilona 'Baby' Szmik whose father was executive secretary of a Budapest bank. She was 16 and he was 34 when they married at St Anne's Church in Budapest. In an interview in 1931 he said: 'In all his life a man finds only one mate. Other women may bring happiness close to him but there is just one mate. This girl was mine.'

Unfortunately, the marriage was not to last. But in the meantime, the film industry in Hungary was beginning to take off, and in 1917 Lugosi appeared in his first film *The Leopard*, where he took the stage name of

Arisztid Olt. A year later he took the lead in a version of Oscar Wilde's *The Picture of Dorian Gray*.

In the instability that followed the First World War, Lugosi seems to have become highly politicised and was a committee member of the Free Organisation of Theatre Employees. In an article in 1919 he wrote:

> Ninety five per cent of the actors' community has been more proletarian than the most exploited labourer. After putting aside the glamorous trappings of his trade at the end of each performance the actor has, with few exceptions to face worry and poverty. He was obliged either to bend himself to stultifying odd jobs to keep body and soul together … or he has to sponge off his friends, get into debt or prostitute his art.

Under the counter-revolutionary government of Miklos Horthy, which banned communism, the arts were under scrutiny. Many in the film industry were imprisoned or tortured, or both. The film director Alexander Korda and the actor Paul Lukas, who would make their names in Hollywood, were among those who fled. Lugosi and his wife escaped hidden in a hay cart, crossed the border and fled to Vienna in August 1919.

Lugosi moved on to Berlin where he found work in films, appearing (in a minor role) in F. W. Murnau's *Der Januskopf*, a 1920 silent horror film that was an unauthorised adaptation of Robert Louis Stevenson's *The Strange Case of Dr Jekyll and Mr Hyde*. It also starred Conrad Veidt. The same year Lugosi appeared in *Der Letzte der Mohicaner* (The Last of the Mohicans) playing the Mohican chief Chingachgook.

Ilona, meanwhile, had returned to her family in Budapest. Her family had had enough of Lugosi. He wrote to her 'every second day' but never received an answer. He later found out that Ilona's parents were confiscating her mail and were insistent that she divorced. She was to remarry the day after the divorce was finalised.

With no ties and hardly any money, Lugosi sailed to America. He docked in New Orleans, made his way to New York and introduced himself to the immigration authorities at Ellis Island. He finally became an American citizen in 1930.

There was a sizeable Hungarian community in New York and Lugosi appeared in some plays in small venues. In 1922, theatre manager

Henry Baron offered him a part in *The Red Poppy*, which opened at the Greenwich Village Theatre and ran for just a couple of weeks. At the time, Lugosi spoke no English and learned his part phonetically, memorising the sounds without being entirely sure what they meant.

He married again, a Viennese woman, Ilona Montagh de Nagyabanyhegyes. However, the marriage was short-lived and it was dissolved in 1924 on grounds of adultery (Bela's).

But while his personal life was, as usual, fairly disastrous, he was becoming a successful actor and appeared in his first American film in 1923. It was called *The Silent Command* and Lugosi played the chief of the bad guys. It was a change of direction. Up until now he had tended to play romantic parts.

At the time, an actor/writer called Hamilton Deane was considering a stage version of Bram Stoker's *Dracula*.

In 1921 the German director F. W. Murnau had made *Nosferatu*, a retelling of the vampire story. Despite many changes to Stoker's original, this incurred the wrath of Stoker's widow Florence who had prevented the film from being screened in Britain and the United States. But Deane's version was approved and premiered in the provinces in 1924, opening in London in 1927 at the Little Theatre off the Strand.

This theatre was already known for grisly Grand Guignol productions produced by José Levy. Audiences could watch Sybil Thorndike having her eyes put out or seeing her lover being eaten by a wolfhound. The director was her husband, Lewis Casson.

In what was a foretaste of the lofty critical reaction to all things 'horror', the reviewers panned it, though the weekly paper *The Era* admitted it was 'very thrilling'. The audiences loved it.

Horace Liveright, an American producer and publisher, saw the production in London and snapped up the US rights. He cast Lugosi as Count Dracula, paying him $100 a week, and the show opened on Broadway at the Fulton Theatre, on West 46th Street in October 1927. The show ran until May 1928 to packed houses and Bela received a lot of fan mail, almost all of it from women. 'It is women who love horror,' said Lugosi years later in an interview, 'Gloat over it. Feed on it. Are nourished by it. Shudder and cling and cry out for more.'

Dracula went on tour in the States and when it opened in Los Angeles, Lugosi was invited to audition for a role in *Queen Kelly*, which was to be directed by Erich von Stroheim. But Lugosi (who was over 6 foot) was considered too tall for Gloria Swanson, who was just 5 foot. It was a lucky escape. The silent film was an expensive disaster, with Stroheim fired and the ending rewritten. It was released in Europe and South America but not in the United States.

He had other distractions in LA. Clara Bow, then one of Hollywood's most luminous stars, threw a mink coat over her swimsuit and went off to see *Dracula* at the Biltmore Theatre. Then she went backstage to introduce herself. She and Lugosi had a brief affair in the summer of 1928 and he commissioned the Hungarian artist Geza Kende to paint a nude portrait of Bow, which he kept prominently displayed until his death.

Bizarrely, Lugosi also married again – another disastrous union – to Beatrice Woodruff Weeks, a wealthy 31-year-old widow. Weeks told the *New York Daily Mirror* that her new husband 'slapped me in the face because I ate a lamb chop which he had hidden in the icebox for his after theatre midnight lunch.' She headed to Reno for a divorce, which was granted in 1929.

Not many kids get given a film studio for their twenty-first birthday. But that was the fortune of Carl Laemmle Jr who was given Universal Studios to play with. Mae Clarke (the actress who gets half a grapefruit pressed in her face by James Cagney in *The Public Enemy*) described him as 'retarded'. And Lucille Lund (who would star opposite Lugosi and Boris Karloff in *The Black Cat* in 1934) said of Junior: 'He was after all the girls and if you didn't co-operate you didn't last too long at Universal.'

Yet for all his shortcomings, Junior produced *Dracula* in 1931 – the first horror film with sound – directed by Tod Browning and starring Lugosi in the title role. He was paid the modest sum of $3,500 in total. Lon Chaney had been the first choice but he had died suddenly in 1930. Lugosi was a natural for the part as he had played the count on stage for so long, but William Courtney and Paul Muni were also considered. What's more, Universal was oddly timid about promoting a vampire film. A full-page ad in *Variety* in August 1930 avoided the 'v' word altogether. It ran thus: 'There's more than just mystery to this classic tale and famous stage play. There's the unconquerable love of a man for a maid – his flaming passion bringing light to a city o'er shadowed by evil and dread.'

No mention of vampires at all. What were they on about?

Universal need not have been so cautious. *Dracula* was an instant box-office hit. Lugosi's interpretation of the count – an old-world European aristocrat whose courtesy and melancholy masked indomitable evil – would define him for the rest of his life. So much so that, even as early as 1934, he would say: 'Every actor's greatest ambition is to create his own definite and original role – a character with which he will always be identified, but on the screen I found this almost fatal.'

Curiously, the film does not do justice to his looks. As the count, he appears heavier and puffier than he was in real life. Obviously, a black-and-white film could not reveal his blue eyes which – with his dark hair – made him so striking. He was tall and slim and had beautiful hands with long elegant fingers. In 1932, he took part in *Intimate Interviews*, a series of staged 'at-home' encounters featuring a reporter called Dorothy West. Lugosi, in white shirt and light trousers, with a cigar, walks Miss West round his garden. He is at his most debonair and charming, claiming that he is mastering American slang – 'OK', 'Cat's whiskers' and 'Baloney'. Years later, the actress Carol Borland, who appeared with him in MGM's *Mark of the Vampire* in 1935, described him as 'The most sexually attractive male I have ever known in my life.'

With the success of *Dracula*, Lugosi was being considered as Universal's main horror star. Its next project was *Frankenstein*, to be directed by James Whale. Lugosi assumed he'd be offered the part of Dr Frankenstein but when he found out that he was to be the monster, hidden under layers of make-up and with very few lines, he turned it down. Lugosi hardly turned anything down because he was usually broke. But he turned down *Frankenstein*. He would cite it throughout his life as his greatest mistake. The part went to relative newcomer Boris Karloff, as did Junior's interest in horror stars. Junior was determined to find a 'new Chaney' and Karloff fitted the bill.

Lugosi, instead, appeared in *Murders in the Rue Morgue* (1932) playing a mad scientist. Robert Florey (who had been originally slated to make *Frankenstein*) directed. But the film did not do well and Bela Lugosi's contract with Universal was not renewed.

The ongoing rivalry between Lugosi and Karloff was partly movie hype and partly real. In 1936, the two big stars made another mad scientist movie called *The Invisible Ray*. Karloff was paid $3,000 a week while Lugosi received a derisory flat fee of $4,000. Suddenly Lugosi was not the big star he had been. He had become used to luxuries and was hopeless at economising. He regularly ordered crates of imported goose liver, Bull's Blood wine, scotch, cigars, Roquefort cheese and Hungarian sausages. He stayed up half the night (he kept Dracula hours) and woke at midday. Throughout his career, he never managed to find himself a good agent and was frequently underpaid because everyone knew he needed the money.

Matters had come to a head in 1932 when he filed for bankruptcy in order to get his affairs in some sort of order. By now he had taken on a young secretary called Lillian Arch who was the daughter of Hungarian immigrants, paying her $16.50 a week. In 1933, the 21-year-old married Lugosi who was, by now, 50.

He was an old-school macho man, insisting that his wife run his house perfectly and that he would pick out her clothes. 'I do not like exotic things on women,' he said.

In 1932, the British Board of Film Censors created the H certificate for films. H for Horrific. These films could not be viewed by anyone under the age of 16. The knock-on effect in Hollywood was devastating. The American studios ceased production of what had been lucrative horror films. What became known as the golden age of classic horror movies was well and truly over. In 1935, Lugosi appeared with Boris Karloff in *The Raven* and, though Karloff has the smaller role, he was billed as simply Karloff in lettering much bigger than that of Lugosi, who plays a deranged doctor obsessed with Edgar Allen Poe.

By 1937, Lugosi was very down on his luck. He had only achieved real stardom in his late forties – pretty late in rapacious, youth-obsessed Hollywood. His wife Lillian was pregnant and gave birth to their son, Bela Lugosi Jr, on 5 January 1938. Lugosi could not even pay the doctor's bill and had to give up his house the following year. He was drinking heavily and was becoming addicted to prescription drugs for sciatica.

There were some straws to cling to though. Universal was amazed when, in 1938, a double bill of the original *Frankenstein* and *Dracula* movies did good business at the box office. As a result, it rehired Lugosi for *Son of Frankenstein* (1939). He finally cast off his objections to heavy make-up in the role of 'broken-necked Igor', a role he would reprise in *Ghost of Frankenstein* (1942).

In 1939, he went to London to make *The Dark Eyes of London*, adapted from an Edgar Wallace novel which would be Britain's first home-made

H-certificate film. In America, it was titled *The Human Monster. The New York Times* observed: 'even connoisseurs of the horror film will doubtless be constrained to admit that nothing quite so consistently horrid as *The Human Monster* has ever befallen this hapless city.'

The same year, he played the Russian commissar Comrade Razinin in *Ninotchka*, starring Greta Garbo and directed by Ernst Lubitsch. Lugosi was pleased not to be in a horror film and said that Lubitsch had changed 'the course of my whole screen existence'.

When America joined the war following the Japanese attack on Pearl Harbour on 7 December 1941, Lugosi made personal appearances at military bases and factories. As America's favourite screen vampire, he urged the public to give blood to help the troops. He joined anti-fascist groups and was involved in setting up the Screen Actors' Guild (along with Boris Karloff), evoking memories of his political activism in Hungary. Unsurprisingly, Lugosi was suspected of being a communist but did not live long enough to be caught up in the McCarthyist witch trials of the 1950s.

Lugosi was nothing if not a trouper. In January 1940, he sent an ingratiating note to the formidable gossip columnist Hedda Hopper who had written a flattering piece. 'I can't find words that would adequately express my thanks to you for the break you gave me. I am sure it will increase my popularity and cement my comeback,' he wrote hopefully. He became busy making B-movies for Monogram Pictures, films such as *The Ape Man* and *Voodoo Man*, which were shot in three weeks.

In April 1951, he came to the UK for another stage tour of *Dracula*, but it did not go well. 'There was giggling in Golders Green,' said his co-star Sheila Wynne who played Lucy. His vampire act was seen as old hat. He was becoming a figure of fun, but for the sake of earning a living – and paying for his fare home – he was prepared to put up with the humiliation of appearing in the 1952 film *Old Mother Riley Meets the Vampire* along with Dora Bryan, Richard Wattis and Hattie Jacques. 'It's enough to make a bat laugh,' read the poster.

On returning to LA he began a three-picture association with the film-maker Ed Wood, who specialised in low-budget sci-fi and horror. Some say Wood exploited Lugosi but it seems likely that the ageing star was grateful for Wood's friendship. He was also, by now, addicted to morphine, which he took for chronic sciatica. In 1955, he checked himself in to the Metropolitan State Hospital in Norwalk, Los Angeles for three months. He was the first Hollywood star to own up to a drug problem and received headlines such as 'Dracula is a Dope Addict'.

Frank Sinatra, moved by his plight, helped out with expenses and visited Lugosi in hospital.

Within three weeks of leaving hospital he married his fifth wife, Hope Lininger, an obsessive fan who had written to him for years.

Lugosi claimed that he was cured and said that withdrawal from drugs was 'the greatest pain in the world'. He was looking forward to working with Wood and some footage was shot, but it appeared in *Plan 9 from Outer Space*, released long after Lugosi's death and routinely referred to as 'the worst movie ever made'.

'Dracula is Hamlet to me,' Lugosi once said. There is something very touching about that. For it's clear that he put so much into any part that came his way. *Dracula* brought him fame and also imprisoned him. But he has the most extraordinary screen presence; the strange rhythms of his Hungarian-inflected accent give his lines a melancholy and poetic resonance. His biographer Arthur Lennig said: 'He seems to speak with great effort as if forcing a mouth long dead to move again.'

Bela Lugosi died at home on 16 August 1956. He was found clutching a script entitled *The Final Curtain*. He was buried, as he had wished, in his Dracula cape.

Chapter Three

Lon Chaney and Lon Chaney Jr – 'To endure pain brought him a strange joy.'

My father, who died at the age of 100 in 2016, reckoned he must have been one of the last people on the planet who had confidently predicted that 'talkies' would never catch on. He would have been 11 when the first talkie, *The Jazz Singer*, came out in 1927 and was repeating the views of his own parents who didn't think much of these new-fangled films.

With the benefit of hindsight, it looks like an inevitable technical progression from still to moving pictures, with synchronised sound as the next step. And even when silent films are shown at the correct speed with appropriate music, it is difficult for a modern viewer to appreciate just how magical those early cinematic experiences must have been. We lost our innocence long ago.

When talking pictures arrived, voice coaches in Hollywood were in high demand with even the most seasoned stars unsure how they would come across, nervous of being exposed by the new medium.

Only a few of the galaxy of silent stars are known by name today, partly because once talkies became established there was a reaction against silent films and they were seen as being old hat and slightly ridiculous. They stopped being shown in cinemas and had no place in TV schedules. Yet Lon Chaney is one of the stars of the silent screen who is still known today, because he appeared in two great films, *The Hunchback of Notre Dame* (1923) and *The Phantom of the Opera* (1925).

Both are 'horror' films in the way that *Frankenstein* is a horror film, with the monstrous protagonist in all three arousing both terror and pity. Curiously, silent horror films still exerted their power even once the silent era had passed.

Chaney himself was very dubious about talkies and his early death in 1930 more or less coincided with the demise of silent films. He said:

> The talkies are making pictures more realistic, shattering that optical vacuity, that romantic make-believe which camera magic has made possible to a degree, far beyond the stage's possibilities ... . In some respects I welcome sound. It adds depth and actuality to situations and individuals. For myself I regret it.

Chaney lived in a silent world long before he became a film star. He was the child of deaf-mute parents, born on 1 April 1883 in Colorado Springs.

His maternal grandfather Jonathan R. Kennedy had founded the Colorado Institute for the Education of Mutes in 1874, which still exists today as the Colorado School for the Deaf and Blind. Kennedy's daughter Emma attended and taught at the school where she met Lon's father Frank, who became a barber.

Emma also suffered badly from inflammatory rheumatism and Lon dropped out of school early to look after his invalid mother.

He was fluent in sign language and would act out the local news for her using signing and his own comedic, pantomime skills.

His older brother John was working as a stagehand at the local opera house and got the 14-year-old Lon a job as props boy. In 1902 Lon became a full-time employee of the theatre, working backstage and as a performer.

The *Colorado Springs Gazette* reviewed him favourably saying that he, 'provoked laughter whenever he appeared on the stage and his dancing was received with loud acclamations of approval. As a comedian he is irresistible, and it would be hard to find his equal in dancing among many first class vaudeville performers.'

On a tour to Oklahoma City, he met a 16-year-old chorus girl called Cleva Creighton. It was a whirlwind romance. The pair married within days of meeting and within a year had a son, Creighton Tull, born in 1906.

They moved to Los Angeles and joined the Ferris Hartman Company where Chaney found himself playing opposite Roscoe 'Fatty' Arbuckle, who would be one of the most popular silent screen stars until he was put on trial for the rape and manslaughter of Virginia Rappe at a party at the St Francis Hotel in San Francisco in 1921.

Hartman was a San Francisco impresario who worked his troupers hard, as did most of the itinerant theatre companies. Some performed three matinees and two nightly performances, seven days a week.

Chaney, always worried about having no job and no money, was a hard worker, but Cleva's popularity as a cabaret singer was soaring and she seemed destined to outshine her husband. The marriage was in trouble. He was jealous and she drank too much.

One night at the Majestic Theatre in Los Angeles, while Lon was working backstage, Cleva stood in the wings and swallowed dichloride of mercury, a poison which was easily available and commonly used for treating syphilis. She survived but lost her singing voice as a result.

Lon waited until she had recovered, but then filed for divorce in 1913 and also won custody of his son. But he was damaged by the scandal and permanently wary of the press digging it up again. It also prompted him to move out of live theatre, where he and Cleva were too well known as a couple, and try his luck at Universal Studios.

He was helped in this by his friend Lee Moran from Chicago, another of those silent film actors who appeared in hundreds of films but is unknown today.

Most early movies tend to be slapstick, westerns or melodrama and were usually two or three reelers. They often – before the Hays code was brought in – dealt with surprisingly risqué themes such as illegitimacy, abortion or alcoholism. But at first Chaney was convinced his career lay in comedy shorts.

In a TV interview in 1969, his son Lon Chaney Jr explained:

> He used to sit in the 'bullpen' at Universal, which was a room the size of this TV studio. He'd sit there and an assistant director would come to them and say, 'Anybody here who can play a college boy?' Dad would say, 'Yeah I can play a college boy.' Then he'd come back and they'd come out and say, 'Anyone here who can play a Chinaman?' Well this went on a few times and there wasn't anybody who could. So my Dad, being a natural artist from the word go, got his make-up kit and his own stuff together and took it to Universal. And when they'd ask, 'Can anyone play a

Chinaman?' he'd say, 'Yeah, I can play a Chinaman.' He'd make himself up as a Chinaman, go to work for ten minutes, come back, then go out and play a Greek. And this way make three or four pictures a day.

Lon Chaney made hundreds of films, most of them long lost. The first of his films, which has survived, is a western called *By The Sun's Rays* (1914).

Universal was a film factory, established by Carl Laemmle in 1912 and first known as the Universal Film Manufacturing Company. Originally it was intended to bankroll and distribute films for independent producers. In 1914, Laemmle expanded by buying a 250-acre chicken ranch for $165,000 and in doing so created the 'studio system', which would be an all-inclusive movie-making resource. Like the 'talkies', the 'studio system' seems like an obvious progression. But at the time it was, like the film business itself, a leap into the unknown.

Hazel Hastings was a chorus girl. She and other members of the troupe used to look after Chaney's son Creighton. At the time, she was married to a legless man who ran a cigar shop in San Francisco. After her divorce, she and Chaney were married in Santa Anna, California on 26 November 1915.

That year he appeared in a melodrama called *A Mother's Atonement* playing an old man but also the same character when younger. He would often play two roles in a film, a chance to showcase his abilities with make-up and as a character actor.

The Scarlet Car (1917) is a crime thriller and *Riddle Gawne* (1918), made by Paramount, is a western. This film was thought to be entirely lost for decades until one of the five reels turned up in a Russian archive.

In 1918, Chaney asked Universal for a pay rise. He was earning $5 a day and asked for $125 a week. This was refused. He was 35 by now and had yet to make his name. He was not matinee idol material and his belief in himself as a comedian had not proved correct.

Yet 1919 saw a change in fortunes when he appeared in *The Wicked Darling*, directed by Tod Browning with whom he would make ten pictures. Chaney plays Stoop Connors, a pickpocket. Priscilla Dean plays his partner in crime who falls for a real gentleman, much to Connors' dismay. This was another film that was thought lost until the 1990s when a mildewed print was discovered in the Netherlands.

He also made *The False Faces*, a First World War drama *Victory* (an adaptation of Joseph Conrad's novel) and *The Miracle Man*, all in 1919.

The Miracle Man, based on a novel by Frank L. Packard and a successful stage play, saw Chaney use his skill for portraying deformity in the story of a man who pretends to be crippled to win the sympathy of the public. It was directed by George Loane Tucker.

In an interview in 1928, Chaney said:

> Tucker didn't really want me for the role of the cripple in *The Miracle Man*. He wanted a professional contortionist but the five he had tried couldn't act it. Tucker explained to me that the first scene he would shoot would be the one where the fake cripple unwound himself in front of his pals. If I could do that I got the job. I went home to try it out. I'm not a contortionist of course. It would have been a lot easier in my subsequent work if I had been. While I was sitting pondering over the part I unconsciously did a trick I've done since childhood. I crossed my legs, then double-crossed them, wrapping my left foot round my right ankle. When I came to the studio on the test day Tucker was already behind the camera ... I flopped down, dragging myself forward along the floor, my eyes rolling, my face twitching and my legs wrapped tighter and tighter around each other. Tucker didn't speak and the sweat rolled off me. Finally I heard a single whispered word from him. 'God,' Tucker said. I wanted to say that too, but not for the same reason.

In *The Penalty* (1920) directed by Wallace Worsley, Chaney plays a criminal mastermind who plans a big heist in San Francisco and also his revenge on the doctor who mistakenly amputated both his legs. For this role, Chaney devised a leather harness which would strap his legs up at the knee so he would seem to be walking on stumps. He was in agony.

The themes of amputation and disfigurement run through Chaney's career (and there is the strange coincidence of Hazel's first husband being a double amputee).

It was the aftermath of the First World War, which had seen mutilation of bodies and faces on a scale hitherto unknown in war. Amputation was the most common operation performed by orthopaedic surgeons during the war. It has been estimated that in Germany, amputations totalled 67,000, and 41,000 in Britain. Many soldiers had multiple amputations. Masks made of tin, enamel or silver – carefully painted to resemble flesh tones – were produced to help those with the worst facial disfigurements. Many who would see Chaney masked in *The Phantom of the Opera* when it was first released would have been wearing masks themselves.

In Tod Browning's *Outside the Law* (1920), another vehicle for Priscilla Dean as a gangster's moll, Chaney plays both a gangster and a scholarly Chinaman. When he made *The Trap* (1922), the tag of 'the man of a thousand faces' was used for the first time. He plays a man cheated out of his girl and his mine. Chaney never ever got the girl.

In *Flesh and Blood* (1922), he plays a man falsely imprisoned who escapes disguised as a cripple to see his wife and child again.

While in *Shadows* (1922), he plays an elderly Chinese man who is, unusually, the hero of the film.

A Blind Bargain (1922) is a horror film in which Chaney plays a mad surgeon, Dr Lamb, who believes he can use animals to prolong human life. One of his less successful experiments is an ape/man hybrid who is also played by Chaney.

Moving Picture World's review said:

> It appears to have been the aim of all connected with this production to accent the weird, mysterious and uncanny elements and to make the picture so that it would thrill and fascinate spectators because of its horror and mystery... .
> Lon Chaney's work in this picture is really marvellous and he again demonstrates that he is one of the best if not the very best character actor on the screen. As the ape-man, his portrayal and likeness to a huge chimpanzee is wonderful and sends chills up and down your spine.

In *The Shock* (1923), he plays a disabled gangster who regains the use of his legs after surviving the San Francisco earthquake of 1906.

Lon Chaney had long been interested in making an adaptation of Victor Hugo's 1831 novel *The Hunchback of Notre Dame* (there had already been a version made in 1911). Wallace Worsley was chosen as director for this new Universal version. Chaney had made several films with him and said: 'Worsley, by the way, is as good as any of the second raters or better but for God's sake don't tell them so.' The competition to play Esmeralda was intense but Lon wanted Patsy Ruth Miller (once described as 'the most engaged girl in Hollywood' on account of her lively love life) and she got the part.

The Hunchback of Notre Dame (1923) was an epic production, involving a vast reconstruction of fifteenth-century Paris. There were thousands of extras, and a special building was erected to house the costumes while 200 people oversaw the wardrobe. The frequent night shoots required 230 electricians, used five miles of cable and seven generators. The traditional director's megaphone gave way to a full public-address system.

Chaney took care of his own make-up for the part of Quasimodo, the hunchback who was also half blind and half deaf (as a result of so many years of ringing the bells of Notre Dame). He had a prosthetic mandible made to give him an oversized bottom jaw, which made him unable to close his mouth. He had a heavy rubber hump made that attached to a leather harness, which in turn connected to a breastplate and leg pads leaving him unable to stand up straight. Over this he wore a flesh-coloured rubber suit covered with animal hair.

He followed Hugo's description almost to the letter:

> We shall not try to give the reader an idea of that tetrahedral nose, that horseshoe mouth; that little left eye obstructed with a red, bushy, bristling eyebrow, while the right eye disappeared entirely beneath an enormous wart; of those teeth in disarray, broken here and there, like the embattled parapet of a fortress; of that callous lip, upon which one of these teeth encroached, like the tusk of an elephant; of that forked chin; and above all, of the expression spread over the whole; of that mixture of malice, amazement, and sadness. Let the reader dream of this whole, if he can.
>
> A huge head, bristling with red hair; between his shoulders an enormous hump, a counterpart perceptible in front; a system of thighs and legs so strangely astray that they could touch each other only at the knees, and, viewed from the front, resembled the crescents of two scythes joined by the handles; large feet, monstrous hands; and,

with all this deformity, an indescribable and redoubtable air of vigour, agility, and courage – strange exception to the eternal rule which wills that force as well as beauty shall be the result of harmony.

The film propelled Chaney to international stardom though, typically, he was anxious about the film's reception and had to be coaxed to attend the New York premiere. Universal hoped to take him across the country from LA to New York with a string of public appearances. Chaney cancelled many of the dates and was met at Grand Central Station by a mass of fans and a brass band.

Moving Picture World found the reluctant star a deeply impressive individual. Their correspondent wrote: 'Chaney personifies sincerity intelligently directed; and it is a first impression that goes with each moment of conversation. Not merely a few pat parrot-like phrases but real evidence of a deep love of his art, wholehearted desire to play fair with it, and boundless ambition for its betterment.' Admiring sentiments, but you suspect Lon might have been hard work on a TV chat show.

In April 1924, Metro Pictures, Goldwyn Pictures and Louis B. Mayer Production merged to make the all-powerful MGM, which cemented the 'studio system' as Hollywood's way of working. The catchline for the new super company was 'More stars than there are in heaven'.

Chaney appeared in MGM's very first picture *He Who Gets Slapped* (1924) – a psychological thriller in which he plays a scientist who becomes a clown and ends up being stabbed to death in the circus ring by the love interest's wicked father. As per usual, Chaney didn't get the girl (played in this film by Norma Shearer). Bela Lugosi, the future Dracula, had a small part in the film as a clown.

The Monster (1925) from MGM is an old dark house movie, some years before James Whale made *The Old Dark House* (1932). It is also a mad scientist film with Chaney playing Dr Ziska who has a gadget which can transfer souls from one person to another. It's quite funny and campily entertaining. The director was Roland West who also made *The Bat* (1926) and *The Bat Whispers* (1930) which inspired Bob Kane, creator of *Batman*.

The 1925 screen adaptation of Gaston Leroux's novel *The Phantom of the Opera* was as epic a production as *The Hunchback of Notre Dame*, starring Chaney in the role of the lovelorn phantom who haunts the building. The vast concrete and steel set built by Universal to replicate the Paris Opera House was only demolished in 2014.

Chaney's skull-like appearance as the phantom was one of his greatest achievements, involving two loops of wire inserted into his nose to pull back and spread the nostrils, as well as padding to accentuate his cheekbones. The wires caused severe bleeding. Prongs attached to protruding false teeth pulled his mouth back at the corners.

It was not a happy production by all accounts. Director Rupert Julian did not get on with either his cast or crew and he was barely on speaking terms with Chaney. Reaction to a sneak preview in January 1925 was unfavourable so a new ending was shot, with scenes directed by Edward Sedgwick who made several Buster Keaton comedies for MGM.

Moving Picture World reported on the New York premiere on 6 September:

> Despite a continuous rain, traffic was halted in Times Square by the thousands who crowded around the front of the Astor. Police reserves called from the West 47th Street police station had little effect in clearing the situation ... .
> Everything about the presentation of *The Phantom of the Opera* was in keeping with the 'spirit'. Entering the lobby, the guests were initiated into the weirdness and mystery ... .
> The walls were covered with plaster 'stone' and from the low ceiling hung wrought iron lamps giving forth one eerie glow. Above the entrance, lying in a niche, was the full length figure of the 'Phantom' robed in the red silk of the Bal Masque scene. His skeleton face grinning at the throng sent cold shivers up and down the spines of those who caught sight of him for the first time.

True to form, Chaney did not attend the premiere but he arranged for a special screening for the pupils at the Colorado Institute for the Education of Mutes.

The Unholy Three (1925) directed by Tod Browning is extraordinary. Three sideshow performers go on a crime spree. Professor Echo (Chaney) is a ventriloquist who disguises himself as an old lady, while a circus dwarf (Harry Earles) plays her baby grandson. Victor McLaglen completes the trio as the strongman.

In *The Blackbird* (1926), with a complex plot, Chaney disguises himself as his character's non-existent twin brother, a crippled bishop. In *The Road to Mandalay* (1926) he plays Singapore Joe, a man so ashamed of his scarred appearance that he cannot bear to face his own daughter. He also plays his younger, unscarred self.

Tell it to the Marines (1926) saw Chaney playing a hero in uniform with no make-up tricks – a sort of prototype of the characters John Wayne would monopolise. But he still doesn't get the girl, a Navy nurse (played by Eleanor Boardman). *Tell it to The Marines* became MGM's highest-grossing film of 1926–27.

In *Mr Wu* (1927), he is both an elderly Chinese man and his grandson. In the same year, he was in Tod Browning's *The Unknown* (also known as *Alonzo the Armless*) playing a carnival knife thrower who is in love with his partner Nanon (Joan Crawford). He pretends he has no arms and throws the knives with his feet. When he discovers that Nanon has a phobia about being touched by a man's hands he has his arms amputated. Unfortunately, Nanon gets over her phobia and falls for the circus strongman.

Burt Lancaster said that the moment when Chaney discovers he had done the horrible deed to no avail was 'the most compelling scene I've ever seen an actor do'.

Tod Browning directed Chaney in *London After Midnight* (1927), a thriller involving hypnosis and vampires that was lost when MGM's film vaults were destroyed by fire in 1965. Just a few frames survive.

In 1928 and 1929, Chaney was voted the most popular male star by theatre exhibitors even though silent films were, by now, on their way out.

He was known as an actor's actor who was always generous to studio staff. He would make sure there were places for extras to sit comfortably during the long hours of filming and he was helpful to young actors. He avoided press junkets wherever possible. Once asked by MGM's publicity department to fill out a questionnaire asking what he had for breakfast, he replied: 'I can just hear them saying "Eat Lon Chaney's favourite cereal and look like the Hunchback of Notre Dame".'

He and Hazel lived in a relatively modest house in Beverly Hills with only a housekeeper and a chauffeur. He escaped to his cabin in the Eastern Sierra Nevada where he loved to go fishing. Tod Browning said he was 'the star who lived like a clerk'. He was also described as looking 'like a carpenter or stage hand'.

He continued to play tortured souls, disabled and anguished. The film critic Ruth Waterbury wrote in *Photoplay* magazine in 1928: 'To endure pain for his work brought him a strange joy.'

In *West of Zanzibar* (1928), directed by Tod Browning, he plays Phroso, a magician, whose wife Anna runs off with Crane (Lionel Barrymore). Crane pushes Phroso over a railing so he is unable to walk and pulls himself along on a wheeled platform. When Anna dies leaving a baby, Phroso plans to take his revenge on the child, not realising she is his daughter.

His characters are always morally ambiguous, often redeemed, rarely achieving happiness. He said: 'I've tried to show that the lowliest people frequently have the highest ideals. In the lower depths when life hasn't been too pleasant for me I've always had that gentleness of feeling, that compassion of an underdog for a fellow sufferer.'

That compassion shines through in his films. The science fiction author Ray Bradbury wrote of Chaney:

> He somehow got inside the shadows inside our bodies. He was able to nail some of our secret fears and put them on the screen. The history of Lon Chaney is the history of unrequited loves. He brings that part of you into the open, because you fear that you are not loved, you fear that you never will be loved, you fear there is some part of you that is grotesque, that the world will turn away from you.

Chaney agreed to appear in a remake (with sound) of *The Unholy Three*, released in 1930. *The Bioscope* said, 'Lon Chaney's first appearance [in a talkie] is an event in film history. It is pleasing to state that he speaks with remarkable distinction.'

While making *Thunder* (1929), his last silent film, Chaney caught a cold and developed a persistent cough. It has been said that one of the asbestos flakes used as fake snow in the film caught in his throat and gave him cancer. But he was also a heavy smoker, which is more likely to have caused the lung cancer which killed him.

He was admitted to hospital in New York and died on 26 August 1930, aged 47. In his last days, unable to speak, he used sign language to communicate with his wife and son, just as he had with his parents in his childhood.

Lon Chaney had not wanted his son Creighton to follow him into the film business. 'He is 6 feet 2,' he said. 'That's too tall [to be an actor].

31

He would always have had to have parts built around him. He couldn't build himself for the part. Besides, he's happy in business, and he's got a great wife. They are grand kids.'

At the time of Lon Chaney's death, Creighton was working as a plumber, but when the Depression hit he found it hard to get work and he decided to go into films, playing an extra or a stuntman in a variety of thrillers and westerns, using a number of names.

His 'great wife' Dorothy – with whom he had two sons – divorced him in 1936, because of his drinking. In 1937 he married Patsy Beck, but by 1939 the couple were so hard up that their car and their furniture were repossessed.

He changed his name to Lon Chaney Jr, something he had always said he would never do. In an interview in 1973, he said: 'I am most proud of the name Lon Chaney. I am not proud of Lon Chaney Jr because they had to starve me to make me take his name.'

But the famous name helped. His luck changed when he was cast as Lennie in Lewis Milestone's screen version of John Steinbeck's *Of Mice and Men* (1939), opposite Burgess Meredith as George. He was very good in the role of the gentle, slow-witted giant.

His next film was *One Million BC* (1940), a Hal Roach caveman fantasy with Victor Mature and Carole Landis heading the cast.

Universal decided the time was right for a revival of horror films, put Chaney under contract and gave him the starring role in *Man Made Monster* (1941). In this enjoyable piece of hokum, he plays Dan McCormack who is on a bus which crashes into an electrical pylon in the rain, electrocuting the driver and all the passengers. Mysteriously, McCormack is unscathed. Unfortunately, he falls into the hands of a mad scientist (a wonderfully over-the-top Lionel Atwill) who transforms the poor sap into a walking, glowing, electrical menace.

But it was *The Wolf Man* (1941), written by Curt Siodmak and directed by George Waggner, which – as a precursor to all werewolf films – ensures Lon Chaney Jr's place in the annals of horror movies. Chaney plays Larry Talbot who returns to his ancestral home in Wales after the death of his brother and has the misfortune to be bitten by a wolf-like creature (Bela Lugosi), which seals his fate. All the villagers know this ancient rhyme (actually made up by Siodmak): 'Even a man who is pure in heart, and says his prayers by night; May become a wolf when the wolfbane blooms and the autumn moon is bright.'

Chaney would play the wolf man in four more films: *Frankenstein Meets the Wolf Man* (1943), *House of Frankenstein* (1944), *House of Dracula* (1945), and *Abbott and Costello Meet Frankenstein* (1948). And he played Dracula himself in *Son of Dracula* (1943).

In 1946 his contract with Universal was not renewed, but he made a few more passable films. He plays the elderly ex-marshal in *High Noon* (1952) and a former convict who meets up with Tony Curtis and Sydney Poitier in *The Defiant Ones* (1958).

In the 1950s, horror found a new audience when films were shown on late-night TV. But Chaney's drink problem destroyed his career. 'Get everything you can out of me before 1 pm because after that I can't guarantee anything,' he'd say.

He died of throat cancer on 13 July 1973.

Chapter Four

Boris Karloff – 'As British as cricket and tea-time.'

Bramshott in Hampshire – on the old London to Portsmouth road – is said to be the most haunted village in Britain. It was devastated by the Black Death in the fourteenth century and was a haunt for highwaymen in the seventeenth century, for there were many travellers. More than a dozen apparitions are regularly sighted – often in the sunken lanes with their dark mossy banks and arching trees that meet overhead.

Boris Karloff is sometimes seen too – his tall, spare figure walking the lanes at night. So they say, anyway. He made Bramshott his home for the last ten years of his life, living in a pretty cottage with a high-walled garden on the road up to the church of St Mary's.

After his death his widow, Evie, re-dedicated a new set of church bells in his honour and there is a plaque marking this under the bell tower.

I drove there on a sunny afternoon in late summer, as typical an English village as you could hope to find, as English as cricket and tea-time. And despite his exotic stage name and Hollywood career, Boris Karloff was British and very much an anglophile – also devoted to cricket and tea-time.

He was born William Pratt in Camberwell, south London, on 23 November 1887, one of nine children. His father Edward was Anglo-Indian and his mother Eliza also had Indian ancestry. William, or Billy as he was known, was dark-skinned. His daughter Sara Jane Karloff believes he faced prejudice because of his dark colour. While Hollywood liked its stars to have an exotic quality, it tended to be economical with the truth when it came to their back stories. Thus, Merle Oberon who had a Ceylonese mother was described by the publicity machine as 'Tasmanian'.

William's father worked for the Indian Salt Revenue Service and many of his sons followed him into the diplomatic service and followed distinguished careers.

But though relatively privileged, it was a far from happy household. Edward was violent to his wife and his children and eventually Eliza was granted a judicial separation. The family then moved to Enfield and though four of his brothers had attended Dulwich College, William went to Merchant Taylors' School in 1899 and then as a boarder to Uppingham School in Rutland between 1903 and 1906.

His older brother George got the acting bug first. In 1897, in a terrible accident, he shot dead his friend Frederick Lockyear and, in 1904, he died of pneumonia. The family was not keen to see another member go into the theatre and William (who we will call Karloff from now on) said that he always felt he was regarded as 'the black sheep of the family, a nuisance who didn't have any brains and didn't do any work and was always getting into trouble of one sort or another.'

By this time his father Edward had died (in 1900) as had his mother Eliza, which meant that Karloff was brought up by his elder siblings.

He says he attended King's College London but he certainly did not finish his degree, and in 1909, with a £100 legacy from his mother, he bought a steamer ticket to Montreal (it could equally have been Australia as Karloff tossed a coin to decide).

He took labouring jobs and had vague plans to go into farming but in 1910 he moved to Vancouver where he met and married Grace Harding (she'd been born in Croydon so they shared a south London history).

He travelled to Kamloops (also in British Columbia) to join the Jeanne Russell Players, a stock theatre company. He was paid £6 a week, reduced to £4 when it was discovered his previous experience was entirely in school plays. He took on the name of Boris Karloff, claiming that Karloff was a name from his mother's side (there's no evidence that it was) and that he plucked Boris from 'the cold Canadian air'.

In 1913, accompanied by an actress called Margot Beaton, he crossed the border into the United States. He told the officials that his name was Boris Karloff and that he had been born in Odessa, Russia. Margot also claimed to be Mrs Karloff, which wasn't quite true either.

There followed what Karloff would describe as 'years of bitter oblivion', a time when he lived 'on eggs fried on inverted pressing irons in "no cooking" boarding houses'.

Yet for all his hardships he seems to have had an active and rather untidy personal life. In 1917, he arrived in Los Angeles with an actress called Olive de Wilton, but she returned to Britain in 1919 and in 1920 Karloff married a 24-year-old musician called Montana Laurena Williams. In 1924 he married again, a dancer called Helen Vivian Soule, known as Polly. Divorce followed and in 1929 he met a librarian called Dorothy Stine. They married on 12 April 1930 and lived in Karloff's 'shack' in Laurel Canyon in the Hollywood Hills. 'There was very little money,' said Dorothy, 'and it was Prohibition but we always loved to entertain, so we made beer in the bath.'

Boris Karloff's fortunes were about to change. He began working as a film extra and then graduated to a bit-part player, supplementing his earnings as a lorry driver. He played a 'spy' in the 1919 Douglas Fairbanks film *His Majesty*.

But he hadn't finished with live theatre and in 1929 he was cast in *The Criminal Code* at the Belasco Theatre. In the same year, he appeared in his first talkie, which was MGM's *The Unholy Night* directed by Lionel Barrymore, in which he had a small part as 'Abdul, the Hindu Lawyer'. *The Criminal Code* had been such a success that Columbia made it into a movie in 1931 starring Walter Huston with Karloff taking on a different role.

He played an unscrupulous reporter in Mervyn LeRoy's *Five Star Final* (1931), starring Edward G. Robinson. He had a small role in *The Mad Genius* (1931), a Warner Brothers horror film directed by Michael Curtiz and starring John Barrymore.

The story goes that James Whale, the British director, was casting *Frankenstein* when he noticed Karloff eating his lunch in the commissary (the studio canteen). Before the screen test, Karloff worked for weeks with the make-up artist Jack Pierce on the monster's distinctive look – the huge padded body, the high, square-shaped skull, the boots weighted 18 lbs each. Whale was delighted when he saw the results.

In an article in *Picturegoer* from April 1932, Helen Weigel Brown described the make-up regime:

> Each time the monster was created, Karloff had to sit in the make-up chair for three and a half hours. First his eyes had to be given that heavy, half-dead, insane look – a matter of applying coats and coats of wax to his eyelids to weigh them down.
>
> Next invisible wire clamps were fixed over his lips to pull the corners of his mouth out and down. Then the overhanging

brow and high, square shaped crown of the head, supposedly 'grafted' from the head of another man. These, as well as his face and neck, were shaped and built up by means of thin layers of flesh. Then the greyish make-up on top of all. Bolt-like plugs were placed on the side of the neck and held there by means of more layers of cotton and adhesive liquids … . Removing the make-up was not much simpler than putting it on, and certainly more painful. It required an hour and a half of prying, pulling and coaxing, plus special oils and 'a great deal of bad language' adds Karloff.

Filming began on 24 August 1931. It was hot and humid and Karloff broiled in the heavy-padded suit. Producer Carl Laemmle Jr insisted that Karloff wore a veil as he progressed from make-up to the soundstage. 'Because,' he explained, 'some of our nice little secretaries are pregnant and they might be frightened if they saw him.'

The most controversial scene in the film is where the monster, having escaped, meets a little girl. Gentle and intrigued, he watches as she throws flower petals into the lake. Then, intending no harm, he picks her up and throws her into the lake where she drowns. Censors took exception to this scene and on many prints it was cut. Marilyn Smith the 7-year-old who played the child had to do the scene twice. The first time she didn't manage to sink.

In Britain, this scene also prompted the National Society for the Prevention of Cruelty to Children to complain to the Home Office that the British Board of Film Censors (BBFC) was being insufficiently vigilant. Partly as a result of this, the BBFC introduced the H certificate – H for Horrific – which was replaced in 1951 by the X certificate. It was designed to be advisory but many local authorities used it as a reason to exclude children under 16.

We are accustomed to the idea that horror films are unsuitable for children even though they're catnip for teenagers. But in the early days there was no barrier. Children loved *Frankenstein* and understood the pathos of the monster.

In an interview in 1937, Karloff described a letter from a little girl:

She said something like this: 'I always like to see you as Frankenstein's monster, though at home they sometimes tell me it will make me sleep badly at nights. It doesn't. If I lie awake thinking about you I think what a poor, frightened thing you are with all those people chasing you: besides, you didn't mean to be bad, did you? They made you be.'

The filming was arduous for Karloff. In one scene, he has to carry his creator Dr Henry Frankenstein (played by Colin Clive) up a steep hill. There were a dozen takes. Said Karloff's daughter Sara Jane: 'He really suffered for the rest of his life because of the physical difficulties of shooting the film.'

The first low-key preview was held on 29 October 1931 at the Granada Theatre in Santa Barbara. There were a number of walkouts and much was made of the fact that ambulances were outside to treat any members of the audience who were in shock.

The film premiered in New York on 4 December. Karloff was not even invited. 'I was just an unimportant freelance actor,' he told *The Saturday Evening Post* in 1962, 'the animation for the monster costume'.

The film was a huge critical and financial success and Universal put Karloff on contract. 'Maybe for once I'll know where my breakfast is coming from after more than twenty years of acting,' he said. *Frankenstein* was his eighty-first film.

In 1932 Karloff was never off the screens. He had a small role in *Scarface*, one of the gangsters mown down in a burst of automatic fire in the bowling alley. François Truffaut said: 'The most striking scene in the movie is unquestionably Boris Karloff's death.'

Karloff also appeared in another monster role in James Whale's comedy horror *The Old Dark House* playing the terrifying butler Morgan. In the cast were Melvyn Douglas, Gloria Stuart, Charles Laughton, Raymond Massey and Ernest Thesiger. It's a variation on a theme that would be a perennial horror favourite – a group of innocents take shelter from a stormy night in a sinister mansion.

He was in *The Mummy*, covered in blue-green clay (it photographed as ghoulish grey) and said it was like wearing a plaster cast. Yet again Karloff suffered for his art as Imhotep, an Ancient Egyptian priest who comes back to life to find that a young English girl is the reincarnation of the Egyptian princess he loved.

That same year, 1932, Karloff was loaned to MGM for *The Mask of Fu Manchu* co-starring Myrna Loy as the 'sadistic nymphomaniac'

Fah Lo See. 'Boris was a fine actor,' she said, 'a professional who never condescended to his often unworthy material'.

In the same year, the Hollywood Cricket Club was set up for the benefit of the anglophile community, planted with specially imported English grass seed. Its leading light was Charles Aubrey Smith, who had captained England in a test match against South Africa in 1889 and was known for an eccentric 'round the corner' bowling style. He appeared in 113 films during his thirty-year career and was knighted in 1944. Any British star who showed up in Los Angeles was commanded to play and Laurence Olivier (arriving in 1933) found a pair of flannels in his hotel room and a note from C. Aubrey Smith telling him that net practice was at 9 am.

Karloff, who was a passionate cricket fan, generally turned out as wicket keeper but his bandy legs made him susceptible to being called LBW.

In 1933, Karloff returned to England on the SS *Paris* to film *The Ghoul* for Gaumont-British in which he played Professor Henry Morlant, an Egyptologist who thinks that an ancient jewel will give him magical powers of rejuvenation if it is offered up to the god Anubis. The film also starred Cedric Hardwicke, Ernest Thesiger and Ralph Richardson in his first film.

Karloff had been a penniless nobody when he left London and now he was a world-famous film star. He and Dorothy initially stayed at the Dorchester but on their first night they were too excited to sleep and went to the jazzy Kit Cat Club in the Haymarket. Later they took a service flat in Duchess Street, Mayfair. Three of his distinguished brothers – Sir John Pratt of the Foreign Office; Mr Justice E. M. Pratt and Mr F. G. Pratt of the India Civil Service – attended a reception he gave. He had not seen them for more than twenty years.

In 1934, Karloff starred with his horror rival Bela Lugosi in *The Black Cat* directed by Edgar Ulmer, an emigré who'd worked on German Expressionist films. Karloff plays the head of a devil-worshipping cult in a spectacular Art Deco castle. It's a very peculiar and disturbing film which ends with Lugosi skinning Karloff, which he probably did with some relish as Karloff's career was soaring whereas Lugosi's was stalling.

In 1992, the great *Observer* film critic Philip French described *The Black Cat* thus:

> The first (and best) of seven Karloff/Lugosi joint appearances. The movie unfolds like a nightmare that involves necrophilia,

ailurophobia, drugs, a deadly game of chess, torture, flaying, and a black mass with a human sacrifice. This bizarre, utterly irrational masterpiece, lasting little more than an hour, has images that bury themselves in the mind.

In 1935, Karloff was back in monster mode in *The Bride of Frankenstein*, also directed by James Whale, which starred Elsa Lanchester as the lucky lady. Said Karloff:

> The watery opening scene was filmed with me wearing a rubber suit under my costume to ward off chill. But air got into the suit. When I was launched into the pond, my legs flew up in the air, and I floated there like some sort of obscene water lily while I, and everyone else, hooted with laughter. They finally fished me out with a boat hook and deflated me.

Karloff made *Son of Frankenstein*, the third in which he plays the monster, in 1938. During the shoot, on his fifty-first birthday, Dorothy gave birth to a daughter, Sara Jane.

When not playing a monster, Karloff would often be cast as a mad scientist. 'The formula was successful, if not original,' he observed. 'The scientist would set out to save mankind. His project would sour and he with it. In the end he'd have to be destroyed regretfully, like a faithful old dog gone mad.'

In 1940, he made a return – with some trepidation – to live theatre in a Broadway production of *Arsenic and Old Lace*. In a 1962 piece for *The Saturday Evening Post* he wrote:

> By the time I arrived in New York, I was almost shaking from sheer fright. I'd rushed through a hard week at Columbia studios, then taken an all-night flight East. At the theatre they handed me a script, and we did something I'd never done in stock or repertory – we sat down, cast and director together, and read cold turkey. I was so tired, and so frightened of my New York role, that I began to stutter – something that always besets me when I'm tired. I rehearsed in stutters for three days, continually thinking

that it would cure itself. But instead it grew worse. The third night I wandered the streets of Manhattan wondering what to do. I thought I'd have to walk up to the management and say, 'I'm very sorry. I've made a mistake, and so have you. I've got to get out of your play. Do I owe you anything?'
I walked some more and thought, If I do that, honest though it is, I've certainly had it in New York and haven't done myself an awful lot of good in Hollywood either. Somehow I've got to go through with the play.

And so he did. He conquered his stammer but his faint lisp remained with him throughout his career. The production of *Arsenic and Old Lace* was a hit, running for 1,400 performances. Later he was to play Captain Hook in a Broadway production of *Peter Pan*.

In Hollywood, he was back in B-movies working on Monogram Pictures' cheap-as-chips productions. He played Chinese detective James Lee Wong in five Charlie Chan spin offs. He parodied himself in *Dick Tracy Meets Gruesome* (1947) and in *Abbott and Costello Meet the Killer, Boris Karloff* (1949). The RKO producer Val Lewton cast him in three rather good films: *Isle of the Dead* (1945), *The Body Snatcher* (1945) and *Bedlam* (1946).

He and his wife Dorothy split in 1945 and the day after the divorce was finalised in 1946, Karloff married again, this time to Dorothy's erstwhile best friend, Evelyn Hope Helmore. This took his daughter Sara Jane by surprise though, loyally, she never said anything negative about her father, even though she barely lived with him after the age of 8. After his death, she and Bela Lugosi's son tirelessly burnished their fathers' images at horror film conventions the world over.

Originally from Putney in West London, the new wife, Evelyn, had been assistant story editor to Darryl F. Zanuck. In 1951 the couple moved to New York, to an apartment in the Dakota building in Manhattan. They flew to Britain every summer and, in 1959, decided to make England their permanent home, living in 43 Cadogan Square in London and then in the little house in Bramshott. Karloff – ever the anglophile – became a Lord's Taverner and a member of the Garrick Club.

He was a regular on TV during the 1950s, always gracefully playing along with the presenter's inevitable monster gags. Typical was CBS's game show *I've Got a Secret* on which Karloff appeared in 1954.

Heavily sponsored by Cavalier Cigarettes, the host Garry Moore smoked throughout the entire show (the poor man died of throat cancer in his sixties). Participants were rewarded with cartons of Cavaliers.

In 1957, he was a guest on *The Rosemary Clooney Show*. 'Oh you startled me,' says Rosemary archly as Boris walks on the set. This time the conceit is that Boris wants to break out of the horror mould and do a storytelling series for children. Wearing what looks like the same luxurious smoking jacket with quilted collar that he wore in *The Black Cat*, he narrates the story of *Little Red Riding Hood* (with Clooney as the heroine). In 1958 – inevitably – he was the subject of an edition of the American version of *This Is Your Life*. A very private and rather shy man, it was not an experience he enjoyed.

He was in constant pain in his later years, suffering terribly from arthritis, no doubt exacerbated by the stresses and strains of playing Frankenstein's monster. After three operations, he would never be able to walk without a cane or leg braces.

In 1966, he was in an episode of *The Girl from U.N.C.L.E.* called 'The Mother Muffin Affair'. In 1991, in a filmed interview, the star Stefanie Powers remembers that, though Karloff was in pain, he was 'a beguilingly lovely man' whose 'timing was impeccable'. The same year, Karloff provided the narration for the Chuck Jones and Ted Geisel animated version of the much-loved Dr Seuss book *How the Grinch Stole Christmas*.

A new generation of film-makers came calling in the 1960s. King of the B-movies Roger Corman cast Karloff in his 1963 film *The Terror*. A fresh-faced Jack Nicholson plays a Napoleonic soldier who has become separated from his regiment, is captivated by a beautiful and elusive girl, and follows her to a sinister castle ('Don't go to the castle!') which is the home of an elderly baron (Karloff in another sumptuous dressing gown).

Corman made the film using sets left over from *The Raven* in which Karloff also starred along with Vincent Price and Peter Lorre. He persuaded Karloff to be available for two days' filming for a small amount of money. Corman says that when he cut together Karloff's footage, he realised that 'it didn't make sense' so he filmed a scene between Jack Nicholson and another actor Dick Miller (in close-up because the sets had been taken down) and had them explain the shaky plot.

The young British director Michael Reeves signed up Karloff for *The Sorcerers* in 1967, set in a swinging mini-skirted London, where actor Ian Ogilvy finds that an elderly couple, Karloff and Catherine Lacey, are plugging into his mind and vicariously enjoying his man-about-town thrills.

In his autobiography *Once a Saint*, Ogilvy recalls what a pleasure it was working with Karloff and that there were some comical moments:

> Early in the shoot, our sound man complained to the director that every time Boris moved, he squeaked.
>
> Boris hooted with laughter and rolled up his trouser leg to reveal a steel brace for his badly arthritic leg. 'Bring me some bicycle oil,' he called, then he greased his squeaky hinge – a bizarre Frankenstein moment.

Peter Bogdanovich directed Boris Karloff in his first feature film, *Targets*, in 1968. Karloff essentially plays himself, an elderly horror film star who, while making a personal appearance at a drive-in cinema, confronts a psychotic Vietnam veteran. It is a poignant swansong of a movie, for his character in the film also represents the golden age of horror of the 1930s and 1940s, before violence and special effects came to dominate the genre.

Boris Karloff died on 2 February 1969 of pneumonia (still working, he had just completed three low-budget films in Mexico). His ashes are interred in Guildford Crematorium.

He had been asked all his life if he minded being typecast. His answer? 'Certainly, I was typed. But what is typing? It is a trademark, a means by which the public recognises you. Actors work all their lives to achieve that. I got mine with just one picture. It was a blessing.'

Chapter Five

F. W. Murnau – 'Here is a man of exceptional nature.'

Nosferatu … does not the word sound like the call of the death bird at midnight? You dare not say it since the pictures of life will fade into dark shadows; ghostly dreams will rise from your heart and feed on your blood.

The opening caption of F. W. Murnau's 1922 classic *Nosferatu*, subtitled 'a symphony of horror', takes us straight into the clammy jaws of German Expressionism, a pulsing miasma of light, shadows and of sickly and unearthly visions. In the aftermath of the First World War, a defeated nation found a sort of brooding solace in its gloomy folklore – the stories collected by the Brothers Grimm infuse the German imagination combined with the caustic and unforgiving stance of a modern art movement, which sought to find a new reality through the distorted and abstract. Expressionism is hard to pin down – but suffice to say – not many laughs.

The German-French film critic Lotte Eisner wrote: 'Mysticism and magic, the dark forces to which Germans have always been more than willing to commit themselves, had flourished in the face of death on the battle fields.' But this tendency goes back further. The woman of letters, Madame De Staël, published a study – *De L'Allemagne* – in 1813 saying: 'We now turn to discuss that inexhaustible source of poetical effects in Germany: terror. Ghosts and wizards please the people as much as men of culture.'

Friedrich Wilhelm Murnau was born on 28 December 1888 in Bielefeld, in Westphalia, described by Eisner as 'a region of vast pastures, where enormous peasants breed heavy-boned plough horses'.

He came from a well-off family in the textile business, who lived on a magnificent estate at Wilhelmshöhe near Kassel. His real family name was Plumpe and he took the pseudonym of Murnau from the town of that name, south of Munich where he lived for a time.

He was highly intelligent and by the age of 12 he was said to be familiar with the works of Schopenhauer, Ibsen, Nietzsche, Dostoevsky and Shakespeare.

As a child, he put on plays at home but his father was not keen to encourage his theatrical ambitions saying, 'I paid for him to become a professor not a starving actor.'

Serious-minded though he was, Murnau did have a taste for the good things in life. When he went to study in Berlin in 1909 he set himself up in an expensive apartment in the smart district of Charlottenburg and his landlady had to demand payment from Murnau's father – which fortunately was forthcoming.

He then went to Heidelberg to study literature and the history of art. Here the director Max Reinhardt spotted him in a student production and invited him to join his actors' school. The influence of the Austrian-born director on theatre, opera and cinema was transformative, not only in Germany but worldwide. Before him the director's role was mostly administrative, but his productions placed the director at the creative heart of a production. His energy was prodigious. Between 1905 and 1930 he oversaw 23,374 performances of 452 plays. In just one year – 1916–1917 – he staged forty-eight productions. His disciples, apart from Murnau, included the film directors Paul Leni, Ernst Lubitsch, William Dieterle, Fritz Lang and Otto Preminger. In 1934, Reinhardt emigrated to the United States where he set up the Reinhardt School of the Theatre on Hollywood's Sunset Boulevard. He died in New York in 1943, aged 70.

The First World War interrupted Murnau's career in theatre. He joined the Imperial German Flying Corps and survived eight crashes without being wounded. When he was forced to make a landing in Switzerland he was held in a prisoner-of-war camp for the duration.

Once the war was over, Murnau returned to acting and in doing so he cut off almost all ties with old friends and family, save for the occasional letter to his mother and brothers.

He set up his own film company in 1919 with the actor Conrad Veidt and his first full-length film (now lost apart from fragments) was *The Boy in Blue*, inspired by the Thomas Gainsborough painting.

Veidt starred in Robert Wiene's film *The Cabinet of Dr Caligari* (1920), a classic of Expressionist horror cinema – about an insane hypnotist, Dr Caligari (played by Werner Krauss), who uses a somnambulist (played by Conrad Veidt) to commit murders. He also appeared in *The Man Who Laughs* (1928) playing a circus performer whose disfigured face is set in a permanent grin, which was an inspiration for the Batman villain the Joker, created in 1940. Veidt was in Wiene's *The Hands of Orlac* and Paul Leni's *Waxworks* (1924) – both horror films. This was the era when an Expressionist setting was enough to confer the label of high art, a label which the horror genre has struggled to retain ever since.

Veidt was bitterly opposed to Nazism and left Germany for Britain in 1933 with his wife Ilona Prager who was Jewish. He moved to Hollywood in 1941, hoping to make films which would persuade the US to join the war. And here he appeared in *Casablanca* (1942) playing the villainous Major Heinrich Strasser. He died in 1943, aged just 50.

Murnau's *Nosferatu* was an unauthorised adaptation of Bram Stoker's novel *Dracula*. Stoker's widow Florence objected strongly and the ensuing legal battle drove the production company – Prana Film – into bankruptcy. At one stage a court ordered that all copies of the film should be destroyed. Fortunately, a few prints survived the legal battle.

There is, though, much in *Nosferatu* that is not a direct steal from Stoker. Albin Grau, the producer and production designer, who had a lively interest in the occult, also took inspiration from a personal war experience. In 1916 a Serbian farmer had confided to him that his father was a vampire.

The screenplay was written by Henrik Galeen, who had also worked on *The Student of Prague* (1913) and on *The Golem* (1920) with Paul Wegener (there are three *Golem* films made in 1915, 1917 and 1920 but the earlier two are lost). *The Golem* is a silent horror film based on Eastern European Jewish folklore. An antiques dealer (Galeen) finds a clay statue – the golem – which has magical powers to protect the Jews from persecution. Paul Wegener plays the resurrected golem who goes on a vengeful murder spree when his love for the antiques dealer is not returned.

In an interview in 1922, Murnau said there are only two possible kinds of films, those dealing with the supernatural and the *Kammerspielfilm*. The latter is a type of film that has intimate portraits of lower middle-class life and derives from Max Reinhardt's Munich Kammerspiele theatre opened in 1906.

If this definition of film seems strangely limited and prescriptive we should remember that Murnau was a pioneer who literally invented the idea of cinema. There was no tradition for him to draw on. Even the notion of the camera moving rather than being fixed and static was one of his innovations, realised with the most basic of equipment and a great deal of ingenuity.

In his film *Faust* (1926), he had Emil Jannings (in the role of Mephisto) with three enormous fans causing his cloak to rise 12 feet in the air. Meanwhile the 'breath of plague' floats over the city, which was shovelfuls of soot driven by a propeller.

One of the conventions on a film set is that the moment the director calls 'action' there is silence. But in the silent era there was no need for that. While filming was going on there would be a tremendous noise as sets were built and everyone went about their business talking as loudly as they liked.

The designer Robert Herlth remembers going to see Murnau on his set and being amazed at how quiet everything was. There he was, 'a tall slim gentleman in his white work coat issuing directions in a low voice'.

Murnau also realised that restraint and understatement were essential when acting for the camera, even though that sometimes clashes with the jumpy theatricality of many Expressionist films.

He also preferred to use actors who were not big names. His choice for Count Orlok in *Nosferatu* (the Dracula character) was Max Schreck, who had been part of Max Reinhardt's company in Berlin. It is an astonishing, mesmerising performance, creating an image of the cadaverous vampire with the bat ears and clawing fingers which is far removed from that of the suave foreign bounder in a cape which became the Dracula norm. But it is equally iconic.

Schreck – a strange man by all accounts and something of a loner – appeared at the Munich Kammerspiele between 1919 and 22 and had a role in Bertolt Brecht's early play *Drums in the Night*. His name means 'fright' and it wasn't a stage name.

Galeen's script sets *Nosferatu* in a fictional German town of Wisborg. The date is 1838. A young estate agent Thomas Hutter (played by Gustav von Wangenheim with puppyish innocence) is sent to Transylvania to negotiate with Count Orlok over the purchase of a house in Wisborg. In Stoker's novel, this character is known as Jonathan Harker.

Blithely unaware of what's going on, Hutter writes to his wife Ellen (played by Greta Schroder) about the mosquitoes that have left two small bites on his neck. Hasn't he ever seen any horror films? Eventually Count Orlok arrives in Wisborg carried by a plague-carrying ship and begins his reign of evil in the small town. Aware of the belief that a vampire can be destroyed if a pure-hearted woman distracts him with her beauty, Ellen gives herself to the monster. Whereas British and American Draculas are, like Stoker's novel, mostly preoccupied with sex and death, this haunting German film is about disease and sacrifice.

According to Paul Wegener, 'light and darkness in the cinema play the same role as rhythm and cadence in music'. The images in Murnau's *Nosferatu* helped establish the visuals of innumerable horror films and psychological thrillers and were equally part of the Expressionist 'look' with its love of distortion and abstraction. Shadows, mirrors, doorways and staircases are everywhere. In *Nosferatu,* the empty swinging ship's hammock is a potent symbol of the plague-stricken sailor who died in it.

Unlike many Expressionist film-makers, Murnau took advantage of the possibilities opened up by location filming, especially in *Nosferatu*. In *The Cabinet of Dr Caligari*, the claustrophobic, distorted set of the mediaeval town is invested with a sinister power and life of its own. But in *Nosferatu* the camera sweeps across the Carpathian Mountains carrying – as the Hungarian film critic Béla Balázs put it – 'the great shadow of the supernatural' and the 'glacial draughts of air from the beyond'.

The success of *Nosferatu* prompted William Fox of Fox Studio to invite Murnau to Hollywood in 1926. His four-year contract with Fox, dated 8 July 1926, says that he will be paid $125,000 in the first year, $150,000 in the second, $170,000 in the third and $200,000 in the fourth.

Murnau made many films which have been lost, or else only fragments remain. In America, he made *Sunrise* (1927) which received several Oscars at the very first Academy Awards ceremony. His next two films were *4 Devils* (1928) which is lost, and *City Girl* (1930), which is said to have inspired Terrence Malick's *Days of Heaven,* with the story of a hardboiled waitress who marries a country boy dreaming of living a rural idyll and is sadly disappointed as the Depression begins to bite.

The last two were not well-received at the time and Murnau consoled himself with a trip to Bora Bora in the South Pacific where he made his last film *Tabu* (1931).

The circumstances of Murnau's premature death at the age of 42 just days before the release of *Tabu* became one of the scandalous stories told by film-maker Kenneth Anger in *Hollywood Babylon,* his 1965 exposé of the dark side of Tinsel Town.

According to Anger, the fatal car accident on the Pacific Coast Highway – Murnau was thrown from his open-top light-blue Packard when it collided with a truck – was the result of Murnau performing a sex act on the young Filipino valet who was driving the car. Murnau died of his injuries on 11 March 1931 at Cottage Hospital, Santa Barbara. Murnau's defenders dispute this claim, regarding it as salacious tittle-tattle.

Kenneth Anger says the valet was 14, whereas it seems he was in his mid-twenties with a wife and three young children. He wasn't Filipino either. Eliazar Stevenson's father was English and his mother was Mexican.

Stevenson and the other passenger, the hired limousine's official chauffeur John Freeland, escaped from the crash with relatively minor injuries.

On 19 March 1931, Murnau's body was taken from the Bagley Mortuary to the Hollywood Lutheran Church. He was in an open coffin surrounded by flowers as the service took place. The German film director Berthold Viertel said: 'Everyone who met him knew it at once. Here is a man of exceptional nature. He had a special dignity and peace about him but also a strangeness, a hint of loneliness.'

On 30 March 1931, the liner *Europa* sailed from New York towards Hamburg with the casket holding Murnau's body. On 5 April, friends including Emil Jannings, screenwriter Carl Meyer and Fritz Lang said farewell in a second funeral. On 13 April, Murnau was finally laid to rest in a cemetery in Stahnsdorf. He had been at the peak of his fame and success, yet even then his future as a film-maker was less certain. The silent era was ending and for all his ingenuity and vision, Murnau had no plans to embrace sound.

In 1979, the German film director Werner Herzog remade *Nosferatu* under the title *Nosferatu the Vampyre* starring Klaus Kinski, Isabelle Adjani and Bruno Ganz. Many of the visuals recreate the look of the original. Herzog admired Murnau and in an interview in 2007 he described him as 'the greatest film-maker in Germany'.

In 2000, John Malkovich played F. W. Murnau with Willem Dafoe as Max Schreck in an amusing 'metafiction' about the making of the original *Nosferatu* called *Shadow of the Vampire.* According to this film, Schreck really was a vampire. The film was produced by Nicolas Cage.

49

Nosferatu had a special place the heart of heavy metal bands. In 1977 Blue Oyster Cult released a track called 'Nosferatu' on the *Spectres* album. It takes up the idea from the film that only a woman 'pure in heart' can destroy the vampire.

> So chaste so calm, she gave herself
> To the pleasure of her dreaded master
> He sucked the precious drops of life
> Throughout the long and cold dark night

Nosferatu lives on.

Chapter Six

James Whale – 'Faun-like charm.'

The headline in the local paper – *The Dudley Herald* – was: 'Dudley Man Who Became a Film Producer Dies in Hollywood'. It was 1957 and the Dudley man, James Whale, had been found dead in his swimming pool on the afternoon of 29 May. A maid named Anna Ryan had discovered the body. Her first thought was to call Pierre Foegel, the young man who lived with Whale, and Whale's business manager George Lovett. The two men pulled the fully dressed body from the pool.

Was it murder, suicide or a terrible accident? There had been rumours of the 'Babylonian' pool parties thrown by Whale in his later years, yet he had also been in poor health for some time. Whatever the truth, he had been no more than a melancholy footnote in Hollywood history for some years.

Like Norma Desmond in Billy Wilder's *Sunset Boulevard* (1950), he was a forgotten star. And as in *Sunset Boulevard*, a body is found in the pool. The perfect Hollywood ending. Yet within a few months, the television release of his movies from the 1930s, *Frankenstein* and *The Invisible Man*, would bring his work to the attention of a younger generation, ensuring that his name would never be forgotten again.

The New York Times obituary was more informative. It read: 'James Whale, who directed the movie *Frankenstein* died today after falling into the swimming pool of his home. He was 60 years old.'

In fact, he was 67 but, out of vanity, he had put it about that he was born in 1896 rather than 1889.

This Englishman abroad was the sixth of seven children. His father William was an ironmonger and secretary of the trade union that he had helped found. His mother Sarah was a nurse. It was a solid, working-class background and one from which Whale was desperate to distance himself at the first opportunity. A brief spell at a sheet metal factory convinced him that physical labour was not for him. But he had a gift for drawing and was able to enrol at the Dudley School of Arts and Crafts. He made money painting signs to supplement his wages as a cobbler.

When war broke out in 1914, Whale was reluctant to enlist and became the recipient of a couple of white feathers. Eventually, in October 1915, he obtained a commission as second lieutenant with the 7th battalion of the Worcestershire Infantry Brigade. In France he was taken prisoner almost immediately.

'My platoon had been told to do a stint at a pill-box at midnight and we had gone straight into a well-laid trap,' he said in an interview many years later. 'It all happened so suddenly I was stupefied and found it impossible to believe myself cut off from everything British and in the hands of the Hun.'

He was held in Holzminden until the end of the war, a prisoner-of-war camp near Hanover with 12,000 inmates. The food was terrible. Whale recalled a stew which consisted of the head of a cow floating in a pot.

To pass the time he played poker and bridge with fellow officers and as there was no money in the camp he collected IOUs from other players, which he took care to cash in after the war. He also staged Saturday night shows in the camp. These were ambitious productions and on one occasion costumes were sent for from Cologne.

Once he was repatriated, Whale joined the Birmingham Repertory Theatre as actor, set designer and stage manager. He appeared in a production of Beaumont and Fletcher's *The Knight of the Burning Pestle*, which was directed by Nigel Playfair. Also in the cast was 19-year-old Noel Coward.

In a 1919 Christmas production of *The Merry Wives of Windsor* at the Gaiety Theatre in Manchester, he met Ernest Thesiger who would star in two of Whale's films, *The Old Dark House* (1932) and *The Bride of Frankenstein* (1935). Thesiger – first cousin of the explorer and author Wilfred Thesiger – described Whale as 'a frail ex-prisoner of war with faun-like charm'.

Whale became an assistant stage manager at the new Regent Theatre in the Euston Road, formerly the Euston Theatre of Varieties, and appeared in *Body and Soul* by Arnold Bennett in the autumn of 1922. At around this time he met the strikingly beautiful and exotic artist Doris Zinkeisen. She and her equally talented sister Anna both won scholarships to the Royal Academy, and Doris's career (she died in 1991), included costume design for film and theatre and working as the official Red Cross war artist at Bergen-Belsen concentration camp. Whale was said to have been engaged to Doris for two years and they remained friends until the end of his life.

This was also the period when Whale, mixing with a glamorous young thespian crowd, knocked seven years off his age. Better to be in your late twenties than your mid-thirties when you're trying to establish yourself. He made his first West End appearance in Richard Hughes' *A Comedy of Good and Evil* at the Ambassadors Theatre in 1925, the year he first met R. C. Sherriff, who attempted to interest Whale in directing his play about life in the trenches called *Journey's End*. Whale, Sherriff noted, wasn't very enthusiastic at the time.

In 1928, Whale starred with Charles Laughton in Hugh Walpole's thriller *The Man with Red Hair*. It was a great success. Whale, aged 38 by now, was cast as Laughton's demented son though Laughton was Whale's junior by ten years. In December, *Journey's End*, directed by Whale, opened at the Apollo Theatre. Originally a 21-year-old Laurence Olivier was offered the role of Stanhope, the captain of the infantry company. But he was contracted elsewhere and, for the bulk of the play's successful run at the Prince of Wales Theatre, the part went to Colin Clive, a descendant of Clive of India. Clive, who died of alcoholism at the age of 37, would play the part of Frankenstein.

Despite the absence of a leading lady (*No Leading Lady* would be the wry title of Sherriff's autobiography), the play was a hit and Whale took it to Broadway.

He went west to Los Angeles where he loved the climate, and the way that the men dressed. 'All the men wear numbers of rings on every finger and (so I believe) amber beads inside their cutie blouses,' he observed. Unusual among gay men at the time, Whale never made any effort to hide his sexual preferences.

He was swept away by Hollywood, claiming that cinema was 'the greatest medium of all time' and that theatre would become a thing of the past. 'One feels the footprints of the immortals are here but one has a terrible feeling that they are in the sand and won't last when civilisation comes this way,' he said cryptically. In 1930, he directed the film version of *Journey's End* with Colin Clive again playing Stanhope. Said the *New York Evening Post*: 'It bears the stamp of all round perfection and James Whale has undoubtedly placed himself along with the foremost screen directors.'

He was also 'dialogue director' for Howard Hughes' 1930 film *Hell's Angels*, which had to be laboriously re-shot as a talkie. He conceived a venomous dislike of Jean Harlow, only 18, and in her first big picture. When she asked him how to act seductive he told her: 'My dear girl I can tell you how to be an actress but I cannot tell you how to be a woman.'

Universal Studios had owned the rights to Peggy Webling's play based on Mary Shelley's *Frankenstein* since 1930 (Mary Shelley's original book was already in the public domain).

Webling had written it at the request of the actor-manager Hamilton Deane, whose adaptation of Bram Stoker's *Dracula* was the basis of Universal's film starring Bela Lugosi. Despite the success of *Dracula*, Universal was not confident that a Frankenstein film would be equally successful. Robert Florey had been expected to direct with Bela Lugosi in the role of the monster. Unfortunately, a screen test with Lugosi had reduced the audience to laughter along with the Universal boss Carl Laemmle Jr.

Florey was furious when Whale made his move on the basis of the success of his Universal film *Waterloo Bridge* (1931). Florey said: 'James Whale, the "ace of Universal" demanded that Carl Laemmle let him film *Frankenstein* which had been promised to me. He satisfied Whale without however, informing me of the change.'

Whale, in an interview with *The New York Times* in December 1931, recalled it this way: 'I chose *Frankenstein* out of about 30 stories because it was the strongest meat and gave me a chance to dabble in the macabre. I thought it would be an amusing thing to try and make what everyone knows to be a physical impossibility into the almost believable for 60 minutes.'

He found Boris Karloff in the Universal canteen and he insisted that Colin Clive took the role of Victor Frankenstein which Laemmle had wanted to go to Leslie Howard. In a letter explaining to Clive how he should play the monster's creator, Whale wrote: 'Frankenstein's nerves are all to pieces. He is a very strong, dominant personality, sometimes quite strange and queer, sometimes very soft and sympathetic.'

By now Whale was involved with David Lewis, a young writer, the son of Russian-Jewish immigrants. Though Lewis was some fifteen years younger than Whale, he found the older man gullible and naive when he first met him over lunch in Hollywood. But they became lovers and later lifelong friends.

Whale gave Lewis a copy of Mary Shelley's *Frankenstein* to read. 'I was sorry for the goddam monster,' said Lewis, thus providing Whale with his guiding motif for the entire film. Critics have also seen a gay subtext in the film – the idea of the outsider who is deemed monstrous by society. But doubtless the film also struck a chord as America slipped into the Depression years and millions felt alienated from the mainstream through poverty.

This was by no means the first *Frankenstein*. There had been a fourteen-minute film made by Thomas Edison's studios in 1910. *Life Without a Soul* from the Ocean Film Corporation flopped in 1915. Italy's Albertini Studios produced *Mostro di Frankenstein* in 1920. Whale was also familiar with, and influenced by, German cinema. He frequently screened films such as *The Cabinet of Dr Caligari*, *The Golem* and *Metropolis*.

Whale was often described as aloof and sardonic. Elsa Lanchester, who had known Whale in London and would star in *The Bride of Frankenstein*, described him as a 'bitter man', ascribing this to the failure of his relationship with Doris Zinkeisen.

He seems to have had more respect for actors who had learnt their craft in live theatre rather than in the movies. He would refer to Boris Karloff as 'just a truck driver' and seemed to compete with him for attention on the studio floor when the publicity photographers were around.

Universal Studios was in deep financial trouble when Whale was shooting *Frankenstein*, but the film – made for $250,000 – was one of the most successful films of all time.

As a movie, *Frankenstein* stands up better than *Dracula*, which is stagey and slow. As John Brosnan says in his book *The Horror People,* it has a genuine sense of 'grandeur'. Whale understood the value of a close-up, of tracking shots and a fast narrative pace.

Following the success of *Frankenstein*, Universal Studios decided that Whale would be their horror man. In his next film *The Old Dark House* (1932), he hired his friends from the London stage, Charles Laughton, Raymond Massey and Ernest Thesiger as well as Boris Karloff.

The Old Dark House is funny and camp. It was thought that the film was lost until it was found in the Universal vaults in 1968. All those films which begin with a party of innocents seeking shelter on a dark and stormy night (such as the 1975 film *The Rocky Horror Picture Show*) owe it a debt. It begins in the mud and rain of the Welsh borders (all shot in California, of course) with two couples ending up in the Femm family's terrifying mansion (Karloff is the butler). Gloria Stuart plays Margaret, chastised for her enjoyment of 'fleshly love' by the menacing lady-of-the-house Rebecca (Eva Moore). 'James had me change into a Jean Harlow-style, bias-cut, pale-pink gown with spaghetti straps,' said Stuart. 'He said I want you to appear as a white flame.' In Whale's next picture, *Kiss Before the Mirror* (1933), Gloria Stuart is bumped off in the opening minutes by her eminent doctor husband who is defended in court by his best friend. Whale presented a tiny role to Stuart as a recognition of her fabulous screen presence.

The part of 102-year-old Sir Roderick Femm in *The Old Dark House* went to Elspeth Dudgeon. Said David Lewis: 'Jimmy couldn't find a male actor who looked old enough to suit him, so he finally used an old stage actress he knew called Elspeth Dudgeon. She looked a thousand.'

R. C. Sherriff was commissioned to adapt H. G. Wells' science fiction novel *The Invisible Man*, which would be James Whale's next film (1933). Boris Karloff had been considered for the role of Dr Jack Griffin, the scientist who can make himself invisible. Colin Clive was offered it but he wanted to return to Britain. So Claude Rains took the role.

Whale had known Rains in London and he also had a beautiful speaking voice, which Whale regarded as essential when the character would be unseen until the end of the film.

John P. Fulton (who would win an Oscar for parting the Red Sea in the 1956 epic *The Ten Commandments*) devised the complex special effects which involved much use of non-reflective black velvet on both the set and the stuntman, who had an air hose running up his trouser leg.

Wires were used to lift the books and bottles that were picked up by Griffin. Said Whale: 'I had to devise bits of business so that the audience would know where the man was, what he was doing, and so on. I made him sit in a rocking chair so that by the movements of the chair the audience would realise he was sitting there.' Artists with small paintbrushes added tiny touches to thousands of feet of film to make it visually perfect.

The Bride of Frankenstein (1935), a sequel to *Frankenstein*, was Whale's last horror film and his greatest. He was earning top dollar from Universal now and lived in a Gothic villa at 788 South Amalfi Drive. But he was always careful with his money. 'That they should pay such fabulous salaries is beyond reason,' said the working-class boy from Dudley.

He had little enthusiasm for *Bride* at the outset saying: 'They've had a script made for a sequel and it stinks to high heaven. In any case I squeezed the idea dry on the original picture and never want to work on it again.'

Mae Clarke, who had played the heroine Elizabeth in the original *Frankenstein*, was not cast. She had been Universal's top female lead but in 1933 she was in a car crash and suffered facial injuries. The part went to 18-year-old Valerie Hobson who would marry Jack Profumo, the British politician.

Whale had known from the start that he wanted his old friend Elsa Lanchester to play the bride. He hired Franz Waxman, a German-Jewish composer who had fled Berlin after a beating by Nazi thugs, to compose the score. Whale had been impressed by Waxman's music for Fritz Lang's *Liliom* (1934), which used echo effects and electronic instruments. He had been introduced to Waxman at one of the salons held by Salka Viertel. She was a Hollywood scriptwriter who gathered around her many of the cultural emigrés from Europe and was a close friend of Greta Garbo.

For *Bride*, Waxman created one of the first Hollywood scores to use a symphony orchestra. Afterwards he was appointed head of music at Universal. He wrote the film score for *Rebecca* (1940) and *Sunset Boulevard* (which won an Oscar in 1951) among many others.

The Bride of Frankenstein went $100,000 over budget and Whale's bosses at Universal were not happy with that or, initially, with the film. But it had good reviews and did well at the box office. Since then its reputation has grown and it was described by *The Observer* film critic Philip French as 'the greatest of Universal's gothic horror flicks'. It is, he wrote, 'a confident mixture of camp comedy, gothic melodrama, casual violence and moral commentary on creation and what is meant by "natural"'.

Whale seemed to many an odd choice to direct Oscar Hammerstein and Jerome Kern's musical *Show Boat* (1936). Said Allan Jones who co-starred with Irene Dunne: 'None of us were very happy with Jimmy Whale. It would have been a much better picture with a different director. He was a very strange man. Stand-offish. I never knew what the hell he was thinking.'

Show Boat includes the song *Ol' Man River*, sung by Paul Robeson who became a close friend of Whale's. Said Whale's biographer Mark Gatiss: 'Like *Frankenstein* it has been so often imitated and parodied that it is easy to forget the original impact of this wonderful song.'

The film did well and *Variety* admitted: 'When James Whale was first suggested as the director it was doubted if an Englishman was the best choice for a subject so thoroughly American. Results look as if Whale had been born in the Mississippi.'

The Road Back (1937), a First World War drama based on Erich Maria Remarque's sequel to his novel, *All Quiet on the Western Front*, marked the start of James Whale's decline. The production manager noted in his weekly reports that the director's 'physical and mental condition was a cause for concern and ... he needed to "speed up".' As a publicity stunt the crew was kitted out in German uniforms appropriate to their status. Whale wore beret, greatcoat and boots.

Universal Studios had a German subsidiary and complaints were made by the Germans about the film. Shamefully, Universal decided to cut the film to gain German approval and distribution.

Whale was fired from *The Man in the Iron Mask* (1939) which included a young Peter Cushing in the cast. *Green Hell* (1940) was a lavish jungle adventure with Joan Bennett and Douglas Fairbanks Jr.

Whale's final film was *They Dare Not Love* (1941), made by Columbia Pictures. But he clashed with studio head Harry Cohn, walked off the set and was replaced by Charles Vidor.

Did James Whale's career suffer because of his homosexuality, or because he was difficult to work with, or because he simply grew bored? The director Robert Aldrich is in no doubt that 'Jimmy Whale was the first guy who was blackballed because he refused to stay in the closet.' Jack Warner, the Warner Brothers' boss, thoroughly disapproved of Whale and made his displeasure known when his employee David Lewis turned up at previews with Whale as his plus one.

Douglas Fairbanks Jr said: 'I don't know why Mr Whale went into decline, but it was very possibly because there were several reports that he was difficult to work with and his employers might well have felt that he was not worth the trouble.'

David Lewis bought Whale painting equipment and an easel to help his partner who suddenly had time on his hands. When America entered the war Lewis, almost 40 by now, joined the air force. Whale did his bit by helping organise entertainment for the enlisted men who passed through Los Angeles.

He began a friendship with Curtis Harrington, who was studying film at UCLA and admired Whale's films. 'The great thing about Jimmy was his huge sense of humour,' said Harrington. 'It was delightful, sly and wicked and you see it in all his films. And that's the way he was in real life.'

Whale visited the young man when he moved to Paris. Said Harrington: 'I could manage to go to cheap Left-bank restaurants and stay in little Left-bank hotels. But when Jimmy arrived he stayed in a grand hotel and took me to some very grand restaurants.'

While in Paris, Whale met Pierre Foegel, a 25-year-old man from Strasbourg. Whale offered him a job as a chauffeur. From Paris, they drove to Italy and Switzerland and then to London. Whale rented a flat in Knightsbridge and Pierre did the cleaning and cooking.

When Whale returned to LA with Foegel as his employee/companion, Lewis was devastated and moved out, ending their twenty-three-year relationship. However, their friendship endured during Whale's last years. Foegel remembers the daily routine:

> His life was pretty much on schedule. He'd get up about 7.30 or so and the maid brought him orange juice. Then he had breakfast and went down to his studio and stayed until lunchtime. At 1 pm the maid would call him up and he'd have cold cuts and salad for lunch with a bottle of beer which he drank out of a silver goblet. He was very particular about keeping his beer cold.

There would be gimlets (gin and lime cocktails) in the evening and dinner guests at 7 pm – the old crowd – Mae Clarke, Angela Lansbury, Gladys Cooper, Judith Anderson, Charles Laughton and his wife Elsa Lanchester. Whale lived well; he had been careful with his money.

But he was suffering from depression – he hated ageing. He also suffered from a number of minor strokes and needed the services of a live-in carer.

It was not until 1987 that David Lewis (who died that year) revealed that Whale had left a suicide note, which he had withheld from the authorities as an act of loyalty to his old friend. It read:

> TO ALL I LOVE,
> Do not grieve for me. My nerves are all shot and for the last year I have been in agony day and night – except when I sleep with sleeping pills – and any peace I have by day is when I am drugged by pills.

I have had a wonderful life but it is over, and my nerves get worse and I am afraid they will have to take me away. So please forgive me, all those I love and may God forgive me too, but I cannot bear the agony and it's best for everyone this way.

The future is just old age and illness and pain. Goodbye and thank you for all your love. I must have peace and this is the only way.

Jimmy

Whale had also left a book by his bedside titled *Don't Go Near the Water* – a typical piece of macabre humour.

Whale had grasped instinctively how fleeting a Hollywood career can be. In 1935, he had been one of the highest paid Hollywood directors but he was forgotten within a decade. Yet television would revive the memories of Universal's golden age horror for subsequent generations of horror fans. And Whale's later life was dramatised in *Gods and Monsters* (1999), a film starring Sir Ian McKellen as Whale. Jimmy would have been amazed by such a tribute.

Chapter Seven

Elsa Lanchester – 'A glittering and satiric sprite.'

Thanks to cinema we know how monsters must look. In Bram Stoker's novel *Dracula*, the count is described as 'a tall thin man with a beaky nose and black moustache and pointed beard'. But the image we have of Dracula – evening wear, theatrical cape, blazing eyes – comes from the movies.

In *Frankenstein*, Mary Shelley describes the creature in some detail:

> His yellow skin scarcely covered the work of muscles and arteries beneath; his hair was of a lustrous black, and flowing; his teeth of a pearly whiteness; but these luxuriances only formed a more horrid contrast with his watery eyes, that seemed almost of the same colour as the dun-white sockets in which they were set, his shrivelled complexion and straight black lips.

That's good but it was left to the great make-up artist Jack Pierce to create the monster's flat-headed look that we all know so well.

In the golden age of horror in the 1930s, when cinema was getting to grips with how evil should look on screen, most of the female stars had a contemporary short hairdo, although the actress Carol Borland was an exception. Her straight, waist-length hair was regarded by the studios as a problem. So, when she turned up at the studio's make-up department playing Luna in *Mark of the Vampire* (1935) with Bela Lugosi, they weren't quite sure what to do with her. In the end, her hair was parted in the middle and spirit gum was used to hold back the curtains. And ta-da! the look of the classic female vampire was created, copied by the character Morticia Addams in *The Addams Family* and Yvonne de Carlo as Lily Munster in *The Munsters* – both popular 1960s TV series – and by anyone who wants to look beautifully evil or evilly beautiful.

Elsa Lanchester was another actress who created a definitive look. In *The Bride of Frankenstein* (1935), her mad hair, like an electrified Nefertiti, is unforgettable. She comes across as an entirely new kind of being. Even after more than eighty years, the shock of her appearance is undiminished.

Like many stars of the early horror films, Lanchester was British. She was born Elsa Sullivan Lanchester in Lewisham, south London in 1902.

Her parents James Sullivan and Edith Lanchester were bohemian, free thinkers and unmarried. Edith, the daughter of a prosperous architect, worked as a teacher and then as a secretary to Karl Marx's daughter Eleanor. She was a prominent member of the Marxist Social Democratic Federation (SDF).

When Edith (always called Biddy) was 24, she announced that she planned to live with her lover James 'Shamus' Sullivan, a self-educated Irish socialist who worked in a black lead factory. Her family was appalled.

Biddy insisted that marriage was immoral and that she could not countenance losing her independence. She was subjected to an examination by a leading psychiatrist of the time, Dr George Fielding Blandford, and committed under the 1890 Lunacy Act. After being forcibly restrained and bundled off to the Priory Hospital in Roehampton, the SDF mobilised and members stood outside the asylum singing *The Red Flag*.

As it turned out Biddy wasn't kept in for long, though after her release she refused to see her father again and the 'Lanchester Kidnapping Case' made headlines round the world. The Marquess of Queensberry (of Queensberry Rules fame) offered the couple £100 if they'd marry at a big church then get up on the altar to deny their vows. The lovers ignored the offer.

Their first child, Waldo, was born in 1897. Elsa followed in 1902. Some of her first memories were of meeting the comrades at May Day marches from Charing Cross Embankment to Hyde Park. There wasn't much money.

'Wherever we lived', writes Elsa in her autobiography *Elsa Lanchester – Herself*, 'we had The Kitchen and not much more – with luck, two bedrooms or a front room with two camp beds. The bathroom and WC we shared with the people above us or below us.' A flat in Clapham 'had that cabbage smell that goes with no money'. Her parents' unmarried status ensured that 'a vague scent of notoriety seemed to be in the air we breathed'. The Kitchen was where comrades and friends gathered to plan the revolution or have tea.

Biddy was ever one of the awkward squad, always anti-authority. She went so far as to take the children camping in the woods so that their names would not be recorded on the 1911 census.

She was a terrible cook and a vegetarian. James often yearned for meat and would sometimes be allowed a pig's head boiled in vinegar or the occasional bloater. Elsa yearned for meat too and would spend her penny pocket money on Oxo or Bovril cubes, which she cut into four and chewed.

Of course, Biddy was a suffragette and Elsa remembered going to the funeral of Emily Wilding Davison who threw herself in front of the king's horse on Derby Day, 1913. Biddy and Shamus also had a parrot who would screech 'Votes for Women' from an open window.

Elsa was always keen on ballet, and Biddy took her to see Anna Pavlova dance *The Dying Swan*. She began to attend free classes at Crosby Hall in Chelsea given by Raymond Duncan, an American businessman who affected a hand-woven gown 'with a Greek filet binding his long hair'. He was also Isadora Duncan's brother. Through this contact Elsa was one of twenty children picked to attend Isadora Duncan's dance school in Bellevue, Paris. The school was based in a hotel which had been given to Duncan by her lover Paris Singer (of the sewing machine family).

The girls danced for three hours in the morning and were then driven to perhaps the Louvres or Versailles in a fleet of Rolls-Royces. Appearing on the *Dick Cavett Show* on TV in 1970, Elsa dismissed Isadora Duncan as 'an untalented bag of beans'. When war threatened, Elsa went back to England, as did most of the children.

She attended a co-educational boarding school in Berkshire for a few days but hated it and caught the train back to London. After that she went to her brother Waldo's school in Clapham but dropped out of full-time education at the age of 13. 'I'm not educated,' she would say, 'but I'm smart'.

She joined the Margaret Morris school of dance in London where she met Angela and Hermione Baddeley. Angela would later play Mrs Bridges, the cook, in the TV series *Upstairs Downstairs*.

There was an ad in the showbiz paper *The Era*: 'Wanted snake dancer. Young, attractive for *A Night in Egypt*. Apply Ida Barr, Edmonton Royal Theatre, £2 a week.' Elsa got the job, her first professional engagement.

When she left, Ida told her, 'You're really too good for this you know, and you'll be a big success, someday, you'll see.'

Elsa was now independent and making a living in a variety of ways. She taught dance once a week at Bedales, the progressive school in Petersfield, Hampshire. From 1918 she ran classes and staged productions for young people, two evenings a week at The Children's Theatre in central London. Though this was closed down by the London County Council claiming it exploited children. She posed nude for artists and photographers. She acted as correspondent for couples who wanted a divorce, which was quite well paid and after all 'it was acting'.

In 1922, she was finally acting on stage in *The Insect Play*, a satire by Karel Capek at London's Regent Theatre with John Gielgud, Claude Rains and Angela Baddeley. She was in a couple of productions at the Lyric Hammersmith, the Garrick and the Everyman Theatre.

In 1924, she – along with her boyfriend Harold Scott, an actor – started up an avant-garde nightclub called the Cave of Harmony in Charlotte Street, Fitzrovia. They performed dramatic readings, exotic dancing and one-act plays after midnight when the West End theatres had closed.

It became a fashionable haunt. Regulars included H. G. Wells, Aldous Huxley, Evelyn Waugh and the film and theatre director James Whale. In his posthumously published diaries, Waugh describes a garret party he attended with her and her 'set' of 'pansies, prostitutes and journalists'. Huxley was so fascinated with the place that he featured it in his novel *Antic Hay*. Lanchester claimed she originated the costume of top hat, fishnet tights and high heels later used by Marlene Dietrich in the film *Blue Angel* (1930).

Elsa was also a founding member of the 1917 Club in Soho's Gerrard Street, attracting socialists and intellectuals. In fact, she was beginning to be noticed. The essayist and travel writer Douglas Goldring said: 'Her flaming red-gold hair, exotic costume and gamine appearance had a startling effect.'

At parties, she wore severe men's suits with a gardenia. She moved to a room in a house in 43 Belsize Park Gardens owned by the writer Mary Butts described by her lover, the composer Virgil Thomson, as 'adept at magic, a smoker of opium, a poet and author of novels and stories'. Elsa remembered the notorious occultist Aleister Crowley turning up on his bike, shaven-headed and wearing a yellow kilt.

She met her husband-to-be Charles Laughton for the first time in 1927 at rehearsals for Arnold Bennett's *Mr Prohack*. His mother had been a Scarborough barmaid who through sheer hard work saved up enough to buy a hotel. She was a devout Catholic and determined that none of her three sons should be 'in trade'. Laughton went to RADA in 1925 and immediately began to make his mark in West End theatre.

He encouraged Lanchester to dress more conservatively and took her to Hermine of Bond Street for some new bespoke lingerie.

They lived together in a tiny flat in Percy Street off the Tottenham Court Road. Notwithstanding Elsa's fancy underwear, their home was crawling with bed bugs.

She had an abortion before they married in 1929. It was her second. The first time, Tallulah Bankhead had found an abortionist for her. Charles sometimes wished they'd had children but Elsa did not. Their relationship is something of a puzzle and it seems they married because they were becoming a well-known couple and the public demanded that they regularised their relationship. 'Public opinion led us up to the brink of respectability – respectability we weren't living,' wrote Elsa.

In her autobiography, she is frank about Laughton's homosexuality and less so about her own leanings. The reader is left with the impression that she was more or less indifferent to sex.

Nevertheless, Charles's infidelity distressed her. They had been married two years when he came home one evening and the police stopped him at the door. A boy had been demanding money. Laughton was in tears but Elsa comforted him: 'It's perfectly all right, it doesn't matter. I understand it. Don't worry about it.'

In 1931, the couple went to New York when the Jeffrey Dell play *Payment Deferred* (based on a crime novel by C. S. Forester) transferred to Broadway. They then went to Hollywood when Laughton was cast in James Whale's film *The Old Dark House*, released in 1932. Whale, originally from Dudley, told him: 'You will love it here in Hollywood, Charles. I'm pouring money through my hair and enjoying every minute of it.'

A film version of *Payment Deferred* was also made. Laughton plays a married bank clerk who murders his rich young nephew. On stage Elsa had played Laughton's 12-year-old daughter Winnie. A rather queasy piece of casting. But when it came to the film version, Maureen O'Sullivan was offered the role. Lanchester was humiliated and angry and – for a time – very anti-Hollywood.

She returned to London, living over the L'Etoile restaurant in Charlotte Street and then in a flat in Gordon Square in the heart of Bloomsbury.

Her next project with Laughton was in Alexander Korda's *The Private Life of Henry VIII*. Lanchester played Anne of Cleves to Laughton's Henry. The British film was a huge international success and cemented Laughton as a film star. He won an Academy Award for Best Actor.

But it wasn't much of a calling card for Elsa. She wrote:

> As Anne of Cleves I had done my best to look like hell in order to keep the character of Henry VIII at arm's length. I made myself look as ugly as possible and in addition the cameraman lit my nose so that it would look like a potato – knobbier than usual at the top.

Hollywood never knew quite what to make of Elsa Lanchester. She was not conventionally beautiful but she had a mesmerising presence. When she played Peter Pan on stage, chosen by Sir James Barrie himself, Tyrone Guthrie described her as 'a glittering and satiric sprite'.

The playwright Bertolt Brecht said she was the only person 'who filled the frame of a proscenium arch in the same way that the Japanese did in a print'. She, meanwhile, objected to Brecht's smelly cigars.

For someone who was so independent, it feels as though she subjugated her own career to Laughton's, always happy to appear with him in a small role. Her first book of memoirs, published in 1937, was tellingly called *Charles Laughton and I*. He always came first.

The couple returned to London to do a season at the Old Vic along with Roger Livesey, Athene Seyler, James Mason, Flora Robson and Marius Goring. There was a production of *The Tempest* with Elsa playing Ariel to Laughton's Prospero – very much as she did in life.

Back again in Los Angeles, James Whale offered her the part which, like it or not, would define her. The 1931 *Frankenstein* with Boris Karloff had been a money-spinner for Universal and a follow-up was expected to do as well. In fact, many critics still regard *The Bride of Frankenstein* as the better film.

Lanchester plays Mary Shelley at the beginning of the film, looking demure and pretty. She wore a white net dress embroidered with sequins of butterflies, stars, and moons, which had taken seventeen women twelve weeks to make. After the prologue, she then appears for no more than a few minutes as the monster's unearthly bride.

In her autobiography, she writes:

> I think James Whale felt that if this beautiful and innocent
> Mary Shelley could write such a horror story as *Frankenstein*
> then somewhere she must have the fiend within, dominating
> a part of her thoughts and her spirit – like ectoplasm flowing
> out of her to activate a monster. In this delicate little thing
> was an unexploded atom bomb. My playing both parts
> cemented the idea.

She didn't get on well with Jack Pierce, Universal's make-up artist. 'He
would be dressed in a full hospital doctor's operating outfit. At five in
the morning that made me dislike him intensely. Then for three or four
hours the "Lord" would do his creative work with never a word spoke.'

To achieve the Nefertiti hair, four tiny, tight plaits were made on
top of her head. On these was anchored a wired horsehair cage about
five inches high. Then her own hair was brushed over this structure and
two white hair pieces (the lightning bolts) were attached – one from the
right temple and one from the left cheekbone. She was also wrapped in
bandages and a shroud-like robe. Going to the loo was a terrible palaver
so Elsa drank as little tea as possible on set.

The effect was fantastic. The film historian Carlos Clarens wrote in
An Illustrated History of the Horror Film: 'A delicate suggestion of both
the wedding bed and the grave.'

Elsa Lanchester made many films after *The Bride of Frankenstein*,
often with Laughton. They included *Rembrandt* (1936), *The
Beachcomber* (1938), *Tales of Manhattan* (1942), *The Big Clock* (1948)
and *Witness for the Prosecution* (1957). She also appeared in *The Ghost
Goes West* (1935), *The Spiral Staircase* (1945), *The Inspector General*
(1949), *Androcles and the Lion* (1953), *Bell, Book and Candle* (1958),
Mary Poppins (1964), *Willard* (1971) and *Murder by Death* (1976).

But her great love was cabaret, and from the early 1940s she appeared
at the Turnabout Theatre in Los Angeles, playing characters who danced
and sang in her own quirky vaudeville show. She gave more than 3,200
performances in the 1940s and 1950s, always insisting that the women's roles
she took on were upbeat, but seeing her perform was an edgy experience.

The New Yorker critic summed it up like this: 'There is a desperate
quality about her art; in some curious way she taker her listeners out of

a close, tidy world and into a disquieting place filled with sharp winds and unsteady laughter.'

Settled in Hollywood, the Laughtons were criticised for deserting Britain during the Second World War. When she took her cabaret show to the Café de Paris in London for four weeks after the war, a cabbie harangued her.

Their marriage continued as it had started, with Charles usually having a young male lover who helped with domestic admin and Elsa making the best of it.

Later in his career, when they were living in Santa Monica (next door to Christopher Isherwood), Charles met Peter Jones, whom he bankrolled through drama school, lying to Elsa about how much he had been paid for the 1960 war film *Under Ten Flags* so he could funnel some of the money towards Peter.

'Charles really didn't have to lie to me,' she says in her autobiography. 'I had always said that he should do everything he wanted with the money he earned. But Charles's guilt about me was eating him through. I was not aware of it. If only we could have talked to each other.'

She didn't dislike Peter, though she complained about how much he ate. 'He had a bottomless stomach,' she grumbled.

Charles died of bone cancer, aged 63, in December 1962. A heavily built man, he weighed less than 90 lbs at the end. It was a long, painful death and Elsa felt a sense of release when it was over: 'I was a kind of Ariel who was being freed from Prospero.'

She lived on until 1986, but she suffered a series of strokes and was virtually comatose in her last years.

Her life had been extraordinary, partly because she lived through two world wars but also because she was at the heart of intellectual and artistic life in both London and Hollywood. Writing about the Bloomsbury Group (she knew all of them) she says: 'It seems a great thing to have been born when I was and to have tasted at this feast without knowing it. I wish now that I'd tried harder.'

Yet she will always be remembered for *The Bride of Frankenstein* and without that she would be merely a footnote, one of the cast of extraordinarily creative people in 1920s London. Making the film occupied her for less than a fortnight. And brought her immortality.

Chapter Eight

Val Lewton – 'The sultan of shudders.'

What does a film producer do exactly? It's a title which covers many aspects of film-making and includes co-ordinating scripts, editors, directors and putting the financing in place. It can vary but it's usually the director who we think of as being the creative force behind a film. The director gets the all-important end credit, not the producer. But producer Val Lewton was something of an exception in that he put his very personal stamp on the distinctive and influential horror films he made for RKO in the 1940s.

Vladimir Ivanovich Hofschneider was born in 1904 in Yalta (then in Russia, now in Ukraine) the son of moneylender Max Hofschneider and Anna 'Nina' Leventon, a pharmacist's daughter. Max died of pneumonia when Val was a small boy and Nina took her two children first to Berlin and then to New York. Here Nina, who had retained her surname of Leventon, went to work as a housekeeper for her well-known actress sister Alla Nazimova.

Catapulted from a life of relative poverty in Berlin to his aunt's flamboyant New York establishment, young Val seems to have been an eccentric little boy. He would recite poems loudly at bus stops and was sent to the New York Military Academy to learn a little discipline.

His first job was as a reporter at New York's night court. He was fired from a job as the gossip columnist for the *Darien-Stamford Review* when it was discovered that he had invented a story about a truckload of chickens dying during a heatwave. He then went on to study at Columbia University's School of Journalism, though he dropped out without completing his course.

In 1924, he published his first novel *The Improved Road*, and would become a successful writer of pulp fiction novels. His best-known book, written in 1932, is *No Bed of Her Own*, a story of a woman stenographer who loses her job in Depression-hit New York. Written from the woman's point of view it is a powerful novel, one of the first to deal with the Depression, and though dated it stands up well today. Another recommendation is that it was included in the list of books that Hitler ordered to be burned.

By now Val Lewton was married to Ruth Knapp and at the time of the Great Crash in 1929 they were living in Greenwich Village. Ruth gave birth to a daughter, Ruth Nina, on 7 May 1930. A son, Val, would be born in 1937.

Nina Leventon, Val's mother, was by now working for MGM's script department. David O. Selznick had taken over from Irving Thalberg as production head of MGM and was considering making a film adaptation of Gogol's *Taras Bulba*.

He asked Nina to send him a list of five well-known writers of Russian extraction who might write the script. Nina's list included her son Val.

As a result, Lewton and his family moved to Hollywood in 1934. The *Taras Bulba* project was shelved, much to Lewton's disappointment, but Selznick offered him the post of secretary and assistant at $75 a week.

Val Lewton became Selznick's Man Friday, involved in opulent productions such as *Anna Karenina* (1935) starring Greta Garbo and Fredric March and *A Tale of Two Cities* (1935) with Ronald Colman.

Selznick then set up Selznick International Pictures which, though it was dissolved in 1943, made an outstanding crop of Hollywood hits including *A Star is Born* (1937), *The Prisoner of Zenda* (1937), *Nothing Sacred* (1937), *The Adventures of Tom Sawyer* (1938) and *Intermezzo* (1939) with Leslie Howard and Ingrid Bergman. In 1939, Selznick teamed up with MGM to make the historical epic *Gone with the Wind*.

Lewton bought the rights to Daphne Du Maurier's novel *Rebecca* for $50,000. Alfred Hitchcock was invited to direct it and in an interview in the 5 November 1938 edition of *Film Weekly* he said:

> I shall treat this more or less as a horror film, building up
> my violent situations from incidents such as one in which
> the young wife innocently appears at the annual fancy-dress
> ball given by her husband in a frock identical with the one
> worn by his first wife a year previously.

Such phrases as 'horror film' would not have endeared Hitchcock to Selznick, who was as passionate about literary classics as Lewton and demanded that Hitchcock ditch his first 'vulgarised' script and produce a more faithful and respectful rewrite. *Rebecca* was released in 1940 and won an Oscar for best picture.

In 1942, following the expensive box-office disaster that was Orson Welles's *Citizen Kane*, RKO hired Val Lewton to help get them out of the red. The studio had made *King Kong* in 1933, the Fred Astaire and Ginger Rogers musicals, and a host of screwball comedies. But the old gag doing the rounds was, 'In case of an air raid, go directly to RKO. They haven't had a hit in years.'

RKO needed a rescue strategy and Charles Koerner, vice president of the company, believed that a slew of cheap-to-make, box-office friendly horror moves would do the job. Universal Studios, who had cashed in on the first horror boom with *Frankenstein* and *Dracula,* were still making them but the product had become increasingly trashy.

Lewton's contract with RKO stipulated that his films would cost no more than $150,00 and none would exceed seventy-five minutes. He would be paid $250 a week and would be obliged to work from 'pre-tested titles'.

Lewton began screening old horror movies to get a handle on his new job. His melancholy disposition meant that he was attracted to the atmosphere of German Expressionist films and he also liked Gothic novels and Victorian ghost stories.

He knew that RKO expected him to produce cheap schlock horror. But Lewton had other ideas. The limitations of the tight budgets meant that monsters and effects could not be shown in their full glory. They had to be suggested by a combination of setting, shadow, light, sound and silence. He was also accustomed to turning jobs around quickly – he wrote his pulp fiction novels by checking into cheap hotel rooms for the weekend and writing the whole time.

He made eleven films for RKO. The first was *Cat People* (1942), directed by Jacques Tourneur. Lewton quickly established a team that worked together closely. Screenwriter DeWitt Bodeen wrote a script inspired by a magazine layout that showed fashion models wearing cat masks. Bodeen recalled that Lewton 'would move to the light switch of his office, turn off the lights quickly, and continue recounting the story in the darkened room.'

According to Ruth Lewton, Val drew on an atavistic fear of cats that he traced back to his Russian Jewish heritage. 'Of course, he knew better,' she says in Joel Siegel's book *Val Lewton: The Reality of Terror*.

'He was a very intellectual man and not a superstitious person – and so he was both frightened and fascinated by fear.'

Set in New York, Simone Simon plays Irena, a Serbian fashion designer recently married to marine engineer Oliver (Kent Smith). They are unable to consummate their marriage because of Irena's belief in an old legend that if she gives herself to her husband she will turn into a panther and kill him.

The film contains two of the most famous scenes in the horror genre. In one, Alice (played by Jane Randolph), who is Oliver's assistant (and secretly in love with him), is walking home by Central Park and is increasingly afraid that she is being followed.

The tension mounts and suddenly a terrifying hiss makes the audience jump out of their seats. But it's not the supernatural panther, it's the airbrakes of a bus pulling up beside her – an idea which came from the film's editor Mark Robson. Hereafter, this technique of ramping up tension and diffusing it was known as a 'Lewton bus'.

In the other scene, Alice is swimming happily in an indoor pool when suddenly shadows surround her. We see nothing clearly, only her growing terror. The shadow of the 'panther' on the wall was Tourneur's fist. He had experienced something similar while swimming in an outdoor pool when a cheetah had started to prowl round the edge only to be shooed away by a gardener.

When Koerner saw the first cut of *Cat People*, he was disappointed. There were not enough shots of the black panther that the studio had rented at considerable expense. Yet the film had been finished in twenty-four days and it was $7,000 under budget. It was also a box office hit and was quickly established as a cult classic. Paul Schrader would remake the film in 1982.

In *I Walked with a Zombie* (1943), also directed by Tourneur, Lewton made a voodoo version of Charlotte Bronte's *Jane Eyre* set on the fictional Caribbean island of Saint Sebastian. It's a beautiful, elegant film. Particularly memorable is the eerie night walk of Betsy and Jessica through the sugarcane fields.

Tourneur's final film with Lewton was *The Leopard Man* (1943), an adaptation of Cornell Woolrich's novel *Black Alibi* – about a series of deaths which may be caused by an escaped leopard.

Another key visual scene here is when a young girl, forced by her cruel mother to go on an errand, screams to be let back in her home.

The clue to her fate is the thick pool of blood seeping under the front door. Monochrome blood would never look as good again until the shower scene in Hitchcock's *Psycho* (1960).

The Ghost Ship (1943) ran into a copywriting dispute and was withdrawn and unseen until a print turned up in the 1990s. A sailor (played by Russell Wade) realises that the captain of the ship (played by Richard Dix) is a psychopathic killer. Again, in *Psycho*, Hitchcock would take up the theme of the madman who seems entirely normal, a recurring theme in modern psychological horror films.

Mark Robson moved into the director's chair for *The Seventh Victim* (1943) in which Mary Gibson (played by Kim Hunter) goes to New York to find her missing sister, who has fallen in with a cult called the Palladists who pose such lofty questions as 'what proof can you bring that good is superior to evil?'

DeWitt Bodeen, who would work with Charles O'Neal (father of Ryan O'Neal) on the script, went to a meeting of New York satanists. They were mostly old people, he reported, drinking tea and doing knitting and crochet. In fact, years later he would say they were 'exactly like the devil worshippers in *Rosemary's Baby*'.

This chilling, morbid film ends with a suicide and a quote from John Donne's *Holy Sonnets*: 'I run to death and death meets me as fast, and all my pleasures are like yesterday.'

Val Lewton paid almost no attention to the 'pre-tested title' in his next film *Curse of the Cat People* (1944), a melodrama about a little girl's disturbed fantasies. She, Amy (played by Ann Carter), is the daughter of Alice and Ollie from *Cat People* who sees visions of Irena (Simone Simon).

The RKO promotion team never held back when publicising Lewton's horror films and often misrepresented them with garish slogans and pictures. Lewton would be called the 'sultan of shudders', 'the titan of terror' and the 'maharajah of mayhem'. Mark Robson said: 'We would ask the heads of the advertising unit to please not use the god-damned "fur" letters and other trick lettering that gave one a supposed sense of horror.'

The distinguished film critic James Agee – who championed Lewton's films – wrote:

> And when the picture ended and it was clear beyond further
> suspense that anyone who had come to see a story about

curses and were-cats should have stayed away, they clearly did not feel sold out: for an hour they had been captivated by the poetry and danger of childhood and showed it in their applause.

The director of *Curse of the Cat People* was Robert Wise who would go on to make *West Side Story* (1961) and *The Sound of Music* (1965). He said: 'When we finished the film and showed it for groups of teachers and child psychologists they all loved it.'

Reluctant at first, Lewton had to use Boris Karloff in *Isle of the Dead* (1945). Inspiration for the film came from Arnold Böcklin's painting of the same name, reproduced many times in the late nineteenth and early twentieth century. In his novel *Despair*, Vladimir Nabokov says that a print could be 'found in every Berlin home'.

It's a creepy painting, a tiny island dominated by dark cypress trees. A small boat is drawing up. There's a mysterious figure in white and something that looks like a coffin. It was also used as set dressing in *I Walked with a Zombie*.

A group of travellers is trapped on a Greek island because of an outbreak of the plague. Karloff plays General Pherides, an obsessive hand-washer who cracks under pressure. The scene where the British consul's wife wakes up in her coffin is particularly memorable.

Despite early reservations, Lewton came to admire Karloff greatly and in *The Body Snatchers* (1945), directed by Robert Wise, he also gave a role to the elderly and infirm Bela Lugosi – the two grand old men of Universal horror, reunited. It's a period drama, an adaptation of the Robert Louis Stevenson story, based on the infamous doings of Burke and Hare in Edinburgh. It proved to be Lewton's biggest box-office success since *Cat People* and it was very popular in the UK.

Youth Runs Wild (1944) and *Mademoiselle Fifi* (1944) were not horror films but Lewton returned to the genre for the final time with *Bedlam* (1946), again starring Boris Karloff and directed by Mark Robson. Horror was once more falling out of fashion – Lewton's view was that after the war the public wanted comedies and spectaculars, while during wartime they liked horror as long as it was not the mass slaughter of war.

But films about mental illness were very much on trend with this eighteenth-century historical drama set in London's St Mary of Bethlehem asylum where the heroine, a courtesan called Nell Bowen (played by Anna Lee), is wrongly incarcerated. Lee found herself costumed in Vivien Leigh's dress from *Gone with the Wind* which Scarlett makes out of the curtains.

With such a rich body of work, you would imagine that Val Lewton would have been happy with his achievement. But he was a difficult, sometimes paranoid man who felt that his bosses at RKO were out to get him, and he was also aware that the studio system was failing and that television threatened to completely change the way that people found their entertainment.

He could be charming and patient but he also had a terrible temper. Mark Robson said, 'In a way, I think [Val] was a man who needed an enemy.'

Apart from his (real) phobia of cats, it has been said that he had a problem with women and hated to be touched. He seems to have been in awe of his highly intelligent mother, and of Aunt Alla who could never understand why he was making low-budget horror films and refused to go and see them. His wife Ruth was very much under his thumb, and though he got on well with his son he did not get on well with his daughter.

DeWitt Bodeen said that Lewton didn't like working with women writers. The only one he would tolerate was Ardel Wray who co-wrote *I Walked with a Zombie* with Curt Siodmak.

He left RKO and moved to Paramount where he produced *My Own True Love* (1949) starring Phyllis Calvert and Melvyn Douglas. Calvert detested Lewton.

His final film was *Apache Drums* (1951) directed by Hugo Fregonese. But his health was failing and he died of a heart attack on 14 March 1951 aged 46.

Like many who make horror films or appear in them, Lewton would probably not have wanted to go down in history as a horror guy. Yet his disposition fitted the brief. His son Val said of him: 'I think my father was really very pessimistic and that came out in his films. The whole dialogue with death – he was obsessed with it.'

His influence can be seen in any horror film where a heroine must take a long walk lit by pools of light from street lamps, such as *Phantom of the Rue Morgue* (1954). *Cat Girl* (1957), a British horror film starring Barbara Shelley, was an unofficial but effective remake of *Cat People*.

Richard Matheson, who wrote horror novels and scripts including *I Am Legend* and *The Incredible Shrinking Man*, was a fan of Lewton's work. He said, 'I remember distinctly, when I was 17, seeing *Cat People* and being incredibly impressed. I loved Val Lewton's movies.'

He even wrote a letter to Lewton identifying some of the techniques that he'd observed in his films, such as leading the viewer's eyes to one side of the screen and then having something pop out on the other side of the screen. Or the technique of having a long silence broken by a sudden noise. These were tricks used by John Carpenter in his film *Halloween* (1978) before he abandoned 'less is more' and the comically gruesome *Halloween* cycle became associated with slasher films where 'more is more'.

'Horror spots must be well planned and there should be no more than four or five in a picture,' said Lewton. 'Most of them are caused by the fundamental fears: sudden sound, wild animals, darkness. The horror addicts will populate the darkness with more horrors than all the horror writers in Hollywood could think of.'

At the meeting where Lewton was told he had to work with Karloff, the news came from a studio boss who was new to RKO called Jack Gross. 'I now find myself working for an abysmally ignorant and stupid gentleman called Jack Gross,' Lewton wrote to his mother.

As Gross ended the meeting about Karloff, an executive called Holt spoke up: 'Remember!,' he said, pointing at Lewton. 'No messages!' What he meant was that films should be pure entertainment and nothing deeper or more demanding. Lewton left without a word, but he was furious. He had his secretary get Holt on the line. 'I'm sorry, but we do have a message, Mr. Holt,' he shouted down the phone. 'And our message is that death is good!'

Chapter Nine

Terence Fisher – 'A director for hire.'

In David Thomson's *A Biographical Dictionary of the Cinema*, first published in 1975, he wrote that Hammer horror films 'have always seemed the work of decent men who tended their gardens at weekends. This is sadly true of Terence Fisher, the man responsible for most of them.' Thomson wasn't a fan of Fisher's nor, possibly, gardens.

Yet no history of the horror genre can ignore Terence Fisher, though it's true that he was resolutely unpretentious about what he did. 'It is no good going into a long spiel of intellectual bullshit about why you do things and why do don't,' he said. He was, he always insisted, merely 'a director for hire'.

In his foreword to Wheeler Winston Dixon's biography of Fisher, John Carpenter, director of the original *Halloween* (1978), writes: 'Anybody who has made a horror picture since 1957 has been influenced by Terence Fisher.'

Fisher directed fifty films in all, not all horror by any means, but it was *The Curse of Frankenstein*, made in 1957, which kickstarted his career in horror with the Hammer studio.

Hammer films were very much the product of teamwork and a team that stuck together for many years. There were the producers Michael Carreras and Anthony Hinds, the writers Jimmy Sangster and John Elder (Elder was Hinds' pen name), the cinematographer Jack Asher, the editor James Needs, the production designer Bernard Robinson, the composer James Bernard and of course actors Christopher Lee and Peter Cushing.

So why is Fisher's role as director so significant? Before we look at that we must ask why film directors as a whole are considered so crucial to the tone, the look and the vision of a film. It isn't the same in live theatre. There are a few theatre directors – such as Trevor Nunn, for instance – who become household names. But usually it's the playwright and the cast which get the lion's share of the critical attention.

The pre-eminent role of the film director rests with the auteur theory, which was defined by the critics who wrote for the French film magazine *Cahiers du Cinéma*, founded in 1951 by André Bazin. In January 1954, an article by François Truffaut attacked 'la qualité francaise', the tradition of dutiful literary adaptations in French cinema for being plodding and simplistic. He and other critics insisted that the vision of the director was the crucial element in a film and this is what the American film critic Andrew Sarris then termed the auteur theory.

These critics who went on to become dazzling young film-makers included Claude Chabrol, Jean-Luc Godard, Eric Rohmer and Jacques Rivette. But auteur theory also became a way of re-evaluating films by Hollywood directors such as John Ford, Howard Hawks and John Huston.

Though modern critical theory tends to place less importance on the guiding hand of an individual and more on socio-political factors that shape a film, auteur theory is still influential. We have expectations of a Hitchcock thriller, the latest film from the Spanish director Pedro Almodóvar, the new horror movie from Jordan Peele. Cinemagoers who don't really know what a director does technically will still claim to admire certain directors and have an idea of what to expect from their work.

Terence Fisher, out of modesty perhaps and a typically British reluctance to intellectualise what he did, insisted: 'All a director is, please, is an interpreter of the written word.'

Yet as it turns out, Fisher became one of the few British directors to attract real critical attention, though only when his career was virtually over. David Pirie, in his important book *A Heritage of Horror*, first published in 1973, championed Terence Fisher's work against the charges that it was crudely sensational and yet pedestrian at the same time. Of his films Pirie writes: 'They have a quality of robustness, a peculiarly bizarre and English form of logic within fantasy and a powerful atmosphere augmented by underlying sexuality.'

Fisher was an only child born in Maida Vale, London on 3 February 1904 and educated at Christ's Hospital School in Horsham, Sussex. His father had died when he was 4 and, with the encouragement of his mother, he left school at the age of 16 to join the Merchant Navy.

He said in an interview in 1974: 'I went to sea for three years' apprenticeship, as it was called then, joined the P&O as a junior officer, and decided that a lifetime at sea wasn't for me.'

A stint with the John Lewis department store followed and it was during this period that he began to go to the cinema as often as he could. But it wasn't until 1933 that he went to work for Gaumont-British at the Lime Grove Studios in Shepherd's Bush (acquired by the BBC in 1949) as possibly the oldest clapper boy in the business.

He slowly worked his way up as third assistant director, assistant director and in 1936 he was the editor on *Tudor Rose*, directed by Robert Stevenson, the story of Lady Jane Grey starring Cedric Hardwicke, Nova Pilbeam and a young John Mills. Film editors were classified as a reservist occupation so Fisher was never in uniform during the war.

In 1945, he edited *The Wicked Lady* for Gainsborough, directed by Leslie Arliss and starring Margaret Lockwood as a nobleman's wife who becomes a highwaywoman for kicks. But he had met his wife Morag during the war years and she encouraged him to apply for the Rank Organisation's programme for film directors.

Once he was with Rank, Fisher's directorial debut came in 1947 with *Colonel Bogey*, a fifty-one-minute supernatural comedy produced at Highbury Studios, intended as a second feature. *To the Public Danger* (1948) was based on a radio play by Patrick Hamilton, a very effective short on drunk driving and the post-war blues of the late 1940s starring Dermot Walsh, Susan Shaw and baby-faced Roy Plomley as a committed drunk: 'Whisky every time! Gin's for women and children.' His next film was *Song for Tomorrow* (1948) about a fighter pilot suffering from amnesia with Christopher Lee in a small role.

Fisher's many years as an editor stood him in good stead. According to Morag:

> Being an editor he 'worked to the cut' so to speak so that there was no wasted film and everything was all there. He never storyboarded things. He basically had all the continuity in his head ... . He looked at the rushes every evening. He would leave at six in the morning and get home at eight at night. And he didn't do any reshooting or practically none.

He moved from Rank to Gainsborough where he co-directed four feature films with Antony Darnborough, who had been a gossip columnist with the *Daily Mail* and whose father Bill Darnborough claimed to have been one of the men who broke the bank at Monte Carlo.

So Long at the Fair (1950) was Fisher's final film with Gainsborough. It is a costume drama starring Jean Simmons as Vicky Barton, visiting Paris with her brother during the World Fair of 1889. The pair book into a hotel but the next morning Vicky can find no trace of her brother or of his room. Desperate, she enlists the help of George Hathaway (played by Dirk Bogarde), a British artist living in Paris. Eventually the puzzle is solved. Johnny had contracted the bubonic plague and the authorities had done their utmost to conceal this horror, even to the extent of sealing up his hotel room. The themes of pestilence, corruption and a sealed room take this film into classic horror territory.

Gainsborough closed in the early 1950s and Fisher spent several years directing low-budget support features, mostly for Eros Films Ltd (named after the company's proximity to the statue at Piccadilly Circus rather than for any erotic content).

His first film for Hammer was *The Last Page* (released in 1952 with the come-hitherish title *Man Bait* in the US), a film noir starring Diana Dors. Fisher admired Dors: 'She had been one of the Rank starlets and I can very well remember being impressed at the time by her great potential talent. I've never known her give a bad performance.'

He was always generous about actors, liked being with them and regretted how little time the tight production schedules allowed for rehearsal. Sometimes, he acknowledged, there was barely time for a complete read through with the cast before filming began.

Stolen Face (1952) stars Paul Henreid as a plastic surgeon who falls in love with a woman (Lizabeth Scott) who is engaged to another man. The surgeon recreates her face and grafts it on to the face of a woman criminal suffering from a facial deformity. Big mistake.

In *Four Sided Triangle* (1953), Lena, Bill and Robin are childhood chums in a sleepy English village. Bill is a genius and with Robin's help, in a makeshift laboratory, invents a 'reproducer' which can duplicate anything. It's rather like the machine in the sci-fi horror movie *The Fly*.

Lena chooses Robin over Bill. In despair, Bill asks Lena for permission to reproduce her so he can have her too. And as we know, any attempt by man to play God will not end well.

Fisher was never greatly interested in science fiction – though he made several sci-fi films in the 1960s – but the moral and philosophical implications appear again and again in his work. James Hayter plays the village doctor who observes these goings-on. Stephen Murray, John Van Eyssen and Barbara Peyton play the troubled threesome.

Many directors and actors seemed to resent working in the horror genre, nervous of being trapped and pigeonholed, aware of the critical opprobrium that the films attracted. But Fisher seemed to relish the direction he was taking, as though it offered a sort of freedom.

In the early 1950s he also worked in television. There was a series called *Colonel March Investigates* with Boris Karloff as Colonel March, heading Scotland Yard's Department of Queer Complaints. He also directed episodes of *The Adventures of Robin Hood* starring Richard Greene. He never cared to venture into live TV saying that: 'In cinema there is a fascination about working out of sequence.'

Following the success of the *Quatermass* films, Hammer conducted a survey of viewers' attitudes and found that it was the horror element which appealed to audiences rather than the sci-fi. Having dabbled in a variety of genres since its inception in 1935 with *The Public Life of Henry the Ninth* (a spoof of Alexander Korda's *The Private Life of Henry the Eighth* two years earlier), Hammer was now ready to begin making the movies that would define it forever in the public consciousness – horror films. And in Fisher it had a director who, as his biographer Wheeler Winston Dixon states, would make 'a cycle of films that would stand as one of the great achievements of the British cinema. These films amounted to nothing less than a complete revitalisation of the horror film.'

The Curse of Frankenstein (1957), directed by Fisher, was the first. Originally it was going to be shot in black and white. There were even doubts that it could be filmed at all when Universal Studios, who had made the original *Frankenstein* film in the 1930s, attempted to halt production.

Universal objected to the registration of the title even though 'Frankenstein' was in the public domain. The monster's make-up, devised by Jack Pierce for Boris Karloff, was under copyright. It was stipulated by Universal that in Hammer's production there were to be 'no nuts and bolts protruding from the neck. No ungainly shuffling walk'.

In the Hammer film, the character of Baron Frankenstein (played by Peter Cushing) is more interesting than in Mary Shelley's book and quite different from Colin Clive's mad, feverish portrayal in Universal's film. Cushing's Baron Victor Frankenstein is an arrogant dandy.

The use of colour is not merely an add-on. Fisher said: 'I can remember painting leaves or twigs red because I wanted in the foreground a suggestion of red. If people were conscious of it I don't know. The red leaves indicating danger and blood.'

Christopher Lee was cast as the monster. It was his first appearance with Peter Cushing in what would become Hammer's memorable double act.

With mismatched eyes and a disintegrating face, Lee's monster, billed as the 'creature', has the brain of a brilliant professor, harvested by Frankenstein but damaged in the process. On first sight of his creator, Baron Frankenstein, the monster attempts to strangle him.

Later in an interview with Harry Ringel, Fisher said: 'Up to that moment, my career had been attempting to find a line of direction which I was good at. *The Curse of Frankenstein* culminated what I was trying to do. It put my career in perspective.'

It was no accident that Fisher was appointed director of this, his first horror film at the relatively advanced age of 52. Producer Anthony Hinds would later say in *Fangoria* magazine:

> I asked to have him. We had worked on two shows together before and got on so well that I knew he would at least understand the sort of films I wanted the Hammer horror shows to be – rich-looking, slow, deliberately paced, bursting with unstated sex but with nothing overt … and he did.

The critics, however, were not impressed. C. A. Lejeune of *The Observer* described it as: 'Among the half-dozen most repulsive films I have encountered in the course of some 10,000 miles of reviewing.' George Campbell Dixon of *The Telegraph* advised a new category for films on the basis of seeing it. SO standing for Sadists Only.

But the audiences loved it. Its commercial success boosted Hammer's fortunes and brought an injection of American cash, though it didn't mean that Hammer production schedules (between six and eight weeks) were any more leisurely or luxurious. For instance, shooting finished on Terence Fisher's *Dracula* on 3 January 1958 and he was back in the director's chair on 6 January for *The Revenge of Frankenstein*.

Just as Universal had capitalised on the success of its version of Dracula with its production of Frankenstein, Hammer moved swiftly to produce its own *Dracula* (1958). The gout of red blood that splashes across the opening credits announced another horror hit with Christopher Lee as the sexy count and Peter Cushing as his implacable pursuer Doctor Van Helsing.

This was followed by *The Revenge of Frankenstein* (1958), *The Mummy* (1959), *The Hound of the Baskervilles* (1959), *The Brides of Dracula* (1960), *The Two Faces of Dr Jekyll* (1960), *The Curse of the Werewolf* (1961) and *The Phantom of the Opera* (1962). The last, starring Herbert Lom, was not a great success and Fisher, always a gun for hire, briefly parted company with Hammer to make *Sherlock Holmes and the Deadly Necklace* (1962) for the German film company CCC and *The Horror of it All* (1963) for Lippert Pictures. This was a horror comedy starring Pat Boone, and best forgotten. In 1964 Fisher returned to Hammer to make *The Gorgon*.

With this workload, it's surprising that he could find time to write an article titled 'Horror is My Business' in *Films and Filming* magazine (July 1964). It gives an inkling as to his way of working. 'Continental film critics acknowledge the English as the world experts in horror,' he wrote. 'It's because we're timid. Shyness breeds shadows and shadows breed vampires. The Americans are different. They're brash and their audiences don't like ghosts they like monsters.'

Hammer films were sexy and resolutely heterosexual apart from some implied girl-on-girl action. And on this Fisher says: 'Certainly Dracula did bring a hell of a lot of joy to a hell of a lot of women. And if this erotic quality hadn't come out we'd have been very disappointed.'

When the actress Melissa Stribling appeared as Nina in *Brides of Dracula*, she asked how she should play a scene where she returns home after a night with the count. Fisher told her: 'You should imagine you have had one hell of a sexual night … . Give me that in your face.'

In the *Films and Filming* article, Fisher also explains that he never tried to avoid showing or unnecessarily delaying the arrival of the monster. In an interview in 1975 with Sue and Colin Cowie, he explained further: 'The horror film requires the creation of the monster, the unleashing of the monster and then ultimately requires the monster's annihilation. This ritual cycle cannot be broken.'

Some critics have found in Fisher's films a staunch Christian viewpoint with their insistence on the dangerousness of desire and of succumbing to the temptations of the flesh.

Fisher himself said: 'I wouldn't claim to be much of a Christian.' But it's true that most of his films feature a battle between good and evil, often raging within a single character. Though the critic Robin Wood dismissed this with: 'His conception of evil is scarcely more interesting or more adult than his conception of good.'

He is a methodical storyteller, though some have called him plodding and un-cinematic because he doesn't move the camera much. For his part Fisher was against flashy camera action. John Carpenter watched his films with a director's eye and tells us: 'His staging of action, usually in medium-to-wide shots from background to foreground and his economy of framing and movement was very much on my mind when I made *Halloween*.'

Comedy plays a small part in Fisher's film. There is sometimes a comic character, an old peasant or something similar, who offers comic relief. But Fisher was very aware that unintended comedy could destroy a film: 'I always do my utmost to make sure that the audience won't laugh at the wrong moment. One laugh at the wrong moment and you're lost.'

By the mid-1960s Fisher was directing less for Hammer and its output became, frankly, trashy.

Three of Fisher's later films are particularly memorable. In *Frankenstein Created Woman* (1967), a woman with a scarred face and her lover – Christina and Hans – are killed. Frankenstein merges the two of them into a single perfect body and the new look Christina (played by Susan Denberg) sets about seducing and murdering the men responsible for her father's and Hans's death. *The Devil Rides Out* (1968) is a powerful adaptation of a Dennis Wheatley novel starring Charles Gray – Fisher got his wish in the casting – as the evil Mocata, pitting his satanic wiles against Christopher Lee as the Duc de Richleau.

In *Frankenstein Must Be Destroyed* (1969) – one of Fisher's personal favourites – he cast Freddie Jones, an actor he much admired, as one of the most touchingly sympathetic monsters. Peter Cushing is, as ever, Baron Frankenstein, still illegally harvesting brains with enthusiasm.

Fisher and his wife Morag lived quietly in Holly Cottage in Twickenham. Terry, she said, was happiest 'being a homebody'. The couple couldn't screen films at home as they didn't have a projector. 'He was absolutely hopeless with any kind of gadgetry,' said Morag. 'Absolutely hopeless. In fact, he couldn't hammer a nail in.'

Daniel Kaluuya senses that all may not be well in Jordan Peele's *Get Out* (2017). *(Moviestore Collection)*

Christopher Lee watches Peter Cushing check out the tarot cards in *Dr Terror's House of Horrors* (1965), an anthology film made by Amicus productions. *(Moviestore Collection)*

Christopher Lee
stakes his claim in
*Dracula Has Risen
from the Grave* (1968).
(Moviestore Collection)

Boris Karloff in
Frankenstein (1931)
directed by James
Whale. *(Moviestore
Collection)*

Director Tod Browning on the set of *Freaks* (1932). *(Moviestore Collection)*

Jamie Lee Curtis spends an uneventful night babysitting in John Carpenter's *Halloween* (1978). *(Moviestore Collection)*

Betsy (Frances Dee) and Jessica (Christine Gordon) in *I Walked with a Zombie* (1943), directed by Jacques Tourneur. *(Moviestore Collection)*

Max Schreck on the plague ship in F. W. Murnau's *Nosferatu* (1922). *(Moviestore Collection)*

Alfred Hitchcock directs Janet Leigh in the shower scene of *Psycho* (1960). *(Moviestore Collection)*

Catherine Deneuve finds horror in a flat in South Kensington in Roman Polanski's *Repulsion* (1965). *(Moviestore Collection)*

Mia Farrow reacts
badly to motherhood in
Rosemary's Baby (1968).
(Moviestore Collection)

Peter Cushing, as Van Helsing,
inspects Gina (Andrée Melly)
in a Transylvanian tavern in
The Brides of Dracula (1960),
directed by Terence Fisher.
(Moviestore Collection)

Werner Krauss in *The Cabinet of Dr Caligari* (1920), directed by Robert Wiene. *(Moviestore Collection)*

Linda Blair takes to the air, watched by Max von Sydow and Jason Miller, in *The Exorcist* (1973). *(Moviestore Collection)*

André (played by David Hedison) has trouble adjusting to life as a bluebottle with wife Hélène (Patricia Owens) in *The Fly* (1958). *(Moviestore Collection)*

Jane Asher and David Weston as Francesca and Gino in Roger Corman's *The Masque of the Red Death* (1964). *(Moviestore Collection)*

Gloria Stuart and Boris Karloff in James Whale's *The Old Dark House* (1932). *(Moviestore Collection)*

Professor Quatermass (Brian Donlevy) wonders what's bugging astronaut Victor Carroon (Richard Wordsworth) in *The Quatermasss Xperiment* (1955). *(Moviestore Collection)*

Jack Nicholson, Peter Lorre, Vincent Price and Olive Sturgess in *The Raven* (1963), one of Roger Corman's Edgar Allen Poe films. *(Moviestore Collection)*

Victor McLaglen (the strongman), Harry Earles (the baby), Mae Busch and Lon Chaney in *The Unholy Three* (1925), directed by Tod Browning. *(Moviestore Collection)*

Madeleine Smith and Ingrid Pitt in Hammer's *The Vampire Lovers* (1970). *(Moviestore Collection)*

Ingrid Pitt and friends in Robin Hardy's film *The Wicker Man* (1973). *(Moviestore Collection)*

Barbara Shelley as Anthea Zellaby, mother of one of the eerie children in *Village of the Damned* (1960), based on John Wyndham's book *The Midwich Cuckoos*. *(Moviestore Collection)*

The lobby of the Rialto Theatre in Manhattan where Val Lewton's *Cat People* held its premiere on 5 December 1942. *(Wikimedia Commons)*

Will you take this monster? Elsa Lanchester and Boris Karloff in *The Bride of Frankenstein* (1935). *(Wikimedia Commons)*

Bela Lugosi and his first wife Ilona. She was 16 and he was 34 when they married in Budapest. *(Wikimedia Commons)*

Lon Chaney in *Phantom of the Opera* (1925), made by Universal. *(Wikimedia Commons)*

A Hollywood casting call for black cats in 1961 to appear in Roger Corman's *Tales of Terror*. It was a publicity stunt. The role had already been filled. *(Wikimedia Commons)*

Director James Whale
and Boris Karloff
take a cigarette break
during the filming of
Frankenstein in 1931.
(Wikimedia Commons)

Carol Borland perfecting
that undead look in *Mark
of the Vampire* (1935).
(Wikimedia Commons)

Christopher Lee and Jenny Hanley in *Scars of Dracula* (1970). *(With permission from StudioCanal)*

Christopher Lee in *The Wicker Man* (1973). *(With permission from StudioCanal)*

His health declined during the 1970s. He had the misfortune to be run over twice in three years and break his leg on both occasions. He was also suffering from cancer in his later years.

In 1972, he shot *Frankenstein and the Monster from Hell* at Elstree Studios, though the film was not released until 1974. It stars Peter Cushing, David Prowse and Madeline Smith. This was to be Hammer's last Frankenstein film and Fisher's last film, and by all accounts there was an elegiac, melancholy atmosphere on set. Fisher was not well and Morag was constantly at his side.

He still had plans. He wanted to make a love story. He wanted to make a biopic about Dr Barnardo. He wanted to do a Svengali film with the pop singer Sandie Shaw who, he said, reminded him of Garbo. His own favourite film was John Ford's 1939 movie *Stagecoach*. 'I never tire of it,' he said. 'It's full of character development and involvement which is the guts of the whole thing.'

Terence Fisher died on 18 June 1980, aged 76. His favourite record was played at his funeral – Louis Armstrong's *When the Saints Go Marching In*. He was a gentle man, with a dry sense of humour, not a flamboyant movie director intent on sharing his vision with the world. But he was enormously influential and, after enduring a lifetime of sniffy criticism, he understood in the 1970s that his work was valued. Much of this recognition was due to the critic David Pirie.

Let the last word be with Terry Fisher. 'I like period, legend and allegory,' he said, 'because they take you out of your personal, present-day experience. After all, let's face the fact: this is entertainment.'

Chapter Ten

Vincent Price – 'Bring me my pendulum, kiddies … I feel like swingin'!'

Early in 1953 Vincent Price – already in his forties and an established actor of stage and screen – was offered two roles in the same week. One was in a Broadway play, a comedy, called *We're No Angels* to be directed by José Ferrer. The other was in a Warner Brothers remake of the 1933 horror classic *Mystery of the Wax Museum*, which was to be called *House of Wax*.

He couldn't say yes to both, so he chose the movie. It was a 'sliding doors' moment, a decision which would lead to him to becoming America's top horror star of the 1950s and 1960s, or as *People* magazine said after his death: 'the Gable of Gothic'.

In *House of Wax* Price plays Professor Henry Jarrod, a gentle sculptor who makes wax models of famous historical figures for his museum and is rather more attached to his exhibits than is entirely normal.

When his business partner burns down the museum as an insurance scam, Jarrod is hideously burned but creates a wax mask to hide his face. He opens a new museum but now constructs his pieces by murdering people and dipping them in wax. Old Bela Lugosi, wearing his Dracula cape, was wheeled out for the New York premiere. And suddenly the middle-aged actor Vincent Price was a favourite with teen audiences flocking to the new generation of horror films.

Jarrod is typical of many of the characters Price played in horror films – sensitive, anguished, with a refined artistic sensibility, poised to tip over into vengeful madness.

With the benefit of hindsight, Price's lofty presence on screen (he was 6 ft 4 ins), his silkily sinister voice and camp mannerisms seem to make his horror career an inevitability. But it wasn't always thus.

Vincent Price was born to a wealthy middle-class family on 27 May 1911 in St Louis, Missouri. His grandfather Dr V. C. Price had invented baking powder, but lost his fortune through misfortune and bad management in the stock market 'Panic of 1893', leaving his son Vincent Leonard (Vincent's father) to rebuild the family fortune in the sweets business and set up the National Candy Company.

Vincent, known as Bink, was the youngest child. He wasn't particularly interested in school work (more a case of attitude than aptitude) but he loved films and he loved art. One of the first films he saw as a child was the German silent horror film *The Golem* (1920), which was so frightening that he wet his pants. His other lifelong interest in the visual arts was triggered when, aged 12, he saved up $37.50 to buy a small Rembrandt etching.

When he was 17 he travelled to Europe – a cultural visit very much like a nineteenth-century grand tour – arriving in London in July, and proceeding to Holland, Belgium, Germany, Switzerland, Italy, then on to the south of France and finally to Paris.

He got into Yale where – this being the Prohibition era – he made wine in the bathtub. During his senior year he became good friends with a Cambridge exchange student called Alistair Cooke, who would become a celebrated journalist and whose *Letter from America* was a jewel in BBC radio's crown.

In 1934, Price returned to London to study art at the Courtauld Institute and discovered a love of all things British. He lived in lodgings at 20 Upper Wimpole Street and worked on a thesis on Albrecht Dürer under his tutor, the distinguished art historian Campbell Dodgson.

At the time, according to his daughter Victoria Price who wrote his biography, he was 'part bohemian, part social climber, part intellectual, part starstruck kid'. He went to tea with Bram Stoker's widow Florence who had been a great beauty, a close friend of Oscar Wilde's and had had her portrait painted by Edward Burne-Jones.

He saw John Gielgud's *Hamlet* and in 1935 was cast in *Chicago*, a play by Maurine Watkins (eventually adapted into the Broadway musical of the same name), produced by Gielgud at the Gate Theatre Club on Villiers Street, near Charing Cross.

He was then given the role of Prince Albert in *Victoria Regina*, a play by Laurence Housman (the brother of the poet A. E. Housman). Along with Vivien Leigh, Price was nominated by the American producer and critic Sydney Carroll as one of his discoveries of the year.

Carroll had been one of the founders of London's Regent Park Open Air Theatre and Price was offered two roles in the 1935 season – Orsino in *Twelfth Night* and Orlando in *As You Like It*. Unfortunately, the actors' union Equity was not happy about an American actor playing roles that could have been taken by a British actor and Price was refused a work permit.

Abandoning his studies at the Courtauld, he returned to the United States to star in *Victoria Regina* on Broadway with Helen Hayes playing Queen Victoria.

At the time, the portrayal of a monarch (even a dead one) was seen as very daring and the intimate scene where Prince Albert is in his dressing gown, shaving his whiskers, was genuinely shocking. So much so that it created a craze for gentlemen's dressing gowns in New York. In his horror films, Price is often costumed in some sumptuous silk dressing gown. They suited him tremendously well.

Invited to Hollywood for a screen test with David O. Selznick, Price arrived carrying a letter of introduction from Helen Hayes to Joan Crawford.

Crawford invited him to a potluck supper at her home, which turned out to be a sit-down dinner for twenty. 'Everybody you ever heard of was there. Joan was in a fabulously form-fitting bathing costume adorning her fabulous form and swam like a goddess,' recalled the young and impressionable Price.

Price was unsuccessful in his screen test for the part of Ashley Wilkes in *Gone with the Wind* which went to Leslie Howard. 'I think I would have been better than Leslie Howard,' Price said later, 'because I never thought he was anything but English. He was just wrong.'

One interesting footnote to the films is that the woman who played Scarlett O'Hara's mother, Barbara O'Neil, was only three years older than her 'daughter', Vivien Leigh. She had been a childhood friend of Vincent Price, and they had an on-off affair for years.

Though he was confident he would have been better than Leslie Howard in *Gone with the Wind*, Price knew that he was not yet a fully fledged screen actor and even turned down a seven-year contract with Warner Brothers, which would have earned him a million dollars. To improve his skills he took acting lessons at the Benno Schneider Theater School where, among his contemporaries, were Burgess Meredith and Peggy Ashcroft.

When he had been at Yale, he had sent a fan telegram to the actress Tallulah Bankhead inviting her to a Yale and Princetown game. She hadn't come but she had answered him. They now became friends. Price adored her outrageousness. He remembered her visiting him in his dressing room. 'She was sitting on my washbasin and suddenly I realised that she was taking a leak,' he said.

He had a brief affair with the actress Anna May Wong when they appeared together in a dramatised version of *Turandot* at the Westport Country Playhouse. One highly impressed reviewer wrote of Price: 'Physically he is a child of the gods. Exceptionally tall, he is exceptionally handsome, and exceptionally graceful. He is one man who can be called beautiful in the sense that a thoroughbred of 17 hands is beautiful.'

The reviews were less kind for a 1937 play called *The Lady Has a Heart*, even though it confirmed his heartthrob status.

The following year he married an actress called Edith Barrett who was some years older than him. He was also invited by Orson Welles, then only in his early twenties, to join his Mercury Theater. Their relationship was not a great success. 'He was completely undisciplined,' said Price. 'Everybody in the Mercury Theater had a bit of a falling out with Orson.'

Price signed with Universal and he and Edith went to Hollywood where they saw a lot of Barbara O'Neil. 'All is well and she and Edi get along well and we are all friends!,' claimed Price, sounding slightly desperate.

He made his big screen debut with Constance Bennett in a passable romantic comedy called *Service De Luxe* (1938). *Screen & Radio Weekly* noted:

> Hollywood's latest importation from the New York stage: tall dark and handsome. His blue eyes, wavy brown hair, 180 pounds distributed nicely over six foot four inches of well proportioned stature, and a beguiling voice give him the Sex Appeal. Note the capitals. SA is the sine qua non. If you haven't got it you haven't got a thing. Price has it. Price has IT.

He was cast as Sir Walter Raleigh in *The Private Lives of Elizabeth and Essex* (1939) and in *Tower of London* (1939), which is half-horror and half a biopic about Richard III. Price was cast as the Duke of Clarence, with Basil Rathbone as the king and Boris Karloff as his fictitious club-footed executioner Mord.

He was in *Green Hell* (1940), an Amazon adventure (shot entirely in the studio) directed by James Whale, who had made *Frankenstein*. It was not Whale's finest hour and Price said of it: 'About five of the worst pictures ever made were all in that picture.'

He was in *The Invisible Man Returns* (1940) and *The House of the Seven Gables* (1940), based on Nathaniel Hawthorne's Gothic tale of a family feud. It opened in a double bill with *Black Friday* (1940), a psychological thriller horror mishmash starring Bela Lugosi and Boris Karloff.

In 1940, Edith gave birth to a boy, Vincent Barrett. Price was back on Broadway in a play called *Angel Street*, adapted from Patrick Hamilton's *Five Chelsea Lane* which would eventually be remade in 1940 and 1944 as the film *Gaslight*. On stage Price plays Manningham, the apparently kindly husband who is systematically driving his wife insane. Extreme uxoriousness would be an element in the Edgar Allen Poe films that Price would make with Roger Corman, drawing on a disturbingly fine line between love and what we now call coercive control.

Angel Street was a hit and Price felt he was finding his way at last. 'I was launched as a villain,' he said, 'a sadistic heavy, a suave killer, a wife beater, a sexy extrovert, a diabolical introvert. Take your pick.'

He starred with the beautiful Gene Tierney in Otto Preminger's *Laura* (1944) and they were on screen together again in *Dragonwyck* (1946), a costume drama. Price plays a wealthy landowner captivated by his foxy cousin Miranda (Tierney) who is poisoning his frumpy wife because she can't provide him with an heir. In *Shock* (1946), a film noir, he is a psychiatrist who beats his wife to death with a candlestick.

Price's own marriage was on the rocks by now. Edith drank and was a chronic spendthrift. She would never cross Fifth Avenue on foot but always took a taxi. This was just one of her maddening habits which Price – always careful with money – found immensely distressing.

They separated in 1944 and divorced in 1949 following a bitter custody battle over their son. Edith said that his father had 'constantly criticised her, told her it was none of her business where he had been when he came home at 4 or 5 am and said he was sorry he had married her.'

Price himself favoured small cars and – though he was always immaculately kitted out on screen – old clothes. The older and more mismatched the better. He spent money on art rather than himself and invested heavily in the Modern Institute of Art, which opened in Beverly Hills in 1948 but was forced to close a couple of years later.

He did a lot of radio work in this period, including a thirteen-part series of Leslie Charteris's *The Saint*. He was resplendent in scarlet doublet and hose as Cardinal Richelieu in MGM's *The Three Musketeers* (1948) and starred with Ava Gardner in a psychological thriller called *The Bribe* (1949), describing the leading lady as the only one 'who ever seems to me to live up to her reputation as a sex object'.

This was an unsettled period for the actor. His parents died and he rekindled his affair with Barbara O'Neil, writing to her: 'On looking into my heart I find I really have loved only one person – you!' But he also began a relationship with the costume designer Mary Grant and they married in 1949.

Though *House of Wax* was a success and he and his wife moved into a palatial Hollywood home at 580 North Beverly Glen, Price felt that his career had stalled. It was also the period when the House Un-American Activities Committee began to root out communists in show business.

Price, born to a Republican family, had moved politically left throughout his career. He had even shown an unthinking, reflexive anti-Semitism in his youth which he was at pains to distance himself from, and he would go on to do a lot of work with Jewish charities.

He was terrified when he found he was on Eugene McCarthy's list of 'Premature Anti-Nazi Sympathisers'.

This extraordinary phrase effectively meant that if you were against the Nazis *before* America joined the Second World War then that made you a communist. Vincent had been 'greylisted' and for the best part of a year he was offered no work in films or on TV. Eventually a couple of FBI agents came to interview Price and his wife Mary and they were exonerated.

In her biography of her father, Victoria Price writes:

> After my father's death, however, a manila envelope surfaced among his papers containing a five-page FBI document, signed and dated 6 March 1954, in which Vincent described all his political activity and refuted any charges of Communism. In the document, my father not only stated that he had never been a Communist but also declared that he believed anyone who pleaded the Fifth Amendment

was un-American … . I was shocked when I found the documents; shocked that he had saved them all these years; shocked that my liberal father had declared 'un-American' those people I considered heroes, those who pleaded the Fifth, refusing to name names.

Her father's great friend, the actor Eddie Albert, warned her against judging because: 'You don't know what it was like.'

Once exonerated, Vincent Price was keen to get back to work and was cast in Cecil B. DeMille's *The Ten Commandments* (1956) as Baka, the master builder of the pharaoh's pyramids. And he was in the Fritz Lang film noir *While the City Sleeps* (1956) made by RKO.

The Fly was a science fiction short story by George Langelaan who had worked for the Special Operations Executive during the Second World War. Parachuted into France, he had been captured by the Nazis but escaped and received the Croix de Guerre. He was a friend of the preposterous occultist Aleister Crowley, who he claimed was also an intelligence agent for the British.

The Fly featured in the June 1957 edition of *Playboy* magazine, and would be reprinted in the first *Pan Book of Horror Stories* in 1958 and subsequently filmed in the same year.

A scientist, André Delambre, has invented a machine that can transport matter but unwisely uses himself in an experiment and finds his atoms have been mixed up with that of a housefly which had entered the transporter. He asks his wife Hélène (Patricia Owens) to kill him and destroy all evidence of the experiment. Vincent Price plays the scientist's brother François who is in love with Hélène and determined to prove that she is innocent of murder.

In the final scene, the fly (which has the head of poor André) is seen trapped in a spider's web with a giant spider about to devour him. 'Help meee!,' he screams over and over again in his tinny bluebottle voice. While filming this, neither Price nor Marshall was able to keep a straight face and ended up sitting on the ground with tears of mirth streaming down their faces.

There were a couple of sequels to *The Fly* and a remake by sci-fi horror master David Cronenberg in 1986 starring Jeff Goldblum. *The Fly* was a commercial success and certainly boosted Price's horror credentials even though he plays the benign brother-in-law as such a drip.

The story goes that the producer/director William Castle ran across Vincent Price eating a slice of pie at a coffee shop near the Goldwyn Studios and pitched his idea for a film called *House on Haunted Hill* (1959): a millionaire invites five strangers to a haunted house party and offers $10,000 to anyone who will stay all night in the house (where seven murders have taken place in the last 100 years).

Price would describe William Castle as 'one of the last great characters in the movies. A witty man who loved gimmicks and knew how to work them sometimes.'

Castle, born in 1914, adored horror. Aged 13 he went to see the stage version of *Dracula* with Bela Lugosi over and over again. The title of his autobiography was *Step Right Up! I'm Gonna Scare the Pants off America.*

He financed his first horror movie *Macabre* (1958) by mortgaging his house. Addicted to promotional gimmicks and with a great sense of fun, he offered everyone who came to see the film a certificate for $1,000 life insurance from Lloyd's of London in case they died of fright during the film.

To promote *House on Haunted Hill* he filmed it in 'Emergo', setting up glow-in-the-dark skeletons, suspended on wires, which would run out into the audience. The film was made for $150,000 and grossed $4 million.

The Tingler (1959), also directed by Castle and starring Price (as a mad scientist), was filmed in 'Percepto'. He fitted electrical devices on selected seats to cause them to buzz and vibrate. Health and safety would have a field day now. *The Tingler* is an alien form which attaches itself to the human spine and can only be destroyed by screaming. Price warned the audience to 'scream for your lives!'

It's said that Alfred Hitchcock decided to make *Psycho* after seeing the success of the B movies by William Castle. Castle, who died in 1977, continued making fun, gimmicky pictures until the mid-1970s and was also the producer of *Rosemary's Baby* (1968).

According to Victoria Price, Mary and Vincent became a Hollywood institution, famed for their parties and their charm. Unlike many stars of the time, Price was happy to appear on TV even though he didn't own a set. He regularly lectured on modern artists such as Jackson Pollock, Jasper Johns and Andy Warhol.

Price could still be starstruck. He recalled meeting Greta Garbo at a dinner and was so captivated by her beauty that the only thing he could think of to talk about was her alleged fondness for home-baked bread. Stepping out of a hardware store one day, a lady in a car yelled 'Vincent!' It was Ella Fitzgerald. After they'd chatted and she'd driven off, Price said: 'Isn't it amazing she remembered me? I met her a few years ago.'

American International Pictures (AIP) had been set up in 1954 by Samuel Z. Arkoff and James Nicholson who had capitalised on the sci-fi movies of the 1950s and would do the same with a new wave of Gothic horror movies. The success of Britain's Hammer studios was in their sights.

In 1960, the producer Roger Corman approached AIP with the idea of making a cycle of films based on stories by Edgar Allen Poe. The first would be *The Fall of the House of Usher* (1960) and Corman said: 'Vincent Price was my first and only choice of the lead role of Roderick Usher.'

Price was keen. He loved Poe and said: 'Working for Roger was a gamble. But there comes a point in every actor's career when you think money isn't everything.'

Screenwriter Richard Matheson provided the script. Vincent suggested bleaching his hair and assuming the sort of hideous pallor that he had seen in Conrad Veidt's performance in the early German horror film *The Cabinet of Dr Caligari* (1920). The film ran as part of a double bill with Hitchcock's *Psycho*. The *New York Herald Tribune* noted the 'film's restoration of finesse and craftsmanship to the genre of dread'.

Vincent Price went on to make *The Pit and the Pendulum* (1961), *Tales of Terror* (1962), *Tower of London* (1962), *The Haunted Palace* (1963), *The Raven* (1963), *The Masque of the Red Death* (1964) and *The Tomb of Ligeia* (1964). The Poe connection is often tenuous at best. For instance, he gets a credit in *The Haunted Palace* even though it was based on a story by H. P. Lovecraft.

In *Pit and the Pendulum*, Matheson invented a back story about a sixteenth-century Spanish nobleman (played by Price) grieving over the death of his wife. Another opportunity for Price to flex his creepy uxoriousness.

AIP believed that young audiences enjoyed discovering some of the classic stars so for *The Raven*, Price starred with Peter Lorre and Boris Karloff as a trio of rival sorcerers. It's also very funny with moments of high slapstick. Price's character keeps hitting his head, a bit of business that Price introduced himself. Hazel Court, a graduate of the Rank Organisation charm school, who appeared in Hammer and AIP films said of *The Raven*: 'I don't think the picture was really meant to be a comedy; it evolved into one on set.' She also appears in *The Masque of the Red Death*, which like *The Tomb of Ligeia* was filmed in Britain. Set in twelfth-century Italy, she plays the mistress of Prince Prospero (Price), a satanist who terrorises the local peasantry even as the plague rages around them. Jane Asher plays the young peasant girl he would like to debauch. 'I want to help save your soul so you can join me in the glories of hell,' he says persuasively.

The sets and cinematography are by Nicholas Roeg. The preponderance of red reminds you of Roeg's haunting film *Don't Look Now* (1973) and the fleeting glimpses of the homicidal red-hooded figure through a dark and eerie Venice.

In *The Tomb of Ligeia*, with a screenplay by Robert Towne (who wrote *Chinatown*), Price plays another crackpot husband, haunted by the spirit of his dead wife and her unfortunate impact on his second marriage. Elizabeth Shepherd plays both roles. As often happens, Price's character is destroyed by fire.

'The scariest thing about the horror films were all those fires blazing,' he complained. 'Symbolical cleansing of evil by the fire is a horror-tale tradition. I have been singed many times. But then Roger's a fire fiend. He's a firebug.'

The film critic Paul Mayersberg wrote: 'Corman's Poe always offers a Gothic hero – a non virile aesthete. That's why Vincent Price has been the perfect interpreter of them. For Price himself in real life is an aesthete, an expert in the visual arts, an appreciator and a collector.' And as Price himself would say: 'The "heavy" who loves beauty always makes the most terrifying villain.'

Victoria Price, Mary and Vincent's daughter was born on 27 April 1962, just a month before her father turned 51. A year later he starred in the teen movie *Beach Party* (1963) with Annette Funicello and Frankie Avalon in which he plays Big Daddy with the great line: 'The pit! Bring me my pendulum, kiddies – I feel like swingin'!'

In 1968 he made *Witchfinder General*, directed by the very young Michael Reeves. He gives a wonderful performance as Matthew Hopkins, the seventeenth-century witchfinder, but it wasn't a happy experience. 'Reeves hated me,' said Price. 'He didn't want me at all for the part. I didn't like him either. It was just one of the few times in my life that I've been in a picture where the director and I just clashed.'

The Oblong Box (1969), based on a short Poe story, marked the first time that Vincent Price and Christopher Lee worked together and they got on famously. He appeared with Peter Cushing and Christopher Lee in *Scream and Scream Again* (1970).

Variety described Vincent Price as 'the rock generation's Boris Karloff'. In 1971, he starred in *The Abominable Dr Phibes*, playing a scientist avenging his wife's death. The same year this most talented of men hosted a cookery programme on ITV called *Cooking Price-Wise*.

In *Theatre of Blood* (1973) he is Edward Lionheart, an ageing Shakespearean actor who has spent a lifetime being rubbished by the critics and, with the help of his daughter (Diana Rigg), plans to take this murderous revenge.

The Australian actress Coral Browne played the only female critic and she and Price fell madly in love. Said Diana Rigg: 'I think they fell into bed and I think it was a wildly sexual relationship. Incredibly sexual. I remember Coral saying that they had worked out their combined ages were 120-something.'

After Vincent divorced Mary, he and Coral married in 1974.

They made a great couple. Joan Rivers remembered:

> They were the perfect dinner guests. You knew he was going to be a gentleman, with manners that California still didn't understand. And you also knew that there was something going on at the other end of the table, that Coral was going to be a firecracker. So they were a great combination.

In 1981 Vincent Price appeared in *The Monster Club*, an amiable horror anthology directed by Roy Ward Baker which also starred John Carradine, Britt Ekland and Donald Pleasence. In 1982, he was the voice on Michael Jackson's *Thriller* album and had a cameo role in Tim Burton's film *Edward Scissorhands* (1990).

He died in 1993.

Unlike many actors who were unhappy to be typecast as horror stars, Vincent Price had no such qualms. As Samuel Arkoff of AIP said, comparing Vincent with some other stars of the genre: 'You see, Vincent liked horror. It did something for him and that really wasn't true of the others.'

And when he was at that difficult age for a male lead – middle-aged – he was discovered by the teenagers who flocked to horror films in the 1950s and 1960s. It was partly the camp sensibility he brought to all his films, except perhaps *Witchfinder General* which he played dead straight. He knew comedy and horror could work. 'Comedy and terror are very closely allied,' he said. 'We tried to make audiences enjoy themselves, even as they were being scared. My job as an actor is to make the unbelievable believable and the despicable delectable.'

And the last word should go to his daughter, Victoria, who said, 'By the end of his life, when many of the big stars of his own generation were forgotten, the name of Vincent Price was known and loved by moviegoers of all ages.'

Chapter Eleven

Peter Cushing – 'Acting? You either can or you can't.'

The film critic Roger Ebert described Cushing's work in the Hammer films like this: '[Cushing is] the one in all those British horror films, standing between Vincent Price and Christopher Lee. His dialogue usually runs along the lines of, "But good heavens, man! The person you saw has been dead for more than two centuries!"'

Cushing was a class act in a genre – horror – not always noted for its classiness. Whatever the limitations of the role or the script that he was given, he approached that role with seriousness and dedication. His gaunt face and haunted eyes bring a gravitas to whatever film he is in.

He was very particular about his costume and the props which he used, to the extent of being a bit of a fusspot, possibly driving the production crew mad in the process. The American actor Forrest Tucker, who appeared with him in Hammer's *The Abominable Snowman* (1957), set in the snowy Himalayas, said in an interview in 1974:

> Peter Cushing is a terribly meticulous man. He had to know where the string on his mittens was tied and when he could take his mittens off at that altitude, how long could he have his hands out of his mittens before they would be frostbitten … he does months of research on everything he does, He's a very valuable asset to a producer because he can save you thousands of dollars in research.

Peter Wilton Cushing was born in Kenley in Surrey on 26 May 1913, the second son of George, a quantity surveyor, and his wife Nellie. After the birth of their first son David in 1910, Nellie had longed for a daughter and when Peter arrived she amused herself by frequently dressing him in girl's clothes and curling his hair which was allowed to grow.

A blue English Heritage plaque – put up in 2018 – tells us that between 1925 and 1936, Peter's family home was 32 St James's Road in Purley, a striking art deco detached house.

George was, it seems, a distant father and a very conventional man. But there was a persistent theatrical strain in the family. George's father, Henry William Cushing, had begun his career in theatre with Henry Irving's touring company. Henry's sister Maude had also been an actress. And Peter Cushing's step-uncle, Wilton Herriot, had been a theatrical jack of all trades, working as stage manager for the original production of *Charley's Aunt*.

At his local cinema, the Electric Palace, the young Cushing wasted many happy hours watching Charlie Chaplin and Buster Keaton films. But his favourite was Tom Mix, the first American western star, who appeared in nearly 300 films, of which all but nine were in the silent era.

David and Peter both attended Purley County Secondary School where Peter showed little interest in academic work but was brilliant at art and rugby. When the boys left school, David became a farmer and his father helped him buy a smallholding near Reigate.

George disapproved of acting as a profession but the Cushings had inadvertently stoked their son's dreams by taking him to see a Christmas production of *Peter Pan* when he was a child. Cushing reveals in his autobiography that the idea of a boy who would never grow up had a strong influence on him and throughout his life he loved toys, model soldiers and playing games.

Dutifully he put aside his dreams of acting – and worked as a surveyor's assistant with the Coulsdon and Purley Urban District Council. This didn't stop him buying a copy of *The Stage* almost every week and responding to adverts for theatre jobs. For a while he used the stage name Peter Ling but soon reverted to Cushing.

He also applied to the Guildhall School of Music and Drama but was told that he would need voice coaching to rid him of his 'lazy drawl'. He worked for months on improving his voice and was eventually accepted. His first proper theatrical job was as assistant stage manager with the Worthing Repertory Company – the same company that Christopher Lee would later join early in his career.

He was invited to join the Grand Theatre in Southampton and later the William Brookfield Players who toured Scarborough and Rochdale. His girlfriend at the time was Doreen Lawrence who would go on to marry the film star Jack Hawkins.

While he was with Harry Hanson's Court Players he met his hero Tom Mix. Mix had come to Britain to appear in a variety show in Nottingham where Cushing was appearing in the Theatre Royal. Cushing took the opportunity of introducing himself to the screen cowboy and was asked to read the star's contract to him and be a witness to Mix's signature. This was because Mix, a great Hollywood star, was illiterate.

Meeting Tom Mix set Cushing's career on a new course. In his autobiography Cushing writes: 'I had this great passion to go where Tom Mix lived, he was my hero, you see. So I went to America. My dad, bless him, bought me a one-way ticket.'

Cushing left for New York on 18 January 1939, aboard the SS *Champlain* from Southampton. He had managed to get a letter of recommendation from Larry Goodkind of Columbia Pictures. On reaching Los Angeles, Cushing moved in to the YMCA and took his letter to the Edward Small Studios. It gained him access to the casting director for *The Man in the Iron Mask* (1939) under the direction of James Whale who had made *Frankenstein* in 1931.

The casting director asked Cushing if he fenced. Cushing said he had fenced 'all his life'. On meeting the fencing master, Cushing confessed he had never fenced at all. 'Now that you've been truthful I will teach you to become one of the best swordsmen in Hollywood,' said his teacher, who had known immediately that Cushing was a novice because he had taken hold of the foil as though it was a knife.

Cushing worked on the picture for three months. As 'second officer', he has one line: 'The king wants to see you.' Louis Hayward was the star, playing twin brothers, and Cushing's role was to act with Hayward offscreen. He had to react to the twins' speeches which were then spliced together.

Cushing recalled he learnt much about film acting:

> I don't really like the word but it's a very *technical* medium.
> When I say I don't like the word – I don't like to think there's
> a technique of acting because to me there isn't, you either
> can or you can't. The greatest compliment is that it all looks
> so easy. But as a *medium* it is very technical. You've got not
> only to remember your lines and the character but also where
> you're standing, whether your foot's on a mark and getting
> your own key light and trying to keep your shoulder out of
> the leading lady's light – there's a great deal on your mind

for those few seconds that you're filming. That's where the mental strains come in. You've got to remember a lot at very short notice and you get very little rehearsal time in films.

He had a small part in a Laurel and Hardy comedy, *A Chump at Oxford* (1939). He noted that in a scene where Stan throws students into a pool, both the stars handed out towels and hot drinks to the dripping extras. It was a small example of thoughtfulness which Cushing would often emulate when he was a star.

He was second lead in *Vigil in the Night* (1940), a George Stevens medical drama in which he appeared opposite Carole Lombard. Though by now he was doing well in Hollywood, Cushing made the decision to return to Britain.

'I got fearfully homesick,' he said, 'because war had broken out almost upon my arrival. It wasn't because I wanted to fight, or anything, I'm not really a fighting man – I'm sure hundreds of people weren't – but I did want to be at home.'

Many British actors left Hollywood at the outbreak of war. Cushing was not considered fit for active service because of some old school rugby injuries (torn ligaments on his left knee and a perforated eardrum). It took him eighteen months to find a way to return home, which he did as a deckhand on a cargo ship.

He immediately joined the Entertainments National Service Association, popularly known as Every Night Something Awful. He got into it because an actor in Noel Coward's *Private Lives* was called up and Cushing stepped into the breach. His leading lady was Helen Beck, who would become Cushing's wife on 10 April 1943 at Kensington Register Office. Peter was 29 and Helen was 37. She was the love of his life. He put it this way: 'I always say that I was born in 1913, I started to live in 1941 when I met Helen and I died in 1971 when she died.'

Helen had been married before, to actor Kenton Redgrave (one of the Redgrave clan). The break up of this marriage had been traumatic and left Helen with physical problems resulting from a damaging pregnancy, which made her unable to have other children. In an interview in 1955, she recalled her first meeting with Peter Cushing:

At the coach station I saw a man with an old suitcase listed to starboard and a grubby, ancient mackintosh, wearing a

> very old hat. Yes ... it was Peter. He swept the hat off and greeted me as if I were royalty and seemed unconscious of his appearance. I thought this is the strangest individual I have ever met, but the most attractive!

When the war ended Cushing intended to return to rep, but Helen urged him to set his sights higher and he joined the Kew Theatre, which was something of a showcase and was attended by West End theatre managers. He was offered the part of Osric in Laurence Olivier's film of *Hamlet* (1948) and joined the Old Vic tour of Australia. This film also had the distinction of being the first film in which Cushing and Christopher Lee appeared together.

But it was a low point in his career. He suffered a nervous breakdown that prevented him from working for six months and he was in desperate financial straits, resorting to designing ladies' headscarves. He was forced to borrow money from his father George, who made the devastating comment that his son was '40 and a failure'.

Helen, ever resourceful when it came to her husband's career, pointed out that television was the future. She bought a copy of the *Radio Times* and sent a round robin to all the producers and directors named in the programme credits saying that 'Mr Peter Cushing finds himself unexpectedly available and is free any time you would like to offer him some work.'

As a result, Cushing appeared in his first TV play in 1951 – J. B. Priestley's *Eden End*.

He found the demands of live TV nerve-racking, but he became a big star. There were already a million TV sets in Britain and only one channel. He had the rare opportunity to play a romantic lead – dashing Mr Darcy – in a serialised adaptation of *Pride and Prejudice* (1952). He made a big impression in a dramatised (and, at the time, controversial) version of George Orwell's *Nineteen Eighty-Four* playing Winston Smith, first broadcast on 12 December 1954 and directed by Rudolph Cartier.

Cartier then teamed up with writer Nigel Kneale (author of *Quatermass*) on *The Creature*, which was broadcast on 30 January 1955. It was the story of a Himalayan expedition in search of the Yeti. Cushing starred as the expedition leader Dr John Rollason and the cast also included Stanley Baker. It was very well-received and Hammer Films would make their own version of the script two years later with Cushing in the same role and titled *The Abominable Snowman* (1957).

Hammer also courted Cushing for its new production *The Curse of Frankenstein* (1957), playing Baron Frankenstein.

Said the producer Anthony Hinds: 'Never were any other actors considered. Cushing was one of Britain's first real television stars ... and whatever he was in would empty all the pubs and bring people home to their TV sets. We wanted him and we got him.'

The film was an instant hit, though not (as often happens in horror) with the critics. It opened at the Paramount Theatre in New York on 7 August 1957 and *The New York Times*, loyal to the old Universal films, said:

> This one should be coldcuts for old-timers who remember Boris Karloff ... but it may titillate the blissful youngsters ... .
>
> Anyone not yet acquainted with the monster of Baron Frankenstein – and we wonder if there are many such people, outside of very young kids – may remedy this social shortcoming by hopping in to see *The Curse of Frankenstein*. This British-made film in color opened at the Paramount yesterday. Here, in this routine horror picture, which makes no particular attempt to do anything more important than scare you with corpses and blood, the most famous monster of screen fiction comes to life and goes clomping around again, smashing the baron's apparatus and choking people with gray and bony hands.

And despite the distinctive look of Karloff in the original *Frankenstein*, Christopher Lee won plaudits for his portrayal of the monster.

Of the premiere in London, Hazel Court (who plays Frankenstein's fiancée Elizabeth) said:

> The amazing thing about *The Curse of Frankenstein* was that no one thought it was going to be a success and when we all went to the big premiere at the Empire in Leicester Square with scarves and sunglasses, and we sat there, we just didn't know what to expect. Then, in one scene where we were having breakfast, Peter says, having just cut up

some bodies and put them in pickle jars, 'Pass me the marmalade darling', and the whole of the Empire, Leicester Square roared with laughter and clapped and screamed and yelled, and that was the beginning of the tremendous success of *The Curse of Frankenstein* which has gone on for years. I adored Peter Cushing; he made me laugh and had so many talents.

Says David Pirie in his book *A New Heritage of Horror*:

> The two men who did as much to build Hammer as anyone else (indeed it is difficult to imagine the company without them) remain Peter Cushing and Christopher Lee. It is remarkable that both were discovered and used for the first time together in the key breakthrough picture *Curse of Frankenstein*. For as the years went by and despite repeated attempts, Hammer were never able to find another actor to match either of them, let alone two at once.

And from that moment, the role of Baron Frankenstein and his association with Hammer defined Cushing's career, as did his apparently effortless underplaying of every role. In 1956, *Picturegoer* magazine noted: 'Peter Cushing doesn't act, or so it seems; he just behaves.'

'I don't mind being known as a horror star,' he would say. 'My heavens that would be like socking a gift horse in the mouth … I do the parts now that I think the audience want to see me doing. Who wants to see me do Hamlet? Very few. But millions want to see me do Frankenstein.'

He wasn't always cast as the villain. He played Sherlock Holmes in *The Hound of the Baskervilles* (1959). In the *Dracula* films, he played Dracula's implacable adversary Van Helsing and he took a turn as timelord Doctor Who in two films. He played sympathetic characters in *The Skull* (1965), *Night of the Big Heat* (1967), *The Vampire Lovers* (1970), *Tales from the Crypt* (1972) and *The Creeping Flesh* (1973).

He appeared in twenty-two films with Christopher Lee and they became close friends. In *Dracula* (1958), Cushing's fascination with props paid dividends in one of the most memorable scenes in a Hammer horror.

He recalled:

> In the original script Van Helsing was sort of like a salesman
> for crucifixes. He was pulling them out of every pocket
> .... I remembered seeing a film years ago called *Berkeley
> Square* in which Leslie Howard was thought of as being the
> Devil by this frightened little man who suddenly grabbed
> two big candlesticks and made a sign of the cross with
> them. I remembered this as it impressed me enormously.
>
> I suggested the run along the refectory table to jump
> onto the curtains and hit Dracula square in the face with
> the sunlight. He would of course be trapped. Then I would
> come along like a hero, grab the two candlesticks and make
> the cross with them in his face. They agreed and I think it
> was quite an effective ending to the picture.

Cushing also wanted to leap over the bannister. The director Terence
Fisher thought it was too dangerous but Cushing did it anyway – in one
take.

Playing Van Helsing as something of an action man was Cushing's
decision. In the 1987 documentary *Hammer: The Studio that Dripped
Blood*, he says:

> In the book by Bram Stoker, he's described as a very old,
> little, withered man who speaks almost double-Dutch. And
> this was going back nearly twenty-five years when I was
> younger and prettier. When I was offered the part, I said,
> 'Well, instead of making me up, I think we'd better play it
> as myself' and they agreed to that.

In 1959, Cushing starred as Sherlock Holmes in Hammer's *The Hound
of the Baskervilles* with André Morell as Dr Watson and Christopher Lee
as Sir Henry Baskerville.

The Hammer studio at Bray became very dear to Cushing as it did
for many of the Hammer team. 'I have a great affection for those days
at Bray,' said Cushing. 'When they did move to places like Shepperton
and Elstree the same people were there and the atmosphere was so very
nice but it wasn't home.'

Though never a difficult or temperamental actor, Cushing admitted that he preferred a studio to location work. He said:

> Film is such a make-believe medium that put me on a set where I know behind is all plaster, sandwiches and where the *Daily Mail* is tucked and people are having cigarettes … then I know it's all make believe. But put me against a lovely wood, a real church or along a real road and I find it much more difficult to pretend. Because that's what acting is – let's pretend. Against the real thing I'm not so happy.

It was in this fulfilling period of his life that Cushing bought a house in the seaside town of Whitstable in Kent, which he and Helen had visited since the 1940s. He converted the attic into a studio where he could work on his models and his watercolours. The sea air was good for Helen who, never in the best of health, had suffered from smoking-induced emphysema for many years.

Throughout the 1960s, Cushing dominated horror movies. He was a 'horror star' even though he had a vast and varied experience in television and theatre. He also made several films for Amicus Studio including *Dr Terror's House of Horror* (1965), an anthology movie directed by Freddie Francis and produced by Milton Subotsky, and featuring Christopher Lee. Amicus made a speciality of these anthology films, which told several stories and had starry casts.

In 1968, he returned to the role of Sherlock Holmes in a sixteen-part BBC series starring Nigel Stock as Dr Watson. It was an arduous workload. In a 1970 interview in the *Radio Times*, he came close to moaning. The writer Rosemary Collins observed: 'Cushing sighs, as if it were almost too much for him. His eyes are large, grey and worried. He folds and unfolds his hands, doesn't smile much, but still manages to create an impression of goodwill.'

Frankenstein Must Be Destroyed (1969) turned Cushing's Frankenstein character into a thorough-going villain, very unlike previous iterations of the role. Hammer boss James Carreras insisted on sexing up the story with a gratuitous rape scene. The female star, Veronica Carlson, remembers: 'Peter was disgusted with the scene and he didn't want to do it. He took me to dinner to discuss the scene. I remember he wore white gloves. I had a lovely evening but it didn't make the scene any easier.' (Cushing always wore white gloves when he smoked so that his fingers would not become stained with nicotine.)

The same year Cushing made *Scream and Scream Again*, a sort of political conspiracy thriller which brought together the dream team of Cushing, Christopher Lee and Vincent Price. Though only Lee and Price share a scene together and Cushing's one scene is just a minute long. 'I never knew *what* it was about,' admitted Price. Their next film together would be *House of the Long Shadows* (1983), also starring John Carradine.

He was a regular on TV's *Morecambe and Wise*, with a running gag that he had never been paid the £3 he was owed for his first appearance.

He was in Hammer's *The Vampire Lovers* (1970) with Ingrid Pitt and Kate O'Mara, a version of Sheridan Le Fanu's classic vampire tale *Carmilla* with a lesbian theme.

His wife Helen was very ill during filming and died on 14 January 1971. Deeply depressed, he threw himself into his work. The director Bryan Forbes said: 'When his wife tragically died he went into a decline and in fact became very odd indeed, possibly through guilt. He confessed to me that to his shame he had been unfaithful to her and now wanted to join her in heaven to make amends.'

His first film after Helen's death was *Twins of Evil* (1971), also based on a work by Sheridan Le Fanu. Looking gaunt and pained, he plays Gustav Weil, a religious zealot and witch hunter in a town where men are killed and drained of blood. The evil twins were played by Mary and Madeline Collinson, who had been *Playboy*'s first twin playmates in October 1970.

He played a grief-stricken man in Amicus Studios' *Tales from the Crypt* (1972) in which a group of visitors become trapped in underground catacombs, where their past crimes and grim futures are revealed by the Crypt Keeper (Ralph Richardson). The cast includes Joan Collins, Ian Hendry and Richard Greene. Cushing is memorable as the widower Grimsdyke, whose death is caused by his callous neighbour (played by David Markham), and who returns as a terrifying zombie to take revenge. This was the only time in a film that Cushing changed his appearance with make-up.

Dracula AD 1972 (1972) brought Lee and Cushing together again in what is recognised as a poor film, updating the Dracula myth to the present day. It also marked a dip in the fortunes of Hammer.

He was back with Lee in Eugenio Martin's *Horror Express* (1972) (also known as *Panic on the Trans-Siberian Express)*, filmed in Madrid. It is a witty and likeable film (about a humanoid monster from a Manchurian cave which is being transported on a train), in which both actors are the heroes rather than in conflict with each other. The cast included Telly Savalas. Another creature film was Tigon's *The Creeping Flesh* (1973), directed by Freddie Francis and again starring Lee and Cushing.

Frankenstein and the Monster from Hell (1974) would be Cushing's final outing as the baron, and director Terence Fisher's final film. In *Madhouse* (1974), an Amicus film, he starred with Vincent Price. Price plays Paul Toombes, a successful horror actor to Peter Cushing's screenplay writer, Herbert Flay.

In *The Beast Must Die* (1974), a werewolf film, Cushing was an archaeologist and lycanthropy expert. In Christopher Gullo's book on Cushing, *In All Sincerity*, the director Paul Annett recalled one aspect of Cushing's technical expertise. A young actor was watching the rushes of his day's filming and couldn't pinpoint what he disliked about his performance. 'Shut your mouth when you've spoken,' suggested Cushing. Said Annett: 'I've given that note of advice countless times over the years to actors who love to leave their mouths hanging open when they've delivered their line.'

Cushing's last film for Hammer, partnered with the Hong Kong-based Shaw Brothers, was *Shatter* (1975), a martial arts thriller.

He was back on television that year in *Space 1999*, wearing gold face paint and long white hair as the alien Raan. He never stopped working.

He attended the Famous Monsters Convention in New York in 1975, unsparing with his time and deeply appreciative of his fans. The actress Barbara Leigh remembers meeting with Cushing there: 'One dinner was especially memorable. We were to eat in his hotel suite and the table was already set for three so I asked who else was coming. "It's for my wife. I always set a place for her," he replied.'

When *The Avengers* was brought back to TV in 1976 as *The New Avengers*, Peter Cushing was the first to guest star with Joanna Lumley and Gareth Hunt.

Cushing had made his name in low-budget films but in *Star Wars* (1977), he had the opportunity to star in a big-budget Hollywood vehicle. Originally, he had been going to play Obi-Wan Kenobi before he was recast as the villainous Grand Moff Tarkin.

Curiously, one role was turned down by Cushing's agent in the late 1970s on the grounds of being too low budget. It went to actor Donald Pleasence. That film went on to be an international success and created the slasher genre. It was John Carpenter's *Halloween*.

The new violence did not appeal to Cushing. 'Today's films are called chainsaw films with heads exploding; they are much too gruesome,' he said. His last role for Hammer was for the *Hammer House of Horror* TV series in 1980, in an episode called The Silent Scream, co-starring Brian Cox. Said Cox: 'Working with Peter Cushing was absolutely splendid. He was a wonderfully eccentric gentleman, a chain-smoking vegetarian which seemed a contradiction in terms.'

In 1983, Cushing, Christopher Lee and Vincent Price were together again in *House of the Long Shadows* with Desi Arnaz Jr as a writer who makes a bet with a publisher that he can write a novel as good as *Wuthering Heights* in twenty-four hours. His publisher provides a writing space, a house full of strange characters.

A severe eye problem revealed that Cushing was in fact suffering from prostate cancer. But he made a good recovery. In 1984, aged 71, he played Sherlock Holmes for the last time in *The Masks of Death*, directed by Roy Ward Baker, and co-starring Susan Penhaligon. His last role was in the 1986 film *Biggles*, playing Air Commodore William Raymond. Cushing would meet Prince Charles and Princess Diana at the premiere. Always the gentleman, he kissed Princess Diana's hand.

In 1987, he announced his retirement. The following year, two years after publishing his well-received autobiography, Cushing wrote another book of memoirs called *Past Forgetting*, which focused on his days with Hammer. He received an OBE in 1989.

He spent his final years peacefully, visiting the Tudor Tea Room in Whitstable almost every day. He appeared in TV's *This is Your Life* in 1990, presented by Michael Aspel. In 1992, Whitstable honoured him with a new sea-viewing platform that was named Cushing's View. He died on 11 August 1994 in a hospice in Canterbury.

Chapter Twelve

Nigel Kneale – 'But you can't hear the sea in the kitchen …'

Finding a name for a fictional character is surprisingly hard. The world is full of names that are there for the taking. But it's always more difficult than it should be, a name being either too close to someone you know, or so general and mundane that it sounds phoney. Names acquire resonance in retrospect if they are given to someone of notoriety. Lucrezia Borgia's name now seems as though it could only be attached to a scandalous, depraved woman who poisoned people. It couldn't possibly belong to a self-effacing librarian in the Home Counties. Or maybe it could … and that would be interesting in itself.

Which brings us to *Quatermass*. My parents thought *The Quatermass Experiment* on TV in 1953 was the scariest thing they had ever seen and my mother never forgave me for the fact that she missed the fifth episode because she was in hospital having me. The very word Quatermass chilled my blood, even though I knew it was the name of the professor hero. It must rank as the best fictional name ever.

But where did it come from? Nigel Kneale, creator of the *Quatermass* stories, said he got the name out of the London phone book. It (possibly) originated in France in the eleventh century, when it was Quitrimala, changing to Quatormaus and the Quatermares. It's also been suggested that the name is a corruption of the name Quatermains, which means 'four hands' and therefore grasping and greedy. Or it may be derived from the Belgian crossroad town of Quatre Bras.

Nigel Kneale's family came from the Isle of Man, though he was born in Barrow-in-Furness, Lancashire in 1922, and named Thomas Nigel. Both his parents came from farming stock but when one of the island's banks went bust, they sold up and went into various trades.

Nigel's father William was a journalist when he married Lilian in 1920, and the couple moved to the mainland where William (always

110

known as Tom) got a job on the *Barrow News and Mail*, followed by a move to Bolton and a job on the *Bolton Evening News*. But in 1928 they went back to the Isle of Man. The depression had hit the north west and the island seemed a better prospect. Tom Kneale became editor of an island newspaper called *Mona's Herald* (Mona being an ancient alternative name for the island).

The dreary damp of Lancashire had been bad for young Nigel's health but the Manx light was no better. It was discovered that he had a skin allergy which made it impossible to spend long periods in direct sunlight.

As a child, he loved boys' comics shipped in from the mainland and he devoured short stories. He admired the ghost story writer M. R. James as well as H. G. Wells (particularly *The War of the Worlds* and *The Invisible Man*).

The Isle of Man was a place rich in superstition and myth, with a leaning towards the pagan and white magic rather than conventional religion. 'If you're surrounded by sea,' said Kneale, 'it naturally comes with all sorts of sea monsters starting with mermaids and working up to things a hundred feet high.'

When the Second World War began, the Isle of Man was used as a sort of holding pen for Italians and Germans. These internees didn't have a bad time and the locals made friends with them.

Kneale left school at 17 and became a law student, writing stories in his spare time. He knew he wanted to be a writer and he also knew that he didn't want to be a lawyer. As a result, he took a gamble and didn't sit his final law exam 'for fear of passing it'.

In 1943, he was signed up by publishers Collins who were impressed by his short stories, which tended towards themes of the weird and supernatural. He read one of his stories live on the BBC's Home Service radio in 1946.

After the war, Kneale thought he might try his luck as an actor, moved to London and enrolled at the Royal Academy of Dramatic Art where he was told he had to get rid of his Manx accent. After he graduated in 1948, he won a place at the Royal Shakespeare Company in Stratford-upon-Avon where he was mostly a spear carrier. He soon came to the conclusion that he was 'the kind of actor who should stick to writing'.

In 1949, Collins published a collection of his work in book form – with a foreword by Elizabeth Bowen – called *Tomato Cain and Other Stories*, which is regularly cited as an important work in British horror writing, particularly one story called 'Minuke'. It's a haunted-house tale told by a matter-of-fact estate agent about a spanking new coastal modern bungalow, put up by a speculative builder in the era of ribbon development. First the new tenants, the Pritchards, complain of a faulty tap, then the serving hatch door crashes down on Mrs P's wrists as she's handing through a plate of bacon and eggs. Furniture begins to move about and food decomposes. What's the noise? It must be the sea. 'But you can't hear the sea in the kitchen ...'.

It's a little masterpiece; the details of the very ordinary bumping up against the extraordinary with a growing sense of dread. It's the format in those horror films, about unexceptional suburban houses which turn out to contain a gateway to hell among the fixtures and fittings, such as *The Amityville Horror* (1979 and 2005) and *Poltergeist* (1982).

Pressed to write a full-length novel which he didn't want to do, he wrote a drama for the BBC Home Service based on the Snaefell mining disaster on the Isle of Man in 1897. It was broadcast on 1 March 1950 from the Manchester studios.

Using his RADA contacts Kneale met Michael Barry, recently appointed head of the BBC TV drama group in London. After the war, television transmissions had recommenced on 7 June 1946 from Alexandra Palace, and in 1949 the BBC acquired another studio at Lime Grove, Shepherd's Bush. Kneale had never actually seen any television before the war because it hadn't reached the Isle of Man.

The primitive television industry didn't quite know what it was about in these early days and Kneale found himself doing all sorts of odds and ends for different departments, before he was employed at the BBC TV Script Unit. There were just two of them in the unit, Kneale and a man called George Kerr, in one of the down-at-heel Lime Grove buildings.

In 1952, in the insalubrious Lime Grove canteen, Kneale met Judith Kerr, a friend of one of the BBC secretaries, who had invited her to lunch. She had been born in Berlin in 1923. Her journalist father, born Alfred Kempner, was a Jew and had been an outspoken critic of the Nazis. The family fled Germany in 1933 on the very day that Hitler was elected chancellor, and after staying in Switzerland and France arrived in London in 1936.

Judith studied at the Central School of Arts and Crafts and then took a part-time teaching job at a girls' technical college in Lime Grove. In an interview with *The Times* in 2004, Kerr said of meeting Nigel: 'He rang me a few days later and took me to see a play that was so terrible, it was funny. We knew that night that we would be together.' Judith Kerr would become famous and much loved in her own right as the author of *The Tiger Who Came to Tea* children's stories.

Kneale wrote another radio play called *You Must Listen*, broadcast in 1952. Set in a solicitor's office that's having a new phone line installed (it was very difficult in those days to get a new line), there's a woman's voice on the line saying terrible, lewd things. The engineers can't get rid of it. Even when it's disconnected it carries on, pouring filth. Again, with the idea of a haunted telephone line, we see that juxtaposition of a humdrum modern world with some possibly supernatural malevolence.

He scripted a TV adaptation in 1953 of Charles Irving's novel *Number Three*, about a group of nuclear scientists who fear their work will be put to dangerous use. It starred Terence Alexander and Jack Watling, with a small role for Peter Cushing.

In 1953, TV scheduling, as a skill, was still in its infancy and it was noted with some alarm that there was a half-hour gap on six Saturday evenings between 18 July and 22 August. Kneale was asked to write something. He came up with *Bring Something Back*, about the launch of a three-man space mission. Only one of the crew returns and an alien life form has penetrated the rocket. The survivor – Victor Carroon – begins to slowly turn into a hideous hybrid.

Michael Barry liked the idea but it was felt that the title was weak. The professor character behind the rocket launch was called Bernard, as a tribute to Bernard Lovell, the then director of the Jodrell Bank Observatory. To find the surname, Kneale opened the London phone directory and found a family in the East End under the Qs. And so Bernard Quatermass was born as was the new title, *The Quatermass Experiment*.

Rudolph Cartier was to direct. André Morell turned down the role of Professor Quatermass and it went to Reginald Tate. Details were kept secret from the press and the first episode went out at 8.15 pm on Saturday, 18 July. Holst's *The Planets* suite ('Mars, Bringer of War') provides the alarming theme music. 'One morning the first manned rocket in the history of the world takes off,' says the voiceover. 'And then all contact is lost ...'.

The series began with an audience of over three million, rising to five million with the last episode.

TV's 'horror plays' had been a term for anything that had a supernatural or a thriller element. But nothing like this had ever been see before. The young Queen Elizabeth had just been crowned in Westminster Abbey and the climax of the series is set in a cleverly mocked up Westminster Abbey where the 60 foot alien lurks. Receiving little help from the special effects people at the BBC, who turned their noses up at science fiction, he and Judith bodged something together using foliage and rubber gloves.

Nigel Kneale and Judith Kerr married at Chelsea Register Office on 8 May 1954. That same year Kneale was commissioned by the BBC to write an adaptation of George Orwell's *Nineteen Eighty-Four*, again directed by Rudolph Cartier, and was also hoping to oversee a film version of *The Quatermass Experiment.*

It was Hammer Films which finally made an offer, then a small company making B films. To his dismay, when the BBC sold to Hammer, Kneale received no money because the BBC argued that, as he was a BBC employee, the script was the corporation's property.

Nineteen Eighty-Four was broadcast on 12 December 1954, starring Peter Cushing as Winston Smith, with Yvonne Mitchell – who had starred previously in Kneale's adaptation of *Wuthering Heights* (1953) – as Julia. It was a controversial production because BBC drama did not usually concern itself with such dystopian themes. The *Daily Express* ran a story headlined, 'Wife Dies as She Watches'. Their critic asked of the production, 'Why was this allowed?' But apparently the Queen and Prince Philip had both watched it and enjoyed it.

Kneale had been fascinated by the Yeti fever that gripped the world in the wake of Edmund Hillary and Tenzing Norgay's ascent of Everest and the discovery of 13-inch footprints in the snow. In 1954, the *Daily Mail* would sponsor its own Himalayan expedition to track down the 'Abominable Snowman'.

Kneale's contribution was *The Creature* (1955), an ambitious production starring Peter Cushing and Stanley Baker, which was again directed by Rudolph Cartier.

Meanwhile, Val Guest had been hired by Hammer to direct its film version of Kneale's TV series, now retitled *The Quatermass Xperiment* (1955) with a budget of £42,000 and American financial backing. Brian Donlevy was to play Quatermass, with Richard Wordsworth as the unlucky crew member Victor Carroon.

It was common for American stars past their best to be recycled in British genre films. Donlevy had once been a biggish star in comedies and film noir, but was now known to be downing martinis as though they were going out of fashion.

An American scriptwriter, Richard Landau, was called upon to boil down the script. Hammer had made a virtue of the fact that the film would get an X certificate (which could only be seen by over 18s) by retitling it *The Quatermass Xperiment*. In 1954, the British Board of Film Censors, having seen the script, said that the 'horrific element was so exaggerated as to be nauseating and revolting to adult audiences'. A judgment almost guaranteed to ensure the film's success.

But Kneale hated the end result, saying it was 'dreadful'. Though it isn't. The monster, Kneale complained, looks 'rather like an off-duty octopus'. And he's not entirely wrong about that.

The effective musical score is by the composer James Bernard, who would write the music for many Hammer films. It has been described as the first film score to treat strings in an unconventional, abrasive manner, including the use of tone clusters which create an edgy dissonance.

Writing in *Cahiers du Cinéma,* the critic and future film-maker François Truffaut said the film was 'very, very bad ... the subject could have been turned into a good film, not lacking in spice ... . None of this is in this sadly English film.'

Still employed by the BBC, Kneale was asked to write a six-part sequel to *The Quatermass Experiment*. The BBC had already dispatched Grace in *The Archers* in a fire in order to divert attention from ITV's opening night in 1955 and *Quatermass II* was intended as another salvo in the new ratings war with independent television. In the new series, Professor Quatermass is on the track of an alien invasion which is being covered up by the establishment. It suited the increasingly paranoid Cold War atmosphere of the mid 1950s.

Reginald Tate was again to play the professor but died of a heart attack on 23 August 1955 at the age of 58. John Robinson, 46, a Liverpudlian actor, was hastily given the role.

In many ways *Quatermass II* is more frightening and more plausible. In 1990, Kneale said it was 'about as socially conscious and politically conscious as I ever got in these things'.

Hammer, realising that sci-fi horror and horror in general was a winner, made *X The Unknown* (1956), written by production manager Jimmy Sangster. It concerns a Scottish village terrorised by radioactive slime which has escaped from the centre of the Earth. Joseph Losey was meant to direct until Hammer discovered that he had been blacklisted for communist sympathies by the House Un-American Activities Committee. Leslie Norman, father of the TV film critic Barry Norman, stepped in.

The X in the title obviously played on the popularity of the *Quatermass* film and Kneale (who had now left the BBC) was brought in to write a screenplay for Hammer's *Quatermass 2* (1957). Brian Donlevy starred again, Val Guest directed. Also in the cast you'll find Sid James, Bryan Forbes and William Franklyn.

Kneale, visiting Bray Studios to see how things were going, found Donlevy 'swallowing gin like it had just been invented'. Considering Donlevy's lacklustre performance, it's astonishing what a strong and menacing film *Quatermass 2* turned out to be.

Still shrewdly piggybacking on the TV success of Kneale's work, Hammer then made *The Abominable Snowman* (1957), directed by Val Guest, with Peter Cushing again in the lead. There was location filming in the snowy Pyrenees, which was obviously more effective than shooting live in a TV studio in West London.

Guest and Kneale were at odds over how much of the monster should be seen. It's something endlessly debated in the horror genre. Is it more frightening to suggest rather than show? At this point, the 'less is more' camp reaches for Edmund Burke's *A Philosophical Enquiry into the Origin of Our Ideas of the Sublime and Beautiful* – a key text for the Romantic movement:

> To make anything very terrible, obscurity seems in general to be necessary. When we know the full extent of any danger, when we can accustom our eyes to it, a great deal of the apprehension vanishes. Every one will be sensible of this, who considers how greatly night adds to our dread, in all cases of danger, and how much the notions of ghosts and goblins, of which none can form clear ideas, affects minds which give credit to the popular tales concerning such sorts of beings.

Kneale wanted the yeti to be seen but Guest, who prevailed, only wanted a shot of the creature's eyes. 'We dare you to see the abominable snowman of the Himalayas,' screamed the trailer. But, in fact, even if you dare, you don't.

Tony Richardson, while a director at London's Royal Court Theatre, had staged John Osborne's *Look Back in Anger* and wanted to launch his own career as a film director with a big-screen version. Osborne had written a film script which Kneale suspects was 'too stagey'.

Kneale was brought in and opened up the play. Osborne was not impressed with this, complaining that Kneale and Richardson were 'ripping out its obsessive, personal heart'.

Look Back in Anger (1959) starred Richard Burton as Jimmy Porter who, as the trailer informed us, 'learned at an early age what it was like to be angry'. The film launched any number of what were called 'kitchen-sink dramas' in British cinema. As a result, Kneale and Osborne collaborated on the screenplay for Osborne's play, *The Entertainer* (1960), starring Laurence Olivier.

In his biography, *Into the Unknown, the Fantastic Life of Nigel Kneale*, the writer Andy Murray says that Kneale once explained there were only three possible variations on the alien invasion scenario, namely: 'We go to them; they come to us; they have always been here.' *Quatermass and the Pit*, Kneale's third *Quatermass* serial for the BBC, brilliantly explores the third option.

Scarred by Second World War bombing, there was much rebuilding in the 1950s. Construction workers, digging down, discover a mysterious capsule. The location, Hobbs Lane, is significant, because Hob is an old name for the devil. It's this linking of sci-fi and the supernatural which makes the story so potent.

When a hole opens up in the object, the remains of aliens resembling horned-headed locusts are discovered. It seems that they are from Mars, and came five million years ago when the planet was habitable.

This time, André Morell, who had refused the part of Bernard Quatermass when Kneale wrote the first serial, took the lead.

Seven million watched the first episode on Monday, 22 December 1958 and eleven million watched the final episode. It's said that pubs were emptied on the night that the series was shown.

Quatermass and the Pit had a massive impact. To call it water-cooler TV is to underestimate its power. One accolade was an episode of *Hancock's Half Hour* called 'The Horror Serial' in which Tony Hancock, scared by watching *Quatermass and the Pit*, finds a mysterious object in his garden and alerts the authorities. *Quatermass* spoofs became quite the thing in TV light entertainment.

Sydney Newman, a Canadian, became head of drama at the BBC in 1962. Under him, the BBC invested in long-running and popular series such as *Doctor Who*, *Adam Adamant Lives!* (1966-7) and *The Forsyte Saga* (1967). He also championed the single TV play. In September 1963 he launched *First Night*, a series of new plays written especially for television. Nigel Kneale's play *The Road* was broadcast on Sunday, 29 September 1963, as part of this series.

It has acquired a legendary status, not least because nobody has seen it since, as it fell prey to the BBC's thrifty habit of wiping tapes for re-use.

The setting is a remote village in 1768, where the local squire sets about investigating some unsettling occurrences. The themes are classic Kneale favourites: superstition versus reason, and the past overlapping the present as the villagers are terrified by sounds from the nuclear future.

In an interview with the *News of the World* to promote *The Road*, Kneale insisted (not entirely convincingly): 'One thing I never do is put something in a plot just to frighten the customers. Any effects like fear are demanded by the story. It's not proper to try to horrify the lights out of people. One uses the unknown to stimulate people's thinking. And one points things out.'

Though the original was destroyed, a new radio version of the play was broadcast on BBC Radio 4 in 2018.

Kneale returned to the theme of nuclear Armageddon with *The Crunch* (1964) for ITV, starring Harry Andrews as a prime minister attempting to avert a nuclear catastrophe in London. This was in the era of 'Ban the Bomb' and the Campaign for Nuclear Disarmament. The prospect of a Third World War was, for many, the ultimate in horror.

Kneale's next film for Hammer was *The Witches* (1966), an adaptation of a novel by Norah Lofts (writing under the pseudonym Peter Curtis). Joan Fontaine stars as a schoolteacher, Gwen Mayfield, who returns with nervous exhaustion following a posting in Africa and then finds her quiet English village awash with voodoo black magic.

After much delay, Hammer finally produced a cinema version of *Quatermass and the Pit* (1967). In this adaptation, the pit where the capsule is unearthed was part of a London Underground station where renovation work was being carried out. Roy Ward Baker directed with Andrew Keir cast as a stern and convincing Professor Quatermass. Hammer favourite Barbara Shelley plays Barbara Judd, the palaeontologist who realises the significance of Hobbs Lane.

118

The Year of the Sex Olympics (1968) was a BBC play set in the future where a ruling elite pacify the population by subduing them with endless programmes of live sex. 'Sex is not to do. Sex is to watch.' Astonishingly prescient, Kneale imagined reality TV decades before it happened. Brian Cox and Leonard Rossiter starred. When Kneale died in 2006, horror aficionado Mark Gatiss wrote a tribute in *The Guardian* which opened: 'When Big Brother began on Channel 4 in 2000, I took a principled stand against it. "Don't they know what they're doing?" I screamed at the TV. "It's *The Year of the Sex Olympics*! Nigel Kneale was right!"'

A 'Wednesday Play' for the BBC called *Wine of India* (1970) dealt with another unsettling future, and starred Brian Blessed and Annette Crosbie. Medical technology has made it almost impossible for anyone to die. To keep the population at manageable levels people (who all look young whatever their ages) agree to terminate themselves at a set time. The play imagines a civilised cocktail party which will end with the death of a 'young' couple. Again, it was prescient and not unlike the sci-fi film *Logan's Run* (1976), where Jenny Agutter and Michael York play a couple who try to escape a similar fate.

The Chopper (1971) was about a motorbike haunted by the ghost of a biker recently killed in a crash. At much the same time, Steven Spielberg's early film *Duel* (1971) came out, in which a driver is relentlessly haunted by a supernatural juggernaut. And in 1983 Stephen King's novel *Christine* was published, and filmed the same year by John Carpenter – the story of a malevolent car.

In the mid-1980s, I was working as the TV previewer for *The Observer*. A colleague from *Time Out* and I, who were very keen on Nigel Kneale's work, were offered the opportunity to see his play *The Stone Tape*, which had originally been shown on Christmas Day 1972. We jumped at the chance and watched it in one of the offices at the old BBC TV Centre in White City.

In those days, you couldn't whistle up an old film or TV series on YouTube, and it was remarkable that *The Stone Tape* hadn't been wiped. Maybe, bearing the title in mind, that would have been too much of an irony.

Even in a bland corporate office in the middle of the day, the play sent shivers down the spine. An electronics company has taken on an old mansion as a research centre. One room seems to be haunted by the visible ghost of a Victorian housemaid, screaming as she falls to her death down a flight of stairs that is no longer there. Using their latest technological wizardry, the researchers attempt to record the phenomenon which, they reckon, has imprinted itself on the fabric of the building as though it was a piece of computer tape.

But what made the maid scream and drove her to her death? Could it be some darker, more terrible and very ancient evil that lies beneath this relatively modern phenomenon? Another layer of terror on the stone tape.

Jane Asher played the computer expert who proves unusually sensitive to the manifestations. But is it a scientific anomaly under investigation or something truly supernatural? This question is often at the heart of Kneale's work.

It is now possible to see it on YouTube and I watched it again. While the idea remains powerful, the relationship between Asher's character and the blokey boffins is excruciating. In that respect, it hasn't aged that well.

In 1976, Kneale wrote a six-part horror anthology called *Beasts* for ATV. An episode called *Baby*, starring Jane Wymark and Simon McCorkindale, seems to have been particularly frightening and even the short trailer is terrifying. It concerns a young couple (she's pregnant) who move to a depressing cottage in the middle of nowhere and find a jar containing the remains of an unidentifiable creature hidden in the walls. With its theme of ancient pagan creepiness, and how it persists in modern Britain, it's an example of what would come to be known as 'folk horror'.

It was Euston Films for Thames TV who would make the fourth *Quatermass* series in 1979 (a film version had a limited release). John Mills played Professor Quatermass who is searching for his granddaughter and fears she may have joined a cult known as the Planet People.

The Planet People are mostly young and disaffected, roaming the country and believing that they will be transported to a better life on another planet. It turns out that far from going to a better place they are being harvested by evil aliens.

At the time, it seemed to refer to the dropout culture of the 1970s (Kneale had begun work on the series five years earlier). But, as with so much of Kneale's work, it now seems to prefigure the millennial angst of Extinction Rebellion. The director was Piers Haggard who had made the cult folk horror film *Blood on Satan's Claw* (1971).

In 1981, I interviewed Nigel Kneale for *The Observer* in his lovely family house in south London and met his wife Judith Kerr – two of the nicest people. Though by this time Kneale had a reputation in the TV industry for being somewhat cantankerous.

The interview was to mark the sitcom he wrote for London Weekend Television called *Kinvig* starring Tony Haygarth. The inspiration had been a sci-fi convention that Kneale attend in Brighton, which he hated. 'These sorts of things attract the T-shirt brigade and people dressing up in funny costumes,' he told me. 'I suppose that's harmless, but you felt it was a cheap show that knew itself to be cheap ... . So much SF is the space equivalent of Barbara Cartland, peopled by very dull characters.'

In *Kinvig,* a harmless couple of electrical repairmen are obsessed with UFOs and conspiracy theories as an escape from their dull lives. It wasn't a great success and was consigned to a late-night slot.

Dan O'Bannon, who worked with John Carpenter on *Dark Star* (1974) and wrote the sci-fi horror film *Alien* (1979), had watched the *Quatermass* films in his youth and acknowledges Kneale's influence. Carpenter met Kneale in Hollywood with a view to him writing *Halloween III*. Carpenter too had been influenced by *Quatermass* and would use elements of the story in *The Thing* (1982) and *Prince of Darkness* (1987) – which he wrote himself, using the screenplay credit Martin Quatermass. In *The Mouth of Madness* (1994) there is a 'Hobb's End'.

To Kneale's displeasure, his script for *Halloween III* (1982) was changed out of all recognition, becoming less nuanced and more slasher. In the end, he walked away and asked that his name be taken off the credits.

Like any successful writer, Kneale's career is littered with unmade scripts and projects that never got off the ground. Yet his influence on cinema is immense, as is the affection in which his work is held by writers and directors who were stunned by the originality and daring of those early *Quatermass* stories.

In 1996, *The Quatermass Memoirs* was broadcast on Radio 3, dedicated 'to those who remember hiding behind the sofa when *Quatermass* came on. His adventures have gone down in cultural history,' said the producer Paul Quinn.

Nigel Kneale died in 2006, aged 84. His last script was for an episode of *Kavanagh QC* in 1997. Quatermass, found in the phone book in the early 1950s, remains, astonishingly, a byword for unsettling sci-fi horror of the very best kind.

Chapter Thirteen

Christopher Lee – 'Too tall to be an actor and too old to be a singer.'

Fans would come up to Christopher Lee and say they had seen all his films. 'No you haven't,' he would reply, because in his long career he made 350 films and even he didn't get to see them all. He has been called the 'king of the franchise', and he is the only actor who is the common denominator in *The Lord of the Rings* films, the *Star Wars* films, Hammer horror and the *Bond* films.

Yet it is as Dracula that he was, is and always will be, best known. He acquired a sort of lofty, fastidious distaste for the role and for the term 'horror', complaining that it should be turned 'fantasy' or 'fairy-tale'. His great friend Peter Cushing used to say much the same thing.

He was born in Belgravia on 27 May 1922, during a heatwave. His father Geoffrey was a colonel in the King's Royal Rifles and had served with distinction during the First World War. Geoffrey had married the Contessa Estelle Marie Carandini in 1910, daughter of the Marquis de Sarzano. She came from one of Italy's oldest aristocratic families with links to Charlemagne and the Borgias. She was a society beauty and the couple was a favourite in *Tatler* magazine. She was a fine singer, danced the tango and had had her bottom pinched by Caruso.

Christopher's father, educated at Radley and Sandhurst, had retired from the Army at the age of 40 and 'confined himself to cricket and golf and blazing away at wildlife', and was a member of the Sunningdale Golf Club. But he was also a reckless gambler, which almost certainly led to him leaving the marriage when Christopher was 4, and not long after the birth of his sister Xandra. The couple divorced two years later.

The contessa remarried a banker called Harcourt George St Croix Rose, nicknamed Ingle, an extraordinarily strong man who would bend pokers round his neck to amuse Christopher.

'It began to rain silver fox furs and diamond pendants,' said Lee in his autobiography *Lord of Misrule*.

Ingle knew all sorts of interesting people. Lee recalled being hauled out of bed to meet a couple of Russian emigrés, Prince Yusupov and the Grand Duke Dmitri Pavlovich, who had been among those who had assassinated Rasputin. Lee would play him in the 1966 Hammer film, *Rasputin the Mad Monk*.

From 1931 he attended Summer Fields prep school near Oxford where he was a contemporary of Patrick Macnee. The plan had been for Christopher to go to Eton and at an interview he met the famous ghost story writer M. R. James, who was the college's provost at the time.

Any hopes of enjoying hearing the 'master of the macabre' read his stories were dashed because Ingle decided that he could not afford the fees. Christopher, aged 14, was sent to Wellington College instead. 'It seems I had fallen among barbarians,' he said, after a miserable first term, 'with nothing to do but grit it out for the next four years'.

It turned out to be only three years because Ingle was declared bankrupt and a 17-year-old Lee found himself out of full-time education. He was already 6 ft 4 ins tall and aware that he was doomed to spend a lifetime sleeping diagonally in beds which were never quite long enough. He was good-looking but decidedly foreign looking, which meant he had become accustomed to being called 'wop' and 'dago' at school.

Ingle and the contessa split up and she went to live in a little cottage – Ramblers' Cottage – overlooking Wentworth golf course.

In the face of penury, it seemed that the best thing to do with her son Christopher was to send him off to the south of France for a holiday in Menton.

Stepping off in Paris he met the distinguished war correspondent, Webb Miller (who would die mysteriously on the London Underground a year later). Webb took the young man under his wing and, by way of entertainment, took him to see the last public execution in France – that of the serial killer Eugen Weidmann, who was guillotined in Paris. Lee claimed to have been afflicted by nightmares of this for the rest of his life.

The holiday in Menton was cut short by war jitters, which forced Lee to return to London with all speed. He took a job with a company in the City, working for United States Lines, a transatlantic shipping company, and commuted from Virginia Water to Waterloo each day.

He moved on to a £1-a-week job with Beecham's and once saw Ingle on a bus, apparently down on his luck. He would never see him again.

Geoffrey, Christopher's father, died suddenly of double pneumonia and at this point Christopher, by now working for Beecham's as a messenger for £1 a week, volunteered for the RAF.

Initially he was sent to Elementary Flying Training School in Hillside, Rhodesia, near Bulawayo, learning in Tiger Moths with open cockpits.

During one session, flying at 5,000 feet, Lee developed a blinding headache and could not see out of his left eye. His sight returned but it was found that there was a problem with his optic nerve and, as a result, he was ruled unfit to be a pilot. He was devastated and felt that 'nobody knew what to do with me'.

He was moved into intelligence and seconded into the Rhodesian police force, where he served as a warden in Salisbury Prison.

He was posted to Suez and Cairo and then received orders to report to 260 Squadron, which he viewed as a 'real job' and involved debriefing pilots who had supported the invasion of the Eighth Army.

Following the decisive Battle of Monte Cassino, he was in Rome where he was promoted to flight lieutenant.

Before sailing from Naples to be demobbed in Britain, he served with the Central Registry of War Crimes and Security Suspects, compiling dossiers on men and women wanted for interrogation. His work took him to a number of concentration camps including Dachau.

During the course of the war he won six campaign medals, was mentioned in despatches and received decorations from Poland, Yugoslavia and Czechoslovakia. Later he would say: 'When the Second World War finished I was 23 and already I had seen enough horror to last me a lifetime. I'd seen dreadful, dreadful things, without saying a word. So seeing horror depicted on film doesn't affect me much.'

He had also caught malaria and been injured in a bomb blast, so spent a period in an RAF hospital before he was released back into civilian life. He had no idea what he wanted to do until he had lunch with his cousin Nicolò Carandini, who had fought in the Italian resistance movement and was now the Italian ambassador who said, 'Why don't you become an actor?'

His mother wasn't keen. 'Just think of all the appalling people you'll meet!,' she said. But Nicolò introduced him to a former lawyer called Filippo del Giudice who was head of Two Cities Films. Founded in 1937, it was a production company operating in London and Rome, but it had been subsumed by the Rank Organisation in the mid 1940s. As a result of this meeting, in 1947, Lee was put on a seven-year contract with the Company of Youth, popularly known as the Rank charm school. This was an attempt by J. Arthur Rank to manufacture and nurture stars in the same way as Hollywood.

Christopher Lee's first film was a small role in *Corridor of Mirrors* (1948), a spooky, swooning tale of romance and reincarnation. It was the directorial debut of Terence Young who would direct three James Bond films – *Dr No* (1962), *From Russia With Love* (1963) and *Thunderball* (1965).

This was followed by *One Night with You* (1948), a comedy musical romance involving stolen luggage and a railway station.

Both Lee and Peter Cushing had small roles (though they never met at that time) in Laurence Olivier's film of *Hamlet* (1948). All Lee had to do was shout 'Lights!' while standing in the dark.

He appeared in *Song for Tomorrow* (1948) which was directed by Terence Fisher who would go on to direct many Hammer horror films. Lee played a nightclub MC.

He was living in a basement flat in Chelsea and spent his money combing the record shops of Charing Cross Road for old opera 78s. He began to take singing lessons but, with no sign that his career was about to take off, he began to wonder if he was 'too tall to be an actor and too old to be a singer'.

His height served him well playing villains and aristocratic vampires. But though 'tall, dark and handsome' are usually welcome attributes in a man, 'tall' is not always good for an actor. In his autobiography Lee says, 'a leading lady doesn't like to speak her lines to her lover as if she had a hinge at the back of her neck, nor play to a man's belt buckle.'

In *Scott of the Antarctic* (1948), directed by Charles Frend, with John Mills, Kenneth More and James Robertson Justice, he plays Bernard Day, a member of the British Antarctic Expedition. But he wasn't required for the location filming in Norway, instead working on the Ealing Studios where he recalled blizzards 'made of salt and acrylic resin, minced in a sieve and blown across the set by an aeroplane engine'.

In *Trottie True* (1949), a comedy about a Gaiety Girl in the 1890s starring Jean Kent, he played the Hon Bongo Icklesham and also met another up-and-coming young actor Roger Moore.

As part of his training, Rank sent him to work in rep at the Connaught Theatre in Worthing. He played the butler in *The Constant Nymph*, a popular play by Margaret Kennedy which had been turned into a best-selling novel and filmed in 1928.

He would never be comfortable with live theatre work and remembers how, at the interval, the producer – impatient with the way the butler was upstaging everyone else's performance – came to his dressing room and said: 'Would you be good enough to finish the rest of the play on your own. As you're playing every part, the rest of the cast can go home.'

He overstretched himself by appearing in *The Flat Next Door* at the Whitehall Theatre when he was also filming *Prelude to Fame* (1950) at Pinewood Studios. (He was cast as 'the newsman'.) Unsure of his lines in *The Flat Next Door*, and shaking with nerves, he was additionally humiliated when he put his hand through a window pane supposedly made of glass and the audience erupted in mirth.

Live TV was also hazardous. In an edition of *Kaleidoscope* (a popular TV show of games and sketches, which ran from 1946 to 1953), Lee was cast as a French policeman in a long scene with a very nervous actor who broke wind constantly and deafeningly for ten minutes.

Rank decided not to renew his contract because (in Lee's opinion) he was too tall, too foreign looking and hadn't made a name for himself.

But he felt things were looking up when he was cast in *Captain Horatio Hornblower* (1951) with Gregory Peck and Stanley Baker. And he duelled with Errol Flynn (playing Edward the Black Prince) in *The Dark Avenger* (1955).

A combination of Rank training and his father's skills at fencing that had been passed on to his son ensured that Lee was good for sword-duelling sequences. In *The Dark Avenger* he also performed as Flynn's double in some of the fighting scenes. This big-budget film caused him to observe one critical difference between American and British films. In his autobiography he says, 'Americans always homed in on their secondary characters giving them their moment. The British didn't. Even in those days they didn't have the time.'

Crimson Pirate (1952), directed by Robert Siodmak, was a similarly big-budget film. It was a Technicolor swashbuckler with Burt Lancaster. Christopher Lee had a small role and said that Lancaster taught him everything about screen fighting. 'I don't think I've ever seen a better co-ordinated man,' he said. 'He moved remarkably well, immensely strong and quite fearless.'

He worked on (pre-recorded) television series throughout the 1950s, among them *The Scarlet Pimpernel* (1955), with Marius Goring as Sir Percy Blakeney, in which Lee played a villainous aristocrat. In *The Adventures of William Tell*, first broadcast in 1958, he was cast as the mad Duke Erik.

His old friend Roger Moore won the lead in *Ivanhoe*, the children's series which was first screened in 1958. Lee was a regular guest star and there was more than enough duelling and stunt work to keep him happy.

But he was not getting the breakthrough roles: 'At the age of 35 the men of my family had become cardinals or colonels, chairmen or ambassadors. I had gone into acting without a natural gift for it. After ten years in the cinema I was as tall and foreign and almost as unknown as when I started.'

It seemed no more than yet another faintly undignified role when his agent, John Redway, told him he had heard that Hammer films planned a remake of *Frankenstein* in colour. 'It was self-evident,' thought Lee at the time, 'that this was not a path to glory'.

Coincidentally he had also met Boris Karloff, then in his sixties, for the first time. They would become friends and neighbours in London. Karloff's great film of *Frankenstein* had been made in 1931. Said Lee: 'The great era of the macabre fantasy struck me as essentially being in the Twenties and early Thirties and hardly relevant to my own prospects.'

Lee agreed to play the Creature in *The Curse of Frankenstein* (1957), but there was no question of him looking anything like Boris Karloff's monster. That make-up had been copyrighted by Universal Studios.

In the event Lee's appearance was equally gruesome, if not quite so iconic. Someone wrote, 'Christopher Lee looked like a road accident'. When in full make-up on the set he could only eat mash and mince and drink through a straw. One consolation was meeting Peter Cushing who was playing Baron Frankenstein. They would make twenty-two films together. 'From the moment we met, Cushing and I were friends,' said Lee.

Playing the Creature made Lee appreciate Boris Karloff's skill. 'And perhaps,' he said, 'that helped me adjust to the very notion of working in the horror genre. It was a case of inventing a being who was neither oneself nor anybody else.'

Lee invests his Creature, grotesque as he is, with great pathos. The critics slaughtered it but the public flocked to see it. The usual way with horror films.

He was on straightforward aristocratic-foreign-villain duty in the Rank Organisation's adaptation of Charles Dickens' *A Tale of Two Cities* (1958), cast as the Marquis St Evrémonde. But in the same year, he made the film that would define his career – *Dracula*.

Michael Carreras, boss of Hammer, said:

> He was an obvious choice when you think about it. He had absolutely the right features, the commanding presence and that fantastic voice. I'm quite sure if anybody at all had been sitting in that office and they saw six actors, one of whom was Christopher Lee, they would have chosen him as Dracula too.

Though Bela Lugosi's count conveyed an unsettling menace and was a real presence on screen, he was, as David Pirie writes in *A New Heritage of Horror*, 'the living tableau of a silent stage actor trapped in modern sound movies'.

Lee, by contrast, had an energetic feral sexiness, that seemed modern, even though he swirled his cape through Hammer's vision of Victorian England. He says that when he began filming *Dracula*, directed by Terence Fisher, he had never seen Lugosi's 1931 version but had read and enjoyed Bram Stoker's novel, identifying with the vampire's 'extraordinary stillness punctuated by bouts of manic energy'.

He was, however, troubled by the red contact lenses which were uncomfortable and made it hard to see where he was going. Dracula's death, caused by Peter Cushing pulling down the drapes to let in the daylight and then pinning Dracula to the floor with a crucifix made by crossed candlesticks (his own idea) is terrific. Dracula's disintegration into dust took a whole day to achieve. During each stage of putrefaction, we cut to Cushing's face, as a pained sympathy for the hideous spectacle passes across it.

But, of course, while Dracula might die time after time he would always return.

The part bestowed on Lee was what he described as the 'blessing of Lucifer'. There would be no escape. On the plus side, it brought him 'a name, a fan club and a second-hand car' (a Mercedes). During these early years with Hammer, he used to loan out that Mercedes and his services as a chauffeur for five shillings a time. After all, his fee for playing Dracula in the first Hammer film was only £750.

Purist Dracula fans are sticklers for vampire lore, something which writers Mark Gatiss and Steven Moffat had fun with in the 2019 BBC TV version of *Dracula* starring Claes Bang as the count. Why was Dracula averse to sunlight and stricken by the sight of the cross? So ponders his nemesis, a nun called Agatha Van Helsing. And while vampire purists are always on the alert for signs of the story diverging from Stoker's novel, they also enjoy references to Dracula's cinematic heritage. In the 2019 TV series, Agatha's grand niece, Zoe Van Helsing, is dying of cancer and the number of her ward is AD I 072, a reference for eagle-eyed fans to the Dracula film *Dracula AD 1972*.

Even as early as the 1950s and 1960s, Lee was called to account by buffs who 'popped up to reproach us with an oversight. One grumbled that I cast a shadow', which of course the authentic Stoker-esque Dracula did not do, any more than he had a reflection in a mirror.

The great success of the film, both in Britain and the United States, ought to have secured Lee's position as vampire-in-chief. But according to John Brosnan in his book *The Horror People*: 'His contribution to the success of Dracula was apparently overlooked, and instead of giving him similar roles that utilised his unique sexual attraction he was relegated to a series of supporting roles.' These included *The Hound of the Baskervilles* (1959), *The Man Who Could Cheat Death* (1959) and *The Two Faces of Dr Jekyll* (1960). He is not even seen in the first sequel, *The Brides of Dracula* (1960), also directed by Terence Fisher, which stars Cushing again as Doctor Van Helsing.

Always keen to make use of the many languages he spoke, he went to Italy to make *Tempi Duri Per I Vampiri* (1959), a comedy pastiche of old horror films, which was exported to the English speaking world under the title *Uncle was a Vampire*.

Lee also appeared in *City of the Dead* (1960), his first non-Hammer horror film and the first to be produced by Milton Subotsky and Max Rosenberg who teamed up to form Amicus. This company specialised in portmanteau horror movies such as *Dr Terror's House of Horrors* (1965). *City of the Dead*, released as *Horror Hotel* in the United States, was a tale of witches' sabbaths in Massachusetts and virgins sacrificed on altars.

Lee met and fell in love with Henriette von Rosen, a Swedish aristocrat. Henriette's father wanted the couple to wait a year before they became engaged and hired private detectives to check up on the actor's background. Lee is somewhat unforthcoming about the relationship in his autobiography, but eventually he decided to call it a day and broke the news to Henriette as they sat parked in Eaton Square in the Mercedes.

A Danish friend introduced Lee to Birgit Kroencke, known as Gitte, a painter and model with red hair and green eyes. He was instantly smitten and the couple married at St Michael's Church in London's Chester Square. But they only had a weekend together before Lee had to begin shooting *The Devil's Daffodil* (1961), a German black-and-white crime thriller also starring Klaus Kinski who would play Nosferatu in Werner Herzog's 1978 remake.

Lee fancied himself as a pan-European actor and the couple moved to Switzerland, to Vevey on the north shore of Lake Geneva. Among the many films he appeared in was *Castle of the Living Dead* (1964), in which he played the evil Count Drago directed by American Warren Kiefer and produced by Paul Maslansky. Among the crew was the young Michael Reeves.

Christina, Lee and Gitte's daughter, was born in 1963. It was a traumatic birth and the baby was born with deformed legs. She spent her early years in splints to correct her limbs but eventually the treatment was successful and she was able to walk unaided.

Lee, meanwhile, realised that he was not going to become the European star he had hoped to be. The family moved back to London, living in a house just off the King's Road.

Between 1965 and 1968 Lee played the villainous Fu Manchu five times, always directed by Don Sharp.

Back with Hammer he made *Dracula, Prince of Darkness* (1966) in which he has no lines, and only hisses. 'In the book he hardly ever stops talking,' complained Lee. 'I think he should say something in these films, though when he does speak it has to be something worth saying.' On the bright side, his cloak is now lined in scarlet silk. Hammer liked a lot of red in its films, apart from the fake blood (what those in the know jokingly referred to as 'Kensington Gore').

He liked *The Devil Rides Out* (1968), based on the novel by his friend Dennis Wheatley, directed by Terence Fisher, with Charles

Gray as a compelling villain and Lee, for once, on the side of good as the Duc de Richleau.

Dracula Has Risen from the Grave (1968) followed, then *Taste the Blood of Dracula* (1970) and *Scars of Dracula* (1970). In an interview with *Films Illustrated* in 1972, he complained about his new film *Dracula AD 1972*:

> All I do is get to stand around on unhallowed ground, sweep down corridors and make the odd pounce or two. Nobody can write dialogue for Dracula. Time and again I have suggested they go back to the original Bram Stoker novel. In the new film I have one original Bram Stoker line but that's yelled out at a distance of a hundred years. I've told Hammer that unless certain conditions are met, I shall not play the role again.

But he did, in *The Satanic Rites of Dracula* (1973). He was always a compulsive worker. When he was in his seventies, he said that the longest he had ever been out of work was four months.

In the mid 1970s, partly to get away from 'vampiric overdrive', the family moved to Hollywood where he found he was 'prancing from genre to genre like the devil on stepping stones'.

The move led to an acquaintance joking that 'the population of Los Angeles were dusting out their bomb shelters in anticipation of a barrage of anecdotes'. Lee was known to go on a bit. There is the story of an actress (unnamed) who got off a plane looking exhausted and white as a sheet. Asked by the airport staff if she needed medical attention, she said she had been sitting next to Lee on the plane and he had not stopped talking about himself during the ten-hour flight.

Years before, he had wanted to play *Doctor No*, the Bond villain in the 1962 film which was the first in the Bond series and directed by Terence Young. The part had gone to Joseph Wiseman.

But now Ian Fleming, a cousin of Lee's, wanted him to play the villain Scaramanga in *The Man with the Golden Gun* (1974). He was paid £40,000 for this, which was the highest fee he had ever commanded until he moved into the big-budget franchises of *Star Wars* and *The Lord of the Rings* in his later years.

Living in LA, he became aware of how much the great directors of the time – Steven Spielberg, Brain De Palma, Francis Ford Coppola and Martin Scorsese – had been influenced by Hammer. He felt that, regrettably, Hammer had become 'complacent and careless' and that a great British asset had been squandered.

In Hollywood he was an unexpected success, hosting TV's *Saturday Night Live* and appearing as a U-boat captain in Spielberg's *1941* (1979).

For many, his finest film in the 1970s was *The Wicker Man* (1973), directed by Robin Hardy and written by Anthony Shaffer. Edward Woodward plays the uptight policeman Sergeant Howie who arrives on the remote Scottish island of Summerisle to investigate the case of a missing child. Lee is the laird Lord Summerisle, presiding over a community given over to pagan worship. It is folk horror's masterpiece, described by the magazine *Cinefantastique* as 'the *Citizen Kane* of horror movies'.

'It was the best scripted film I ever took part in,' said Lee, who was paid nothing for appearing in this low-budget (£500,000) film. It was released as a part of a double bill with *Don't Look Now* and such was Lee's belief in the film that he begged critics to go and see it. Meeting Michael Deeley at a screening, producer of *The Italian Job* (1969), *The Deer Hunter* (1978) and *Blade Runner* (1982), Lee was appalled when Deeley said: 'It's one of the worst ten films I've ever seen.'

The film was savagely cut with much of the original footage going missing. Producer Peter Snell spent months investigating. He concluded that the cans of film may well have been dumped in a hollow near Shepperton which had been filled for a new road along with, possibly, 300 other movies.

In 1985, Lee had a heart attack and returned to live in London where he underwent heart surgery but returned quickly to work.

Star Wars and *The Lord of the Rings* franchises beckoned, the well-paid reward for the grand old men of British films and theatre.

Lee won a Bafta fellowship award in 2011. A BFI fellowship in 2013 was presented to him by Johnny Depp. In France, he was made commander of arts and letters. He was made CBE in 2001 and knighted in 2009, shuddering at tabloid headlines which ran 'Fangs For The Memory'.

He was a dedicated golfer, a devout Anglo-Catholic and had a library of occult books, an interest he had developed when he made friends with Dennis Wheatley.

Christopher Lee died aged 93 in 2015. At 50 he had decided to 'Draculate no more'. But he would be Dracula for all time. 'I was drowned, asphyxiated and incinerated,' he said, 'and three times when I was burnt, the barn or studio went up too. I always came back for more. Through clouds of nuclear waste I intoned … . The world shall hear of me again.'

And as he observed, Stoker was wrong about one thing – Dracula casts a very long shadow.

Chapter Fourteen

Roger Corman – 'The Pope of Pop Cinema.'

Roger Corman is often asked which of his films he likes best. *Creature from the Haunted Sea* (1961) may not be one of his best-known pictures, but he says it's a strong contender as his favourite.

It's a comedy horror, spoofing spy and gangster films. The villain begins to bump off the passengers aboard a ship transporting Cuban exiles and a treasure chest, while claiming that a sea monster is to blame.

But here's the twist. There really IS a monster. The film ends (spoiler alert) with the monster sitting on the treasure chest on the seabed, contentedly picking from his teeth the bones of his victims and burping quietly. 'The monster wins!' said Corman.

Now in his nineties, Roger Corman was a child of the Depression, born in Detroit in 1926. He was 3 years old at the time of the Great Crash in 1929 and believes this shaped his attitude towards money. 'My film budgets have always been notoriously lean, while the waste and excess built into the major studios' production have tended to appall me.'

Lean and spare himself, well over 6 foot with the look of a disciplined military man who has somehow stumbled into the louche world of independent, low-budget cinema, Corman has always been a self-proclaimed maverick. His 1990 autobiography is called *How I Made a Hundred Movies in Hollywood and Never Lost a Dime*. In fact, unusually, he sells himself short in the title. He made many more than 100 movies. More like 400.

His father, William, was an engineer and the family moved to a not-very fashionable section of Beverly Hills. Roger went to Beverly Hills High where his classmates had names such as Goldwyn, Warner, Zukor and Laemmle.

He excelled at maths and sciences but read widely as well. Edgar Allen Poe's *The Fall of the House of Usher* made a great impression on him. As a film-maker he would make several adaptations of Poe's works.

He went to Stanford University in California to study engineering and when war began he joined the Navy, but never saw active service. By now he had decided that a career in engineering was not for him and he began to look for work in the film industry, eventually finding a lowly job as a messenger at Twentieth Century Fox.

The major studios – MGM, Twentieth Century Fox, Paramount, Universal and Columbia – still dominated. But a ruling by the Supreme Court in 1948, called the Paramount consent decree, ended their monopoly on distribution.

This anti-trust rule prevented movie studios from owning a significant number of cinemas and banned ticket price fixing and other practices that forced cinemas to purchase movies in bulk packages. This opened the market to small independent producers, though on the downside it led to the closure of hundreds of cinemas. It was also the dawn of the television age. All these changes helped shape Corman's career.

He progressed from delivering packages to being a 'story analyst', which meant reading and reworking scripts. It was frustrating work because Corman wanted to write his own scripts. He applied to Oxford University on the GI Bill, which offered Second World War veterans the chance to attend higher education along with other benefits. He was accepted and studied modern literature at Balliol College for just one term. He moved on to Paris's Left Bank where many other hip American students had gone to enjoy jazz and existentialism.

He made a little easy money smuggling Leica cameras from West Germany into Paris, but when his funds ran out he returned to America.

Corman sold a script to Allied Artists for $3,500 called *Highway Dragnet* (1954), starring Joan Bennett and Richard Conte. But the first film he produced, raising $12,000, was *Monster from the Ocean Floor* (1954), inspired by an article in the *LA Times* about a one-man submarine that was being tested. The submarine, made by Aerojet General, takes a starring role in this story of a one-eyed marine monster, a mutant caused by atomic testing, lurking off the coast of Mexico.

In 1954, he became one of the founders of American International Pictures (AIP) set up by James Nicholson, former sales manager of Realart Pictures Inc, and Samuel Arkoff, an entertainments lawyer. It was aiming at a teenage audience, with low-budget films packaged as double features. Appearing in a chat show in the 1980s, Arkoff expanded on his 'Arkoff' formula for a successful low-budget movie: A for Action;

R for Revolution (a novel or controversial theme); K for Killing (a small amount of screen violence); O for Oratory (a good script); F for Fantasy; F for Fornication (sex appeal).

AIP's publicity department also came up with what they called 'the Peter Pan Syndrome', which stated that:

a) a younger child will watch anything an older child will watch

b) an older child will not watch anything a younger child will watch

c) a girl will watch anything a boy will watch

d) a boy will not watch anything a girl will watch

Therefore: to catch your greatest audience you zero in on the 19-year-old male.

AIP's first film, which Corman wrote and produced, was *The Fast and the Furious* (1955), a crime drama starring John Ireland and Dorothy Malone, filmed in sixteen days. The title itself is an accurate description of Corman's movies, the speed at which he made them and the sheer volume of action – chases, crashes, fires, floods, fights. As someone says in the documentary, *Corman's World*, released in 2011: 'Girls who go skinny dipping and end up being eaten by the crocodiles – that's just so Roger Corman.'

Corman's next movie, which he also directed, was a return to sci-fi with the post nuclear-holocaust *The Day the World Ended* (1955). The opening credits read: 'What you are about to see may never happen ... but to this anxious age in which we live, it presents a fearsome warning.'

It's 1970 and only seven people have survived a nuclear war. They find refuge in a house in an isolated valley shielded by mountains from radiation. The formula of placing an assortment of imperilled and disparate characters under one roof is a mainstay of horror thrillers.

Between 1956 and 1957, Corman made a dozen of these 'exploitation' films. He explains:

Exploitation films were so named because you made a film about something wild with a great deal of action, a little sex, and possibly some sort of strange gimmick; they often come

136

out of the day's headlines. It's interesting how, decades later, when the majors saw they could have enormous commercial success with big-budget exploitation films, they gave them the loftier terms – 'genre' films or 'high concept' films.

Not of This Earth (1957) is about an alien called Paul Johnson (stolidly played by Paul Birch in dark sunglasses) who comes from the planet Davana where everyone is being wiped out by a blood disease. Johnson, a fastidious type, who can kill humans with a glance from his white eyeballs, has arrived to send back samples of blood. The tone is very tongue-in-cheek yet it still packs a punch. The fine balance of horror and humour is a thread that runs through Corman's films.

Also in the cast was Beverly Garland who was close to him but not romantically. 'There was a puritanical side to him, almost like a boy scout,' she said. 'I didn't want a boy scout. Roger debonair? No. Not an Omar Sharif type. He was happiest when he was wheeling and dealing.'

With *The Little Shop of Horrors* (1960), Corman reckoned he had created a new genre – the black comedy horror film. It certainly became a cult classic – very much like *The Rocky Horror Picture Show* (1975) – and over the next thirty years spawned another movie, an award-winning comedy musical and a fanzine (*Little Shoppe of Horrors*) for horror buffs.

In this film, which either strikes you as amusing or plain stupid, a florist's assistant grows a plant that feeds on human blood and wheezes 'feed me' (which became a catchphrase). A very youthful Jack Nicholson appears as Wilbur Force, a creepy young undertaker who loves pain and refuses Novocain at the dentist because it 'dulls the senses'. It was made at breakneck speed between Christmas and New Year in 1959.

The early 1960s were Corman's Edgar Allen Poe years. Between 1960 and 1964, he moved firmly into Gothic horror territory – often recycling the same sets – with eight films based on stories by Poe, which he had first read when he was a child.

His highly sensitive commercial radar also told him that there was money to be made from exploiting the Hammer recipe of lurid period films, made in colour with a literary provenance. Bram Stoker's *Dracula* and Mary Shelley's *Frankenstein* were being retold and reinvented and audiences never seemed to tire of them. Could adaptations of Poe be as successful?

He wanted to make a colour film based on *The Fall of the House of Usher*. 'Poe has a built-in audience,' he told his backers at AIP. 'He's read in every high school.'

Corman was by now the man known for making monster films, so when the producer Samuel Arkoff asked: 'But where's the monster?', Corman replied: 'The house is the monster.' He got the go ahead and a budget of $270,000, with a large proportion of that going to the actor who was Corman's first choice – Vincent Price. The film, entitled simply *House of Usher,* was released in 1960.

The story of siblings Roderick and Madeline Usher, trapped by a house and by their own madness and catalepsy had been filmed before. Curtis Harrington – who became close to the *Frankenstein* director James Whale when he was studying film at UCLA – cast himself as the siblings and directed two films in 1942. A British black-and-white version had been released in 1950 starring Gwendoline Watford.

House of Usher is a magnificent poetic work, hallucinatory in the way the narrator focuses languorously on small details of Roderick Usher's deterioration and the awful house. Then Poe hurries us along with a startling sentence which is almost comic in its briskness. For example: 'One evening, having informed me abruptly that the lady Madeline was no more, he stated his intention of preserving her corpse for a fortnight (previously to its final interment), in one of the numerous vaults within the main walls of the building.' The reader wants to say, 'Hang on! Run that one past me again ...'

Corman was fascinated by the connection between humour and horror, between creating and sustaining tension and by the psychology of fear in general. Drawing on Freud's interpretation of dreams, he wanted his movies to work on an unconscious symbolic plane, comparing the windows, doors, arches and corridors in a horror film to a woman's body.

'The deeper you go into the dark hallways, then, the deeper you are delving into, say, an adolescent boy's first sexual stirrings,' he said. Desire and fear build tension and a horror sequence is – he says – equivalent to the sexual act with the feeling of release from tension the equivalent of an orgasm.

Whereas a comedian ratchets up the tension and gets a laugh with the punch line, a horror director does the same and 'gets a scream'. Sets should always be interiors he thought, and exteriors should only appear at night. Though in *The Tomb of Ligeia* (1964) – his last Poe film – he would make good use of the ruins of Castle Acre Priory in Norfolk.

The Pit and the Pendulum (1961) cast Vincent Price in doublet and hose, as Nicholas Medina, son of an Inquisition torturer whose torture chamber is still in working order downstairs in the family castle. His wife Elizabeth (Barbara Steele) has just died of fright in an iron maiden. Or has she? Elizabeth's brother comes to discover the truth about her death and ends up on Medina's 'ultimate device of torture', the razor-sharp pendulum swinging inexorably towards his body. 'You are about to enter hell,' promises Medina. The last scene is a delicious shocker.

Due to a contractual dispute with AIP, Corman cast Ray Milland rather than Vincent Price in *The Premature Burial* (1962), another Poe adaptation. Milland plays nervy newlywed Guy Carrell (Hazel Court plays his bride), a British aristocrat with a serious laudanum habit and a morbid fear of being buried alive.

Next came a Poe trilogy of short films called *Tales of Terror* (1962) – 'Morella', 'The Black Cat' and 'Facts in the Case of M. Valdemar'. In 'Morella', Vincent Price plays another grieving widower (as in *The Pit and the Pendulum*) who keeps his wife's rotting corpse tucked up in bed.

When his daughter arrives back home, his dead spouse possesses her. It's a rich brew of necrophilia and incest. 'The Black Cat' teams Vincent Price and Peter Lorre as unlikely love rivals. Price and Basil Rathbone star in 'M. Valdemar' about a man hypnotised on his deathbed and then manipulated by the living as his body deteriorates.

Grieving yet again for a dead wife in *The Raven* (1963), Vincent Price, as Dr Erasmus Craven, is a sorcerer visited by a rival magician Dr Bedlo (Peter Lorre), who was turned into a raven by the evil Dr Scarbarus (played by Boris Karloff). Bedlo's son Rexford is played by Jack Nicholson and Hazel Court is the deceased wife.

The Raven is a long, narrative poem published by Poe in 1845, chronicling a descent into madness. A 1935 film by Universal Studios starred Boris Karloff and Bela Lugosi ('Lugosi at his most unhinged' screamed the publicity). In Corman's hands and with a script by Richard Matheson it becomes a high camp horror comedy.

Price also plays a devoted but sinister husband in *The Tomb of Ligeia* (1964). Anyone seeking a biographical handle on Poe's fondness for a dead or dying wife will find it in his strange relationship with his cousin Virginia Clemm. He married her when she was 13 and, apparently, they lived as brother and sister. When she was barely out of her teens she contracted TB and died at the age of 24.

Her years of illness left Poe deeply depressed – especially when she seemed to get better only to relapse yet again. He wrote to a friend:

> Each time I felt all the agonies of her death – and at each accession of the disorder I loved her more dearly and clung to her life with more desperate pertinacity. But I am constitutionally sensitive – nervous in a very unusual degree. I became insane, with long intervals of horrible sanity.

Matheson wrote the screenplays for five of Corman's Poe adaptations including *House of Usher* and *The Pit and the Pendulum*. He also wrote sci-fi and westerns, novels and scripts. His work includes the screenplay for *The Incredible Shrinking Man* (1957), many episodes of TV's *The Twilight Zone* (1959–1964), the Hammer adaptation of *The Devil Rides Out* (1968) and the early Steven Spielberg film *Duel* (1971).

In Corman's *The Terror* (1963), Jack Nicholson plays a young French officer from the Napoleonic wars cut adrift from his regiment who is rescued by a woman who seems to have died twenty years earlier. Boris Karloff was called in for two days' work as the wicked baron. Some of the exterior scenes (a rarity in a Corman film) were shot at Big Sur in California. The assistant director was a youngster called Francis Coppola, fresh out of the UCLA film school.

The most opulent of Corman's Poe cycle is *The Masque of the Red Death* (1964) with Vincent Price, Hazel Court and Jane Asher. Set in mediaeval Italy, Price is a prince and satanist with a cavalier attitude to the plague-infected peasants in the village.

Filming began in November 1963, coinciding with the assassination of President Kennedy. Corman also records what he calls another 'historic moment'. He was seeing Jane Asher at the time but was reasonably friendly towards a young man called Paul McCartney who turned up on set. He had no idea who The Beatles were at the time, nor that his girlfriend was dating one of them when she was in London.

David Pirie, in his book *A New Heritage of Horror*, admires Corman's Poe adaptations with this caveat: 'Poe was a literary genius,' he writes. 'But in the end he was more of a poet than he was a creator of myths. As a result Cushing's Baron Frankenstein and Lee's Dracula are iconic for cinema in a way that Price's doomed hero in a frock coat can never be.'

Admitting that if he had confined himself to gothic horror he would be as mad as Roderick Usher, Corman made many other films in the 1960s (sometimes two at a time) and *The Man with the X-Ray Eyes* (1963) took him into sci-fi horror, opening with eerie music and a bloody eyeball bobbing about in a laboratory flask.

Ray Milland plays a scientist trying to develop X-ray vision who injects himself with an experimental serum. The film won the Best Film prize at the Trieste Science Fiction Film Festival.

Corman's self-proclaimed maverick status naturally led him to work with actors such as Peter Fonda, Dennis Hopper, Jack Nicholson and Bruce Dern, all geniuses at playing alienated characters. Dern and Fonda, along with Nancy Sinatra, starred in the cult biker movie *The Wild Angels* (1966) scripted by Charles B. Griffith and then extensively rewritten by the new kid in Hollywood, Peter Bogdanovich.

After *The Wild Angels*, Corman offered to finance Bogdanovich's first feature film *Targets* (1968) with Boris Karloff as a retired horror film actor.

In December 1970, Corman married Julie Halloran, who had worked as his production assistant, and he set up a new production-distribution company called New World Pictures that would become one of the most successful independents in the film industry.

His target audience was aged between 15 and 30 and his films had a left-of-centre viewpoint, a connection with the counterculture, plus some sex and action. On the walls of his office he had pictures of the May 1968 riots in Paris. In his autobiography he writes: 'It told anyone coming to us where we stood and which side of the barricades they had better be working on in Hollywood.'

Corman didn't want to only be associated with exploitation films, he wanted to make art films too. Ingmar Bergman's *Cries and Whispers* (1972) fitted the bill. The mix of films such as *Night Call Nurses* (1972) with art house movies by Fellini or Bergman seemed, as Corman says, 'hip and smart and rather amusing'. New World also released *The Harder They Come* (1972), the Jamaican reggae film starring Jimmy Cliff and directed by Perry Henzell.

In 1977 he produced *Grand Theft Auto*, which marked the directorial debut of Ron Howard who went on to make films such as *Cocoon* (1985), *Apollo 13* (1995), *Rush* (2013) and the Beatles documentary *Eight Days a Week* (2016).

The following year he produced *Piranha* (1978) directed by Joe Dante, which was followed by the werewolf film *The Howling* (1981). The horror titles keep on coming – *Dinoshark* (2010), *Attack of the 50 Foot Cheerleader* (2012), *Death Race 2050* (2017) – a sequel to the 1975 film, *Death Race 2000*, which he also produced.

In a male-dominated industry Corman has supported women with talent. Gale Anne Hurd, producer of *The Terminator* (1984), *Aliens* (1986) and *The Abyss* (1989) and former executive assistant to Roger Corman at New World Pictures said: 'I never realised sexism existed in Hollywood until I got outside New World.'

Talking about the ideal film for New World, Corman said in an interview:

> There should be a certain amount of action within them, and they had to have a kind of a liberal slant. For instance, a number of them featured women as the leads, and several times the writer would send in a script in which the girl's boyfriend would come in and solve the problem for her, and I said, 'No, the girl must solve her own problem.' So there was a little bit, not a great bit, a little bit of a feminist movement, a liberal movement and a little nudity.

There was a popular myth that Corman often said to New World directors, 'You can do whatever you want, but after ten minutes there must be a shower scene.' It wasn't quite true but the idea was right, he agreed: 'I never said it specifically, but they knew that these pictures were R-rated [Restricted]. In other words, there should be a little bit of nudity but not a great deal because I didn't want to make X films.'

For all his maverick status, Corman is one of the most significant producer/directors of the last sixty years. He gave many of Hollywood's biggest directors their first jobs – such as Ron Howard, Jonathan Demme, Francis Ford Coppola and James Cameron.

Talking about Cameron, Corman said:

> For instance, Jim Cameron who, with *Titanic* made the most expensive picture ever made, and then broke his own record when he did *Avatar* – I can say that he still goes back to the time when he was the head of our Special Effects

Department. I remember the night before starting a picture, it was a science fiction picture, and there was a spaceship. And there was a wall on the spaceship that was just a simple plain wall, and I said to Jim, 'I really like (what we call) articulation of the surface. Can you do something tonight to break up that surface?' And he said, 'It'll be ready. Come and see it tomorrow morning.' And I saw it the next morning, and it was great, and I said 'Jim, what did you do?' He said 'I went to McDonald's and I bought a lot of hamburger cartons. I glued the hamburger cartons to the wall, I sprayed them with aluminum paint and it cost $12.'

Learning through low-budget 'guerilla' film-making, these directors went on to make big-budget Hollywood films, including those in the horror genre. Without Corman's example in low budget but 'cool' movies, blockbusters such as *The Exorcist* (1973), *The Omen* (1976) or the new wave of big-budget horror films might never have been made.

For despite the critics' well-known aversion to horror and exploitation films, Corman has always been admired. The former editor of *Sight & Sound* magazine, Penelope Houston, once wrote of Corman: 'Roger Corman has become if not the darling of the critics, at least their mascot.' The French newspaper *Le Monde* called him the 'Pope of Pop Cinema'.

In the documentary *Corman's World*, Jack Nicholson lounges, smoking on a sofa and observes: 'By mistake he made a good picture once in a while.'

Chapter Fifteen

Roman Polanski – 'Pray for Rosemary's Baby.'

In 1979, I went to the Cannes Film Festival. It was the year that Roman Polanski's film *Tess*, based on Thomas Hardy's *Tess of the D'Urbervilles*, was made and Polanski was at the festival, as was the star of the film Nastassja Kinski. With an optimism that had no basis in reality, I had got on the phone and promised the editor of *Penthouse* an interview with the notorious director.

The year before, Polanski had fled to France from America where he had pleaded guilty to a charge of engaging in unlawful sexual intercourse with 13-year-old Samantha Geimer. He made his escape hours before he was formally sentenced.

Since then, for nearly half a century, he has been periodically arrested, detained, re-interviewed by authorities in France and Poland, threatened with extradition, and taken newspapers and magazines to court. Public disapproval of Polanski has, if anything, increased over the years, particularly with the advent of the Me Too movement, which has prompted more women to come forward to accuse him of rape and assault. Such is his notoriety that his latest film, *An Officer and a Spy* (2019), will not be shown in Britain or the United States.

At that Cannes festival, I found myself in a lift with Polanski in the Carlton Hotel. Nothing ventured, nothing gained. I asked him if I could interview him. He seemed appalled. 'Non,' he said without looking at me. We continued our journey in silence, me trying to come up with a killer question, the answer to which would furnish me with enough material to write an article of 2,000 words or so. No luck. Polanski exited the lift. You can't win 'em all.

Tess is a long, sumptuous and reverential take on a classic. In an interview before the Cannes festival, Polanksi – who was 45 at the time – said:

Tess is a new departure. It is, as I have said, the film of my mature years. I shall be sorry if people have such a limited idea of what my style as a director is like – and my preoccupations – that they cannot accept something different from me. In the cinema, directors can be typecast as well as actors.

He has made all kinds of films – film noir, Shakespeare adaptations, psychological thrillers, swashbucklers, comedies, wartime stories. The film critic Barry Norman once said: 'In an industry that worships the routine, he never brings the same rabbit out of the same hat twice.'

There is no typical Polanski film but there are also very few bad ones. His excursions into horror are few – principally *Repulsion* (1965) and *Rosemary's Baby* (1968) – but very important.

His whole life has been a horror story, and – let's get this straight – that's a matter of fact, not intended in any way as an excuse for his depravity.

Raymond Roman Thierry Polanski was born in Paris on 18 August 1933. His father Ryszard was a Jewish emigré from Krakow who had come to Paris to pursue a career as a painter. His son's mother was his second wife, a half-Jewish Russian called Bula Katz who was beautiful, elegant and wore fox furs at almost all times.

In the summer of 1936, Ryszard decided to take his family back to Krakow which, considering the political situation, was as Ryszard himself would say a 'truly exquisite blunder'. When war became inevitable the family went into exile in Warsaw which was another mistake, as by early September 1939 German panzer forces arrived just outside the city and began relentless bombing raids.

The Polanskis hid in a basement scavenging for food. They lived for some days on a jar of pickles, including the bottling juice – a detail that Polanski would use in the film *The Pianist* (2002), a biographical film about the Polish-Jewish pianist and composer Władysław Szpilman, a Holocaust survivor.

They managed to return to Krakow, living in the 'Jew sector' which would become a sealed-off ghetto. Apart from the daily indignities and privations the small child witnessed terrible sights; an elderly woman shot in the back by German soldiers on a summer day in 1941.

Bula, four months pregnant, was taken to Auschwitz and gassed. The little boy's grandparents were taken away along with his half-sister

Annette, and his uncle Bernard. Ryszard was sent to Mauthausen concentration camp. Roman remained in hiding in Krakow (where he pretended to be German in order to be able to buy cinema tickets) and then made his way to the remote Polish village of Wysoka where he stayed with the Buchala family in a house made of mud and straw and worked the small plot of land. Sometimes he ate stewed flowers or rat pie.

When the war ended he returned to Krakow, living rough. It was chaotic, hellish and the persecution of Jews continued. His father had survived Mauthausen and returned, marrying again in 1946. The 13-year-old regarded this as a betrayal of his mother and refused to live with the couple, keeping himself by dealing on the black market.

He attended school occasionally and went to Krakow's Kino Swit cinema when he could. That summer he went with Scout Troop 22 on a camping holiday in the Pomeranian Hills west of Gdansk. He did a turn at the concert party and proved to be a talented comic and a natural organiser. In his autobiography Polanksi notes: 'I had discovered my vocation.'

He also developed a passion for cycling. In June 1949, he had arranged to meet a man called Janusz Dziuba who was to sell him a new racing bike. Dziuba said the bike was stored in an old air-raid shelter. Once inside, Dziuba hit Polanski five times on the head with a rock wrapped in newspaper. Dziuba was caught and subsequently hanged for this and other crimes. Polanski needed eighteen stitches to his scalp.

When he was 17 he began to attend Krakow's Institute of Fine Arts. But life behind the Iron Curtain held few charms and Polanski announced that he wanted to 'get the fuck out of Poland, grow a beard and become a writer' in Paris. Playing a small boy, he appeared in a propaganda film called *Three Stories* (1953) where he met a young Andrzej Wajda who would become one of Poland's leading film directors, winning an honorary Oscar in 2000 for his contribution to world cinema.

In 1953, desperate to avoid conscription, Polanski was accepted by the National Film School at Lodz. 'It was a relaxed and refined environment,' he said in an interview in *Cahiers du Cinéma*. 'We were able to keep in touch with Western culture since the censor allowed us "specialists" to see a lot of American, Italian and French films.'

He was one of the top students, which would have been a surprise to many. His chaotic childhood may account for his failure to read properly until he was in his early teens. Many family members also thought he had learning difficulties. His kindergarten teacher described him as a 'cretin'.

Annette, his half-sister, had survived the war and was living in Paris when a change in the law allowed Polish citizens to visit family members living abroad. Roman had to wait six months for his visa to come through, but in May 1957, he achieved his ambition of going to Paris.

A quirky, experimental fifteen-minute film, with a melancholy jazz score by Krzysztof Komeda, called *Two Men and a Wardrobe* (1958) made Polanski something of a celebrity in Poland and recognised as a talent in European film-making.

At 26 he married a 19-year-old Polish actress called Barbara Kwiatowska, known as Basia and referred to as the 'Polish Sophia Loren', and for a while she was better known than him.

Early in 1961 Polanski heard that the Polish ministry of culture had given the go ahead to *Knife in the Water*, his first feature-length film about two men and a woman on a tense boating holiday.

Though reviews were lukewarm, it was shown as part of the New York Film Festival in 1963, *Time* magazine put it on the cover and it was nominated for an Oscar in the Best Foreign Film Category.

When his marriage to Basia ended, Polanksi assumed the life of a carefree bachelor in Paris. In a sign of things to come he watched Hitchcock's *Psycho* many times, but was uninterested in the French New Wave and declared Jean-Luc Godard's film *Un Homme et Une Femme* (1966) to be 'unbelievably dreary'.

The left-wing politics of directors such as Godard and François Truffaut exasperated him and he said they were 'like little kids playing at being revolutionaries'. He continued: 'I've passed through this stage. I was raised in a country where these things happened seriously.'

In 1964 he moved to swinging London, which he found very much to his taste. Here he met film producers Michael Klinger and Tony Tenser. Former strip club owner Klinger had teamed up with Tenser in 1960 to open a private members' cinema called the Compton Club dedicated to nudie, exploitation films. They agreed to finance *Repulsion* (1965).

Catherine Deneuve, then aged 21, plays Carol Ledoux. She is a Belgian manicurist sharing a shabby flat in South Kensington with her sister Helen (played by Yvonne Furneaux). When Helen goes on holiday with her married lover Michael (Ian Hendry), Carol loses her already tenuous grip on sanity and the claustrophobic flat becomes the scene for her nightmarish hallucinations and homicidal rampages. A skinned rabbit, left uncooked by Helen, and rotting slowly throughout the film becomes a queasily apt image for Carol's mental disintegration.

At first, we are not entirely surely whether Carol's experiences – the grubby labourer who breaks in and rapes her – are real or fantasy. Seemingly blighted by her own femininity and beauty, she becomes as much a victim as she is a homicidal maniac.

Gradually the grim reality of the flat begins to distort. This was achieved by a specially built set which transforms the cramped sitting room into an echoey cavern in some scenes.

Rather than a precursor to what would become known as 'slasher' films, *Repulsion* with its slow, episodic build-up is more of a psychological thriller. It opens with a close-up of Deneuve's eye, reminiscent of Luis Buñuel's horrific pupil-slicing film in *Un Chien Andalou* (1929). We understand immediately that we are in horror territory. Polanksi, showered with praise for his accuracy in portraying what we would now call 'mental health issues', claimed he'd just made it up: 'To me film-making is what a train set is to a child.'

The film won a Silver Bear at the Berlin festival and Polanski began work on his second film with Klinger and Tenser, the comedy thriller *Cul-de-Sac* (1966) starring Donald Pleasence and Deneuve's sister Françoise Dorléac.

His next film was *The Fearless Vampire Killers* (1967), archly subtitled 'Pardon Me, But Your Teeth are in My Neck', a first-rate horror spoof which starred Sharon Tate and Polanski as Alfred, the endearingly hapless assistant vampire slayer. He and Sharon Tate would fall in love during the shoot in the Italian Dolomites.

It was Robert Evans, in charge of production at Paramount who invited Polanski to read an as-yet unpublished novel by Ira Levin called *Rosemary's Baby*. Polanski agreed to a budget of $1.9 million and a fee of $150,000. He wrote the screenplay himself, his first adaptation. It was Polanski's chance to conquer Hollywood and the horror genre's chance to go big budget.

In a subsequent interview Ira Levin said:

> I've always felt that the film of *Rosemary's Baby* is the single most faithful adaptation of a novel ever to come out

of Hollywood. Not only does it incorporate whole chunks of the book's dialogue, it even follows the colour of clothing (where I mentioned them) and the layout of the apartment. And perhaps more importantly, Polanksi's directorial style of not aiming the camera squarely at the horror but rather letting the audience spot it for themselves off at the side of the screen coincides happily with my own writing style.

Mia Farrow and John Cassavetes play Rosemary and Guy, a very ordinary middle-class young American couple who move to an apartment in New York (it was filmed in the Dakota building, renamed the Bamford in the film). Guy's career as an actor is stalling but their elderly, fussy neighbours show an interest in the couple. Odd things happen. Guy's career takes off when a rival actor goes blind. A young woman neighbour commits suicide.

Rosemary gets pregnant after a strange rape dream which is like an acid trip.

Is she, like Carol in *Repulsion*, going mad in a claustrophobic apartment, or is there really a satanic plot to impregnate her with the devil's baby? Has her husband sold himself to the devil in exchange for career success? As in *Repulsion*, the modern urban environment is a setting for evil and madness. *Rosemary's Baby* would also spawn other devil-child films of the 1970s such as *The Exorcist* (1973) and *The Omen* (1976).

Polanski was a force of energy on set. 'I pep myself up by telling myself I'm the greatest,' he said in a 1986 interview with Pierre-André Boutang. Ruth Gordon, who played one of the satanic neighbours, liked his style and affectionately called him 'the little bastard'.

Polanski went way over budget with the film eventually costing $2.3 million, but it was an immediate hit when it was released in June 1968 with the famous catchline 'Pray for Rosemary's Baby!' The critics loved the film, unusual for a horror picture. Roger Ebert wrote that Polanski 'outdoes Hitchcock'. Though Penelope Gilliatt in *The New Yorker* didn't get it. 'Why on earth does a major film-maker feel seduced by a piece of boo-in-the-night like this story?' she wrote.

Rosemary's Baby seemed to touch a nerve in an America where opposition to the Vietnam War was growing among the young (the old are evil in *Rosemary's Baby*) and where the counterculture dabbled in alternative religions and creeds. In April 1966 *Time* magazine had famously asked on its cover: 'Is God dead?'

The novel itself, published in 1967, created a boom in horror fiction. Truman Capote compared Levin with Henry James. Levin had taken inspiration from his wife's pregnancy but refused to let her read the manuscript. He was also concerned about a backlash, that the book would be viewed as blasphemy, because it turned the story of the nativity on its head. He wondered if he would be blacklisted by publishers as a result.

In 1992 in an interview, Levin, who died in 2007, admitted to having 'mixed feelings about *Rosemary's Baby*'. He felt the book had 'played a significant part in all this popularisation of the occult and belief in witchcraft and Satanism', and added, 'I really feel a certain degree of guilt about having fostered that kind of irrationality.'

Levin's immaculately plotted novels were a gift to cinema. *The Stepford Wives*, published in 1972, is a sort of comic horror science fiction yarn in which women living in an apparently idyllic Connecticut suburb are replaced with submissive robots by their husbands.

The first film adaptation, directed by Bryan Forbes, was made in 1975 and a more recent 2004 version starred Nicole Kidman and Bette Midler. *The Boys from Brazil*, written in 1976, is a sci-fi thriller with nods to horror, with teenage Hitler clones (more devil children) bred to create a new Führer for the neo-Nazi movement. The film version appeared in 1978 with Laurence Olivier, James Mason and Gregory Peck.

The idea that *Rosemary's Baby* was a cursed film has drifted around for decades and inevitably gained traction with the coming of the internet. The composer of the score, Krzysztof Komeda, died of a clot on the brain after injuring his head in a fall. The producer, William Castle, was severely ill with kidney stones and while hallucinating was said to have shouted: 'Rosemary, for God's sake, drop the knife!' John Lennon was shot dead outside the Dakota Building, where *Rosemary's Baby* was filmed. And 'Helter Skelter', a track on The Beatles' *White Album*, was written in blood on the wall of the house where Sharon Tate was murdered in 1969.

Sharon Tate had wanted to play Rosemary and is seen as an unnamed extra in the party scene. Rosemary throws a party to re-establish contact with her old – or rather her *young* friends – as opposed to the elderly neighbours. 'It's going to be a very special party,' she says sarcastically to Guy, 'you have to be under 60 to get in'.

Roman Polanski and Sharon Tate married in London on 20 January 1968 at the Chelsea Register Office with the reception held at the Playboy Club in Mayfair. Guests included Keith Richards, David Bailey, Vidal Sassoon, Joan Collins and Michael Caine as well as Polanski's father and his wife.

Barbara Parkins, the actress who starred in *Valley of the Dolls* (1967) with Sharon Tate, was the maid of honour. The bride wore an ivory silk mini skirt. The photographer Peter Evans would describe the couple as 'the Douglas Fairbanks/Mary Pickford of our time … . Cool, nomadic, talented, and nicely shocking'.

Sharon wanted nothing more than to be a wife and mother and she tolerated her husband's persistent unfaithfulness. She even liked to repeat the story of how Polanski had been driving along Sunset Boulevard and shouted at a girl on the sidewalk, 'Miss you have a beautiful ass.' When she turned around he recognised her as his wife.

Sharon became pregnant late in 1968 and early in 1969 the couple moved to a new Hollywood address, 10050 Cielo Drive. Polanski last saw his heavily pregnant wife in July, when she sailed from Southampton to America on the *QE2*. In his autobiography, he says he had a 'grotesque thought' that he would never see her again.

On 9 August, Sharon Tate was murdered by members of the Manson Family, Charles 'Tex' Watson, Patricia Krenwinkel, Susan Atkins and Linda Kasabian, the young people who had fallen under the malign influence of the drifter and petty criminal Charles Manson and believed that he was the Messiah.

Tate died in the early hours of the morning in a bloodbath along with her unborn son, an 18-year-old called Steven Parent who had been visiting the estate's caretaker, and house guests Jay Sebring, Wojciech Frykowski and Abigail Folger.

It fell to Polanski's agent Bill Tennant to identify the bodies and phone him in London. Polanski flew straight back to Los Angeles and on 13 August moved in to the house of his friend Mike Sarne, the British actor, director and (briefly) pop singer.

The worldwide coverage of the murders was sensational and prurient. Didn't these decadent Hollywood types have it coming? Wasn't it a drug orgy that had gone wrong? Even Polanski, who had been out of the country, came under suspicion as his reputation for excess counted against him. For his part, he believed that one of his circle was responsible and carried out his own obsessive investigations, swabbing his friends' cars for blood stains and leaving microphones in their homes.

The police finally rounded up the Manson Family by December and the trial opened on 24 July 1970. They were sentenced to death, but in 1972 the California Supreme Court voted to abolish the death penalty. Charles Manson was still exerting his malign fascination on the world when he died in prison in 2017, aged 83.

Roman Polanski left America. His next film would be Shakespeare's *Macbeth* and – suggesting they collaborated on an adaptation – he approached Kenneth Tynan, the British theatre critic and writer who had been appointed literary manager of the new National Theatre.

In a 1971 profile for *Esquire* magazine, written while *Macbeth* was being filmed, Tynan – clearly dazzled by Polanski's machismo – described him as an 'imposer'. By that he means someone who imposes his will but also dictates 'the conditions – social, moral, sexual, political – within which one can operate with maximum freedom'.

'Nobody is harder to faze than this cocksure Polish gnome,' he says, admitting that he has also seen him described as 'the original five-foot Pole you wouldn't touch anyone with' (though you suspect Tynan might have come up with this description himself). Polanski's aim, continues this love letter, 'is quite simply to be invulnerable, physically as well as psychologically.' What else? 'He both skis and drives like a maniac and takes pride in the friendship of people (like the racing driver Jackie Stewart) who risk their lives professionally and get away with it.'

Polanksi's take on *Macbeth* was that Macbeth and Lady Macbeth – usually played by middle-aged actors – should be young. Jon Finch and Francesca Annis (who had auditioned for Catherine Deneuve's part in *Repulsion*) took the roles. They are ambitious, optimistic and, crucially, *do not know* until it is too late that they are in a tragedy. It mirrors the insouciance of so many protagonists in horror films, unaware of what is to come, though the audience is completely aware.

It was not an easy shoot. There were even moves at one stage to replace Polanksi. But a sudden injection of cash from the Playboy organisation kept the production afloat. (The coven of comely witches would appear in a *Playboy* centrefold.) Tynan mentions how, while filming the murder of Macduff's wife and children, he questioned the amount of blood which a small boy would shed. 'You didn't see my house in California last summer,' said Polanski.

The reviews were mixed, endlessly commenting on parallels with the Manson murders. In the *Chicago Sun-Times* Robert Ebert wrote: 'It's hard to watch a film directed by Roman Polanski and not react on more than one level to such images as a baby being "untimely ripped from his mothers' womb" ... Polanski's characters all resemble Manson.'

His next film *What?* (1972) – produced by Carlo Ponti and filmed at Ponti's villa – was succinctly and brilliantly described in Vincent Canby's review for *The New York Times* as 'an X-rated nonsense comedy about a Goldilocks marqué, a wide-eyed America girl on the loose in Asia and Europe, and her specific adventures among some mad characters she meets when she takes refuge in an Italian seaside villa to escape three would-be rapists.' Marcello Mastroianni starred.

Chinatown (1974), a masterpiece and a nod to 1930s film noir, which looks as fresh today as when it was made, starred Jack Nicholson and Faye Dunaway. It was nominated for eleven Academy Awards but only won one – Robert Towne for Best Screenplay.

In *The Tenant* (1976), which he both starred in and directed, Polanski returned to the sort of claustrophobic modern horror of *Repulsion* and *Rosemary's Baby*.

The female star was 21-year-old Isabelle Adjani who would star in Werner Herzog's *Nosferatu the Vampyre* (1979) opposite Klaus Kinski – a remake of F. W. Murnau's *Nosferatu* (1922). Roger Ebert was not impressed, saying: '*The Tenant* might have made a decent little 20-minute sketch for one of those British horror anthology films in which Christopher Lee, Peter Cushing and Vincent Price pick up a little loose change. As a film by Polanski, it's unspeakably disappointing.'

By all accounts his arrest in 1977 for having sex with a 13-year-old child completely astonished Polanski. He couldn't believe he had done anything wrong, though he didn't deny the substance of the charges. He fled to Paris and has never returned to America.

Tess won three Oscars at the 1981 Academy Awards.

In 1984, Polanski turned 51 which is when he met Emmanuelle Seigner, just 18, who would become his third wife in 1989. They have a daughter, Morgane, born in 1993 and a younger son, Elvis.

Filmed in Tunisia, *Pirates* (1986) was a jolly swashbuckling comedy with Walter Matthau as the somewhat elderly dashing lead. Polanski's next project was a competent Hitchcockian thriller *Frantic* (1988) with

Harrison Ford desperately searching for his missing wife who disappears from a Paris hotel room. Emmanuelle Seigner helps him out.

Death and the Maiden (1994) is a political thriller, originally a play by Ariel Dorfman which starred Sigourney Weaver and Sir Ben Kingsley. In true Gothic horror style, it opens at a remote beach house, a storm raging.

Paulina Escobar (Weaver) is convinced that the man given a lift by her husband tortured and raped her under the old regime and plans to execute her own sadistic revenge.

The Ninth Gate (1999) is a supernatural thriller with Johnny Depp hired by a satanist to locate two rare volumes of demonological interest. Inevitably there were comparisons with *Rosemary's Baby* and comments on Polanski's apparent obsession with the satanic. It would become one of the most commercially successful films that Polanski has made.

As his career seemed to be drawing to a close, Polanski stormed back with *The Pianist* (2002) which, set in Warsaw during the Second World War, took him back to his childhood. Adrien Brody stars as the Jewish musician Władysław Szpilman struggling to survive in the Warsaw Ghetto. The famous scene in which the Nazi officer asks Szpilman to play the piano, with the understanding that if he doesn't he will be shot, is remarkable.

The film received an eight-minute standing ovation at the Cannes Film Festival in 2002 and Polanski was awarded the Palme d'Or. Though he was talking of retiring, he went on to direct *Oliver Twist* (2005) and the black comedy *Carnage* (2011) with Kate Winslet, Jodie Foster, Christoph Waltz and John C. Reilly.

When *The Pianist* came out, Samantha Geimer generously said: 'Mr Polanski and his film should be honoured according to the quality of his work. What he does for a living and how good he is at it have nothing to do with me or what he did to me.'

By that measure Roman Polanski is very good at what he does. Films such as *Repulsion* and *Rosemary's Baby* redefined the scope and purpose of horror, taking the fantasy genre into the harsh light of the modern world, reflecting preoccupations which still seem relevant even though these films were made more than fifty years ago.

Chapter Sixteen

Ingrid Pitt – 'The most beautiful ghoul in the world.'

Where Eagles Dare regularly appears in any list of the best war films of all time. Made in 1968, with a script by Alistair MacLean, it finds Clint Eastwood and Richard Burton on a daring Alpine mission to rescue an American general from a German fortress. The two female stars are Mary Ure and Ingrid Pitt, as undercover agents, both handy with a machine gun when the action kicks off.

In her autobiography *Life's a Scream* published in 1999, Ingrid Pitt describes a lavish MGM press event for *Where Eagles Dare*, held in Las Vegas.

At a banquet the president of MGM, Bo Poke:

> blasted out a corporate message about *Where Eagles Dare*, swarmed over Clint, threw me a titbit and thanked the Nazis for being the greatest source of entertainment since Nero burned down Rome.
>
> As if on cue some joker smashed through the double doors of the banqueting hall in Adolf Hitler gear: stupid little black moustache, SS hat and Führer uniform. Just in case anyone missed the allusion, he kicked his heels together, shot up his arm in the Nazi salute and shouted 'Heil Hitler!'
>
> Everyone laughed.
>
> I felt sick.

The Nazis, as far as Pitt was concerned, were not a subject for humour.

Ingoushka Petrov was born in a railway station in 1937 as her parents were attempting to flee from Nazi Germany to England via Poland.

Her father, a 'true-blue Prussian' was a scientist, educated at Heidelberg and Oxford where he took up rowing and took part in the first Olympic Games in 1896 in Athens.

He settled in England for twenty years, and, well ahead of his time, he patented a type of electrical battery in 1900 and used it to power a car on a London-to-Brighton run.

He also designed aircraft and worked on a British airship. But as war threatened, he faced the possibility of being detained as an enemy alien or returning to Germany. He went back and served in the Prussian cavalry. He later said that the detention camp would have been the better choice.

After the war, he married Katja, a woman of Lithuanian origin who was thirty years younger than him and the couple lived in Berlin. Ingrid's mother was Jewish and with the Nazis gaining power the couple decided to flee. Unable to make the journey, the family took refuge in Grodno where Ingrid's mother had family. Ingrid's father meanwhile was under pressure from the authorities to use his engineering expertise for the German war effort.

Inevitably – when Ingrid was 5 years old – the family was rounded up and transported to Stutthof concentration camp in Poland where she and her mother would remain for the next three years.

It was the first concentration camp to be set up outside Germany and the last to be liberated by the Allies in May 1945.

Ingrid was sent to the *Kinderschuppen* where the camp's children were groomed to be adopted by childless Germans. Conditions were a little better than they were in the rest of the camp. She was given a smock and a bunk with a mattress and two blankets. The children were given German lessons and allowed out to run around in a makeshift playground.

Occasionally, selected children would be sent off in a truck to the German families. The blond children went first but later they would take the dark-haired children too. Ingrid's friend at the time was a little girl called Rachel with dark curly hair and black eyes who said she was a gypsy. She and Ingrid performed song and dance routines for Fraulein Gloge, the woman in charge of the *Kinderschuppen*. Ingrid would witness Rachel being raped and killed by the SS guards.

On another day, her German teacher, for whom she had no affection, was dragged outside and shot in the head. She saw a woman called Annie, who she adored, taken out and hanged, her broken body left dangling for days.

As the Russian Army approached, the SS began closing down the camps and started a mass gassing of prisoners. About waiting with her mother in Block 5, Ingrid writes: 'I don't think I really comprehended that we were going to die now. The thought of death is a very abstract concept to an eight-year-old.'

But instead of being sent to the gas chambers (they had temporarily broken down), the prisoners were marched into the forest where they expected to be shot. Instead they were locked in a barn. They expected the guards to set it on fire. But they didn't.

The next day they trudged on, attacked by Allied planes who killed some of the guards but more of the prisoners. Ingrid's mother – with Ingrid lying beneath her – played dead. When the column departed, Ingrid and her mother were free. Still in great danger, but free. And eventually they made their way to a partisan camp in the forest where they stayed until the war was over.

Ingrid was suffering from TB and was taken to a hospital run by the Red Cross, as was her mother who had typhus. They stayed for seven months and were then taken to a factory which had been turned into a dormitory for displaced persons.

For the next two years they would travel from one Red Cross camp to another, mostly on foot, searching for Ingrid's father. Once Ingrid's mother, searching through the endless lists of names nailed on fences and boards, found the names of her parents, murdered in Treblinka.

Mother and daughter made their way back to the old home in Berlin which had been assigned to another family, the Totenhoefers, who were very welcoming. And finally the remarkable Katja tracked down her husband, by now – at 77 – a shadow of his former self who would only live another five years.

The two families shared the Berlin house and received a reparation payment from the post-war German government.

Something like normal life resumed and Ingrid's father began to take his daughter to the Gloria Palast cinema every Sunday. Here they watched *Elephant Boy* (1937) and films with Roy Rogers and Johnny Weissmuller. But his health was failing and he died on 16 July 1953.

Ingrid briefly attended medical school but dropped out. She had dreams of acting but her mother insisted she did a typing course.

She first found work with the Berliner Ensemble in East Berlin, founded by Bertolt Brecht in 1949. She stayed with an aunt in East

Berlin and visited her mother once a week, having to pass through Checkpoint Charlie. She would always be searched and invariably made to strip naked. Once the Berlin Wall went up in 1961 she was no longer able to make trips home.

Always outspoken, she was critical of the communist regime and was briefly hauled in for questioning until Helene Weigel, artistic director at the Berliner Ensemble (who had been Brecht's wife), managed to convince the police that Ingrid was mentally unstable and didn't know what she was saying.

On the opening night of *Mother Courage and her Children,* Ingrid was tipped off that the police wanted to question her again. In full costume she made a run for it straight into the freezing waters of the River Spree. Close to drowning, she was pulled out of the water in West Berlin by American GIs and found temporary refuge in a brothel. Until her mother came to take her home.

Six months later she married Laud Roland Pitt Jr, the American lieutenant who had pulled her out of the river. He was transferred to Fort Carson in Colorado and Ingrid became pregnant. She recalls in her autobiography that she was alone at home watching *Rawhide* on TV when her waters broke. Heavy snowfall made it impossible for an ambulance to get through and Ingrid delivered her baby daughter by herself. She called her Steffanie.

Shortly afterwards Laud announced that he'd volunteered to serve in Vietnam, which was when Ingrid called time on the marriage and again pursued her dream of acting. This time with The Playhouse, a touring American 'stock company'.

But she was barely making a living and reneging on her rent so she left town in her Oldsmobile. A burst tyre and an unscheduled stop led to her hanging out on a reservation with native Americans.

She decided to return to Europe and sold her wedding ring for petrol. Then she sold her car and bought a ticket for Madrid.

A photograph in a newspaper of her crying at a bullfight came to the attention of film director Ana Mariscal who invited her to do a screen test for the film *Los Duendes de Andalucia* (1966).

Now with a little money, Ingrid found a flat in Madrid in a building where Geraldine Chaplin also lived. She got a small part in Richard Lester's *A Funny Thing Happened on the Way to the Forum* (1966), which starred Phil Silvers and Zero Mostel.

Dr Zhivago (1965) was being filmed in Spain and she had five small roles in that. She worked as a stunt horse rider in Almeria. Then she heard that Orson Welles was making *Chimes at Midnight* (1965) in Spain and was determined to be in it. Wangling an invitation to a dinner he was attending, she writes: 'I focused on Mr Welles, giving him the full treatment: flashing eyes, a glimpse of leg, cleavage and any other part of my anatomy which might interest him and get me invited to his table.'

Wells was not impressed saying, 'I do not give auditions when I am having dinner.' But her perseverance got her a small walk-on part. She disliked Welles intensely, who called her to his room, greeted her in his underpants and pushed her on to the bed. She managed to heave him off her on to the floor and escaped.

Invited by Twentieth Century Fox to do a screen test she found she had been set up. There was no screen test, but she began doing bar work in Los Angeles until W. Lee Wilder (Billy Wilder's brother) offered her a part in a film called *The Omegans* (1968), a sci-fi horror concerning a radioactive river in the tropics, that was to be filmed in Manila, co-starring with Keith Larsen, husband of Vera Miles.

She moved to LA and, worried by the levels of violence, took karate classes at the Nishijima gym in Hollywood. She worked out with Elvis Presley – a black belt – a few times.

She had a part in the TV series *Ironside* (1967) and then flew to Munich to play Heidi in *Where Eagles Dare*. Arriving at Schloss Adler, the Alpine setting for the film, she recalled later:

> The atmosphere of the war had been so faithfully recreated that I had difficulty not believing I was back in my childhood nightmare and I began to have trouble breathing. I gave myself a good talking to. This was my big chance. The Germans had destroyed part of my life – I mustn't allow them to squash me again.

She sensed resentment from Mary Ure, the bigger star who wanted to be the only blonde in the production. So when Ingrid went to hair and make-up she came out 'some sort of mouse'. Worse still, Robert Shaw, Mary's husband, arrived on set and flirted with Ingrid which she attempted to discourage.

She had an equally awkward meeting on location with Elizabeth Taylor, then married to Burton.

Ingrid Pitt settled in London but wasn't a British citizen and avoided a threat of deportation by marrying George Pinches of the Rank Organisation – a marriage of convenience. She thought it would help her career but the relationship turned sour.

At a film premiere party, she found herself sitting next to James Carreras, head of Hammer Films who invited her to his Wardour Street office the following day.

She describes her entrance like this:

> With a practised movement I swept off my hat and let my carefully prepared hair tumble around my shoulders. Act one. Another deft movement rid me of my maxi-coat. I tossed it negligently on to a chair and let him get a crack at the skimpy sweater and even skimpier micro-skirt I was wearing. He didn't bat an eyelid when I slunk across the Axminster and hitched a thigh on to the corner of his desk.

He did, though, offer her a part in *The Vampire Lovers* (1970), based on a Sheridan le Fanu story of lesbian vampires, *Carmilla*.

From then on Ingrid's reputation as the 'Queen of Horror' or 'The most beautiful Ghoul in the World' was assured. She loved the family at Hammer and was full of praise for Tudor Gates's script and Roy Ward Baker's direction. Wrote Ingrid: 'The film involved nude scenes. I'd never done the full-frontal bit before but I was proud of my body and not reluctant to show it.'

Her 21-year-old co-star Madeline Smith had appeared in *Taste the Blood of Dracula* (1970) and was thrilled to be in another Hammer horror. She featured on the cover of a book called *Hammer Glamour* published in 2009 and in an interview with the BBC about *Vampire Lovers,* Smith said:

> I got a very worried phone call from the producer who said he was concerned about my lack of bosom. He said 'we like you a lot, but we don't think you are voluptuous enough.'
>
> I reassured him, and then I scuttled off to Hornby and Clarke dairy round the corner and I bought every yoghurt I could find and stuffed myself like you might fatten cattle, and it worked!

Asked if she felt exploited, she said:

> I was a very willing exploitee – I didn't mind at all. My main point of existence is to make people laugh and I was able to use those bosoms later for comedy. I was the foil in a lot of comedy shows and sketches and I have absolutely no regret about being 'sexploited'.

Ingrid's other co-star was Kate O'Mara. Ingrid had to lean over Kate and dispatch her, but her false fangs kept dropping into Kate's cleavage. Ingrid requisitioned the clapper boy's chewing gum to keep the fangs in place and kill Kate in the next take.

She became great friends with Peter Cushing and his wife Helen. Cushing plays a general who dispatches Carmilla and then cuts her head off (a scene which the censor objected to strongly).

Although Ingrid Pitt's career with Hammer began as the studio was in decline, she was a marvellous addition, with her extreme beauty and her deep voice and exotic pan-European accent. (She could speak English, Spanish, German, Russian, Italian and French.) Sex and death was Hammer's brand and Pitt fitted the bill perfectly.

She moved swiftly on to Amicus's anthology film called *The House That Dripped Blood* (1971) with Christopher Lee, Peter Cushing, Jon Pertwee, Joss Ackland and Denholm Elliott. Jon Pertwee plays a horror film star who fears his Dracula cloak turns him into a vampire.

Director Peter Sasdy had wanted Diana Rigg to play the notorious eighteenth-century Hungarian countess Elizabeth Báthory (who bathed in the blood of young girls to restore her youth and beauty), but Ingrid persuaded him to give her the role in the 1971 Hammer film *Countess Dracula*.

She read that director Robin Hardy was about to launch a movie called *The Wicker Man* in Scotland. She also read that the role of the nymphomaniac librarian was still not cast. She drove round to Robin Hardy's home in Chelsea on a Sunday morning and a week later was on the sleeper train to Dumfries.

It wasn't an easy shoot, as she recalled:

> *The Wicker Man* was beset by difficulties. British Lion, the production company, changed hands three times during filming ... . The cold got worse as we nudged into

November. We all huddled in blankets, clutching rapidly cooling hot-water bottles until the shot was set, then we'd throw off our coverings and prance about pretending it was spring and the sun was warm.

The Wicker Man (1973) was based on Anthony Shaffer's novel and script and, as David Pirie explains in his book *A New Heritage of Horror*, 'took up a theme that had been used extremely successfully by John Bowen three years earlier in the widely acclaimed BBC TV play *Robin Redbreast*. Bowen's television drama teased its audience with unknown menace in a rural English setting but ultimately proved to be about human sacrifice as pagan ritual.'

In *The Wicker Man*, a policeman (played by Edward Woodward) arrives at a remote Scottish island to solve a murder. Here the pagan laird (played by Christopher Lee) holds sway as Woodward's hapless character is drawn inexorably to his terrible fate.

George, still married to Ingrid, claimed *The Wicker Man* was not commercial and the Rank cinema circuit would not distribute it. It was left to EMI, Britain's other cinema circuit, to put the film out in a double bill with Nic Roeg's masterpiece *Don't Look Now* (1973). Ingrid Pitt wrote: 'Neither film deserved the double-bill treatment – each stood up on its own. And both have become classics.'

On a plane to Switzerland to appear in a children's TV show called *Ski Boy*, she met the racing driver Tony Rudlin. When George Pinches found out about the relationship he taunted her with her failing career and told her to finish with Rudlin. After that Ingrid reports: 'George now dedicated his life to turning mine into a morass of hatred and venom' and threatened to end her career.

He was as good as his word. Pinches was a powerful man in the British film industry and made efforts to ensure that nobody would employ Ingrid. Tony and Ingrid left for Buenos Aires, where they dined with the great racing driver Juan Manuel Fangio, were invited to lunch by Peron's widow Isabel (who was now President of Argentina), to tea with the British ambassador and to a poetry evening at Luis Borges' apartment.

Isabel Peron wanted to see Ingrid's horror films so prints were acquired. Afterwards Isabel took Ingrid to see her own horror show – a sarcophagus with a glass top containing the embalmed Eva Peron.

But then, following a military coup, Isabel Peron was arrested and placed under house arrest. Tony and Ingrid were advised to leave the country. Tony managed to find a small plane which he flew to Uruguay, but after a brief interval they returned to Buenos Aires and spent two years there attempting to raise finance for a film. News that George Pinches had been sacked by Rank made it possible to return to Britain as Ingrid hoped that the vendetta against her would now be at an end.

Back in Britain she was diagnosed with ovarian cancer, but pulled through and took a part in the film *Who Dares Wins* (1982) and in the BBC's *Smiley's People* (1982), followed by *Wild Geese II* (1985). Richard Burton was to star but he died just as filming was to begin. Edward Fox took over the part.

By now Ingrid and Tony were in dire financial straits, full of ideas for films and TV series which were never given the green light. Their home was repossessed and they rented a tiny cottage in Sheen. Ingrid's mother died in 1986.

Her next setback was breast cancer, which she also overcame. She continued writing, making occasional TV and film appearances, and attending horror conventions until the end of her life. She died in 2010 aged 73, in south London, of congestive heart failure.

In a long series of tweets, Tony Rudlin chronicled the ups and downs of Ingrid's health and treatment in the last year of her life. After her death he wrote: 'The nurse came back into the room and looked at Ingrid, picked up her hand and slapped her wrist. No response! She called the other nurse to get the Sister. I stood there staring at Ingrid. She looked beautiful, all the pain and age problems seem to have melted away.'

Chapter Seventeen

Michael Reeves – 'And may God be with you till we meet again.'

The old Playhouse Cinema in Gerrards Cross, Buckinghamshire is still going strong, and is now an Everyman. It was opened in 1925 and designed by the British architect John Stanley Beard, who was responsible for many cinemas in and around London after the First World War. He had a slightly eccentric taste for the baroque and the neo-classical, and the Gerrards Cross Playhouse was notable for an octagonal tower at its entrance, Doric columns within and, of course, an orchestra pit.

What it didn't have (until 1969) was any form of heating and on very cold days I remember blankets being handed out to customers.

My childhood home was a few yards away and from the mid-1960s I was a regular. Among the films I saw was Michael Reeves' *Witchfinder General* (1968) which made a huge impression on me. Apart from anything else I had a crush on the handsome actor Ian Ogilvy, who stars as the Roundhead soldier Richard Marshall in this semi-fictional account of the seventeenth-century witchfinder Matthew Hopkins (played by Vincent Price). I suppose I was 15 or 16 and technically too young to see an X-rated film. Not everyone appreciated it as much as I did either. Had I read *The Listener* (the BBC's magazine), I would have discovered that Alan Bennett called the movie 'persistently sadistic and morally rotten'. If I had read it, I don't suppose it would have deterred me from going.

The film went on to achieve a cult status partly because of the sudden death, less than a year after the film's release, of its 25-year-old director Michael Reeves.

Ogilvy was the star of two of Reeves' films. They had met in 1960 when they were both teenagers – Ogilvy was at Eton and Reeves at Radley College. Says Ogilvy in his autobiography *Once a Saint*: 'He was tall and thin, with a strong narrow jaw and dark hair that flopped into his eyes.' The two floppy-haired public-school boys quickly became close friends.

Reeves was an only child, born to his mother Elizabeth in 1943 when she was in her early forties. She had been a pianist at the Savoy Hotel when she met Derek Leith 'Bungie' Reeves who had been a naval officer and then played the stock market while working as a solicitor. He suffered from depression, as would his only son.

Bungie died suddenly of a heart attack 'in the marital bed' in 1952. Just days after his father's funeral, at the age of 8, Michael Reeves went to King's Mead preparatory boarding school in Sussex. Even at such an early age he was obsessed with movies, taking a keen interest in the programming of the Saturday evening film when the boys were shown suitable family fare.

Contemporaries remembered that if you gave him the name of a film he would instantly recite the whole credits, including distributors and running times. When he later attended Radley College, he would sneak off to the cinema in Newbury. One year he claimed to have seen 212 films.

Ogilvy remembers that in the school holidays he went to stay with Michael at his home, Foxbriar House in Cold Ash, Berkshire. 'We made our first movie, a 20-minute thriller called *Carrion*. Mike shot it all on a little 8mm camera in black and white. It was about a wheelchair-bound girl, alone and vulnerable in her snowbound home. I played a deranged murderer recently escaped from the local lunatic asylum.' To achieve a tracking shot, Michael put his cine camera on his mother's tea trolley.

Reeves and his mother were the poor relations of a wealthy family and at the age of 16, Reeves – to his considerable surprise – inherited a fortune. As a film-maker this was a blessing and a curse. While he could have bankrolled his own films, he wanted to finance them in the usual way so that there could be no suspicion of him being a dilettante movie hobbyist. Vincent Price, who had a difficult relationship with Reeves during the filming of *Witchfinder General*, said of Reeves' wealth: 'I suspect that may have been the reason for his impersonal approach to people.'

But, aged 17, with money in the bank for the first time, Michael Reeves bought a plane ticket to Hollywood and turned up on the doorstep of his hero, the film director Don Siegel. The Reeves' legend machine claims the teenager turned up unannounced. But, in fact, he had already written to Siegel several times.

The American show business writer Bill Kelley recorded an interview with Siegel in 1975. Siegel told the reporter:

> Michael showed up at my house, totally unknown, very brash … . He said, 'I think you're the greatest director in the world today', or something like that. And because we're nuts we just let him come into the house, told him he could go up to the pool-house and live there if he wanted to.

By then Siegel had already made the original *Invasion of the Body Snatchers* (1956). Reeves would always claim that Siegel's *The Killers* (1964) was his favourite film and would screen it again and again on his home projector.

At the time the young English man arrived, Siegel was working on an Elvis Presley vehicle called *Fun in Acapulco* (1963), though in the end it was directed by Richard Thorpe. He took Mike on as 'audition dialogue coach'.

The Reeves family also had a connection with the producer Irving Allen and, on his return to Britain, Mike managed to wangle a job on *The Long Ships* (1964), a Viking saga starring Richard Widmark and Sidney Poitier. He was one of several, uncredited, assistant directors. Irving Allen also employed Reeves on *Genghis Khan* (1965) starring Omar Sharif.

Producer Paul Maslansky (now best known for the *Police Academy* movies) offered Reeves work as assistant director on a low-budget horror film he was making in Italy called *Castle of the Living Dead* (1964). It starred Christopher Lee and marked the film debut of Donald Sutherland. The screenplay was by the director Warren Kiefer. He was a great friend of Sutherland who named his son after him.

Kiefer and Maslansky each put up $10,000 plus the script. 'With those elements,' Kiefer recalled, 'we contacted Chris Lee for ten working days, and shot the film in five weeks at a splendid old castle [the Odescalchi Castle] overlooking Lake Bracciano.'

Maslansky then produced Michael Reeves' first proper feature, *The She Beast* (1966), shot in Rome and starring Ogilvy in his first major role. Made for £15,000 and finished in twenty-one days, it also stars Barbara

Steele, already a horror film veteran who was booked for only a single day. 'I managed to get her for $1,000 for one day's work,' Maslansky recalled, 'but I didn't say how long that day was. I made her work for eighteen hours. She didn't speak to me for twenty years.'

Steele and Ogilvy play Veronica and Philip, a glamorous young couple who have inexplicably chosen to spend their honeymoon in Transylvania. Checking in to a grim hotel (the innkeeper is hilariously called Groper), they fall foul of a hideously deformed witch, Vardella, who was tortured to death two centuries ago and returns to life to exact revenge.

In his biography, Ian Ogilvy explains that: 'at that time the Italian license to shoot a documentary was less expensive than the one they issued for a feature film so we pretended to be making an archaeological movie called *Ruini Etrusci* chalked on the clapperboard.'

It is generally agreed that *The She Beast* (sometimes called *Revenge of the Blood Beast*) is an hilariously terrible film, but in its clumsy, trashy camp way it prefigures the menace that Reeves would use to such effect in *Witchfinder General*.

As the screeching, gibbering Vardella is brutally skewered on a makeshift ducking school, the camera cuts to the face of the watching womenfolk of the village, impassive, blank-faced and utterly chilling. When Vardella lays her curse on the village, we see a shot of Reeves (employing himself as an extra) looking (as John B. Murray notes in his biography) 'for all the world like a cross between a young Dirk Bogarde and a young Cliff Richard'.

Reeves bought a house in Yeoman's Row, Knightsbridge (near Harrods) with a Lotus E Type parked outside. He had all the accoutrements for the good life in swinging London and a girlfriend called Annabelle Webb, to whom he was engaged but somehow the wedding never came off. The house was a magnet for their small circle of friends who came to watch films on Mike's projector and play poker or endless games of Monopoly (according to his particular rules).

He was very young, not very domesticated and utterly single-minded. 'If you weren't interested in cinema you were a bore to Mike,' remembers Ian Ogilvy.

If he felt hungry he'd go to the nearby Carlton Towers Hotel restaurant where he would eat either steak or smoked salmon and drink Coca-Cola. They kept a tie for him, which he would attach to his black polo neck sweater. His friend, the writer Tom Baker, remembers he had an annoying habit of never finishing his food. He had various little verbal affectations including bidding his friends farewell with, 'And may God be with you till we meet again.'

Ogilvy also remembers that Mike had a slightly strained relationship with actors, leading some to think that he didn't like them, whereas the truth was that he was rather in awe of them and preferred to leave them alone to get on with their jobs, without too much direction. He didn't like going to the theatre because he was always 'waiting in trepidation for something to go wrong, which couldn't happen in a film.'

Mike Reeves' next project was *The Sorcerers* (1967) made by Tigon Pictures, led by Shoreditch-born Tony Tenser, who also produced Roman Polanski's first English language films *Repulsion* (1965) and *Cul-de-Sac* (1966). Tenser's other claim to fame was that he coined the term 'sex kitten' about Brigitte Bardot.

Boris Karloff initially rejected the script as 'thoroughly immoral', but after extensive rewrites and the promise of half the film's £34,000 budget as his pay check, the grand old man of horror came on board.

He and Catherine Lacey play an elderly couple who develop a way of tapping into the experiences of a young man-about-town (Ogilvy), driving him into violence and depravity. Filming began late 1966 in a studio in Barnes, in Blaise's nightclub in South Kensington and at Dolphin Square in Pimlico (Mike knew someone who had a flat there).

It was also the actress Susan George's first film. 'She was on set for about two hours,' says Ogilvy, 'until I killed her with a pair of scissors. Mike hurled a lot of blood over her and then she went home.'

Raquel Welch, who had put up money for the film, helped out in the costume department. Mike filmed Ogilvy on a speeding motorbike from the open boot of a car racing along the M4. A Jaguar was exploded on a patch of waste ground with no permission sought or given. 'The blast shattered windows for blocks around,' says Ogilvy. 'Then we ran like hell. We knew that if we didn't get the right shot within minutes, we'd be in jail for sure.'

As usual, Mike was economical with his notes for the actors. 'Could you be a bit more grammar school?' he asked old Etonian Ogilvy.

For all the swinging London setting it's a chillingly nihilistic film, which is perhaps why it doesn't feel dated despite the mini-skirts and pop music. 'How long do you think all this can last?' asks Ogilvy's dead-eyed character as he sits in the nightclub watching the pretty girls gyrating about him.

The Sorcerers was released in the West End in June 1967 and won prizes at science fiction film festivals in Trieste and San Sebastian.

The idea for Mike Reeves' next film, *Witchfinder General*, came from Tony Tenser when he read Ronald Bassett's recent novel of the same name. Scripted by Reeves' friend Tom Baker (not the actor), it was conceived as a kind of revenge western with Roundhead soldier Richard Marshall (Ian Ogilvy) galloping around under the wide skies of Suffolk and Norfolk to avenge the rape of his girlfriend Sara (played by Hilary Dwyer) by Matthew Hopkins (Vincent Price) and his brutish sidekick John Stearne (Robert Russell). Nicky Henson joined the cast as Marshall's loyal friend Swallow. Rupert Davies – who played the lead in TV's original *Maigret* series (1960–1963) – was Sara's uncle, John Lowes, a pastor who defies Hopkins and ends up in a dungeon being nibbled by rats.

Half the money came from Roger Corman's American International Productions (AIP) and with it the insistence that the part of Hopkins went to Price. Reeves wanted Donald Pleasence in the role but he had no choice if he wanted AIP's backing. He refused to go to Heathrow to meet Price when the star landed in Britain.

This marked the start of a very strained relationship. Although Price had worked with the corner-cutting whizzkid Roger Corman, he was used to more luxurious conditions and more deferential treatment than he received in drizzly East Anglia.

At one point in the shoot Price said to Mike: 'Young man, I've made ninety-three films in Hollywood. How many have you made?'

'Two. Good ones,' replied Mike. Apparently everyone laughed at that.

Nobody was spared Price's camp sarcasm. 'Oh my ga-a-a-d,' he drawled on catching sight of the dashing Ogilvy on horseback. 'She's so pretty and she rides that fucking horse so well. I hate her.'

Richard Marshall's rather beautifully shot sex scene with Sara (set to Paul Ferris' lovely score) caused both Ian Ogilvy and Hilary Dwyer some anxiety.

Says Ogilvy in his autobiography: 'I always played my love scenes in bed wearing grey flannel trousers because I knew Mike was quite capable of reaching out in the middle of the scene and whipping the sheets off me and my lover.'

Hilary wondered what her parents would think but Mike promised her it would all be very dark with a blue filter. On seeing the finished product Hilary said: 'It might have been blue, love, but it wasn't dark.'

Problems with the British Board of Film Censors (BBFC) began before a single frame was shot. It was usual for film-makers to send scripts to the BBFC so they wouldn't waste money shooting scenes which would then have to be cut. In his notes of 4 August 1967, the examiner F. N. Crofts describes the film as 'an unseemly story' which 'provides endless chances for brutality, murder and rape'. He concludes his lengthy remarks: 'Personally I should not grieve if this script dropped dead in its tracks.' Another examiner, Newton Branch, wrote: 'This ape Tenser will continue to be a time-wasting nuisance until the Board puts him in his place.' Of the (admittedly) shocking witch-burning scene in Lavenham, when a convicted woman is lowered onto a bonfire he wrote: 'This whole episode is disgusting and designed only for the pleasure of sadists and should be left out or drastically altered.'

The completed film was submitted to the BBFC on 29 March 1968 and some more cuts demanded. Reeves met the secretary of the BBFC John Trevelyan (they were distant cousins) on 3 April and Mike agreed to make a few further cuts. He then wrote Trevelyan a long letter from the Bay Roc Hotel in Montego Bay where he was on holiday. This is the crucial passage:

> In order for the film to retain its point, there <u>must</u> be a level of brutality throughout; thus, by seducing the audience into accepting it, we prime them for the ending, where the stool is whipped right from under their feet, and they are left looking at themselves, and their involvement with the foregoing violence, with, I hope (and am in fact sure) the sense of self-loathing one invariably receives when one has been momentarily involved in a flash of sadism – however slight it may be, no matter be it verbal or physical. If the film is cut to an 'acceptable' level of violence, this ending will lose all point and become merely 'horror-comic', and that is what both you <u>and</u> I so desperately wish to avoid. If the picture is 'reduced' it could well become just an exercise in gratuitous violence … and would have exactly the reverse effect it is intended to have, i.e. an audience having a lovely time revelling in their nice censor-protected 'safe' brutality.

At the end of the film Richard Marshall axes Hopkins to death in an orgy of violence. Continued Reeves:

> Marshall's madness at the end must be motivated, and strongly motivated, to have <u>any</u> effect; so also must the final image of Sara screaming hysterically. And if the sequence … is cut down, this will not be the case. As I say, the morality of the film lies in its whole content; and the fact that in the final 90 seconds, the violence explodes utterly in the face of the 'sympathetic' protagonists (by their own participation in it) is the core of all that is good (morally good) in the film.

The back and forth continued between Reeves and the BBFC, but in the end the cuts to the finished film ran to no more than one and a half minutes.

Many of the reviews, including (as mentioned earlier) that of Alan Bennett in *The Listener*, were very negative. In *The Sunday Times*, Dilys Powell called the film 'peculiarly nauseating' and Margaret Hinxman in *The Sunday Telegraph* called it a 'sadistic extravaganza'. It was, though, a commercial success.

Mike Reeves seemed to lose his way after *Witchfinder*. He split up with Annabelle, he was depressed and was described Largactil. His friend, composer Paul Ferris, who also had mental health problems, describes the effect of the anti-psychotic drug: 'You don't go up, you don't go down, and you're not particularly happy and you're not particularly sad and it drains the life out of you.'

Mike also went to a private clinic in North London for electric shock therapy. Ian Ogilvy wrote: 'He was always prone to mood swings but now he sometimes plunged into deep depression. He became reclusive.'

Reeves was due to start making a film called *The Oblong Box* but walked away the day before shooting was due to start in November 1968. He died of an accidental overdose of barbiturates in February 1969.

Those who die young having shown great promise rob us of what they might have achieved in life but ensure their own immortality. Reeves' output was small but it guaranteed his place as an exceptional director.

He wasn't a cinema intellectual and didn't particularly like art house films. 'Oh Christ, I'm not going to read subtitles all night,' he moaned if an outing was suggested to something foreign. His love of the New Wave

French director Jean-Luc Godard was connected to Godard's excursions into gangster chic rather than anything more cerebral.

Reeves was also a pragmatist and knew it was easier to raise money for a small-budget horror film than any other genre. 'Therefore,' he said, 'until such time as somebody wants us to make something bigger and better let's make the best horror movies that have ever been seen.'

If his films fit into any sub-genre of horror (which is in itself a most elastic species of film), it is that of 'folk horror'. The critic Adam Scovell says these films deal with 'the evil under the soil, the terror in the backwoods of a forgotten lane, and the ghosts that haunt stones and patches of dark, lonely water.' *Witchfinder General*, Piers Haggard's *The Blood on Satan's Claw* (1971) and *The Wicker Man* (1973) are sometimes called The Unholy Trilogy. 'The trilogy,' wrote Scovell, 'follows an alternative vision of Albion, unearthing a darker past often kept on its little-visited, uncanny copse-ways.' It is the battle for the soul of England. You see the same theme in several episodes of *The Avengers* (1961–1969), when Steed and Mrs Peel travel to a quiet rural backwater and find horror of some sort afoot. As Britain became more homogenised in the 1960s, these excursions into what remained of ancient Britain were presented with a haunting mixture of dread and nostalgia.

Tom Milne gave a sense of this in his *Observer* review of *Witchfinder General*, noting 'the subtle use of colour in which the delicate patchwork of greens of the English countryside is shot through by the colours of death and decay.'

And if Mike Reeves had lived, what then? Writing some years ago in *The Guardian*, Tom Baker recalled:

> What Reeves might have gone on to achieve is hinted at by a letter from his old cinematographer [John] Coquillon to the American director Jeff Burr, written in 1983. Coquillon recalls a telephone conversation with Reeves when he was in Los Angeles, shortly before he died. 'One day he called me full of excitement. He'd found the story. We were going to ride around the US, shoot in 16mm and shoot every which way, into the sun and out of the sun – on motorcycles. The actor was to be a long-time LA buddy – a completely unknown son of an actor – name of Peter Fonda. The film was to be called *Easy Rider*. It was while planning this movie that Michael Reeves died.

Chapter Eighteen

John Carpenter – 'Too much of the monster.'

In a small way, I like to think I was crucial to John Carpenter's success. In the 1970s, I worked briefly as a publicist for a film producer and distributor who specialised in soft porn. David Grant of Oppidan Films called himself the 'king of sexploitation'. He was sent to prison over a video nasty (defended by the human rights barrister Geoffrey Robertson) and died in mysterious circumstances in 1991. It wasn't the most rewarding of jobs, nor the most arduous. The film critics were not interested in carefully crafted synopses of *Sinderella* (1972) or *Secrets of a Door-to-Door Salesman* (1973) or *Girls Come First* (1975), so I never bothered to watch them either.

Unexpectedly, my boss acquired another low-budget film to distribute. The fact that it was low budget wasn't unexpected. All his films were low budget. The lower the better as far as he was concerned. The surprise was that this latest addition to our far-from prestigious roster of movies wasn't porn, and it was actually very good.

It was called *Dark Star* (1974). It was a spoof of Stanley Kubrick's *2001: A Space Odyssey* (1968). It followed the ill-kempt crew of a spaceship, twenty years into their mission to destroy unstable planets. It was written by John Carpenter and Dan O'Bannon – who would write *Alien* (1979) – starting life as a short student film made at the University of California, gradually extended to feature-film length as and when money became available.

Our little company went into overdrive with this classy product to promote. I wrote a proper press pack and we showed the film to the proper film critics in a proper screening room in Wardour Street. We had warm white wine, and canapés. It was tremendously exciting and rather pleasing to be respectable for once. And over time the film itself has become a cult favourite.

The 'cult' label has always hung around Carpenter. In his 1981 book, *Cult Movies*, Danny Peary says: 'Cultists believe they are among the blessed few who have discovered something in particular that the average moviegoer and critic have missed – the something that makes the pictures extraordinary.'

And there's always been a sense that there are those who love and appreciate Carpenter's early films and his music and those who are outside the club and therefore missing out.

He emerged in the 1970s, a contemporary of mainstream directors such as Steven Spielberg, Martin Scorsese, Francis Ford Coppola and George Lucas. But like Brian de Palma or Robert Altman he has maintained his idiosyncratic approach to making movies and, where possible, exerted total control by directing, screenwriting, editing, scoring and using a favoured team of actors and technicians.

Many of his films are stylish homages to old Hollywood. For instance, *Assault on Precinct 13* (1976) is (notwithstanding its modern urban setting) a remake of Howard Hawks' siege western *Rio Bravo* (1959), set in an abandoned LA police station.

Yet he is also credited for – or depending on your viewpoint stands accused of – inventing the teen slasher movie with *Halloween* (1978) and its many sequels and offshoots.

His 1982 film *The Thing* was a remake of a Howard Hawks and Christian Nyby film *The Thing From Another World* (1951). Set on an Arctic base, a merciless monster threatens to take over a group of research scientists. In *Halloween*, the children are seen to be watching *The Thing From Another World* on the television, a nice touch for Carpenter's fans who like a little homage with their horror.

In Carpenter's hands, the story of *The Thing* becomes far more visceral than the 1950s original, and is what came to be known as 'body horror', a term coined in 1986 in the University of Glasgow film journal *Screen*.

Body horror means special effects recreating decomposition, suppuration, mutation, deformity, parasitical infestations, exploding heads, evisceration – the works. Animatronics, latex, prosthetics and the goriest make-up all have their grisly part to play. In body horror, the threat does not come from outside, it lurks within, under your skin.

Film-makers such as David Cronenberg, David Lynch, Tobe Hooper and George A. Romero are the other masters of body horror, but have always had an art house following. Carpenter's films played in mainstream cinemas and multiplexes.

John Carpenter was born in Carthage, New York on 16 January 1948 to Howard and Milton Jean. His father was a musician and an academic. Howard was offered a job at Western Kentucky University and the family moved to Bowling Green, Kentucky in 1953. Even at such a young age John experienced a severe culture shock at being uprooted from Democrat-inclined, liberal New York and transplanted to the deep south.

In an interview in 2000, published in *The Cinema of John Carpenter: the Technique of Terror* and edited by Ian Conrich and David Woods, he explained: 'My dad was a kind of intellectual, and here we are in yahoo land with all these country boys, and I was completely out of place.' This was the Jim Crow south before the civil rights movement gained momentum and he says he saw things he would never forget. 'Everything I know about evil I learnt in that little town,' he said.

His father also worked as a session player for artists such as Brenda Lee, Roy Orbison and Johnny Cash, and was one of the founding members of a band called the Nashville Strings. John would sometimes accompany his father on recording trips to Nashville. Music has always played a big part in his life but movies were his first love, and his father gave him an 8mm camera to encourage his early attempts at film making.

The first film he remembers seeing when he was 5 years old was *It Came from Outer Space* (1953), which was black and white but in 3D, with a widescreen format, based on a Ray Bradbury story and directed by Jack Arnold for Universal. A meteorite crashes near a small town in Arizona but further investigation reveals it is an alien spacecraft. The aliens are satisfyingly amorphous and slimy until they take on the shape of humans. Richard Carlson plays the author and astronomer who makes contact with them. Once their spaceship is repaired they fly away. 'They'll be back,' Carlson tells his fiancée (played by Barbara Rush).

Another film that impressed Carpenter at a very early age was John Huston's adventure *The African Queen* (1951) with Humphrey Bogart and Katharine Hepburn. He particularly enjoyed the scene where Bogart peels off his shirt to find that he is covered with black leeches, which Hepburn heroically attempts to remove. Whether this was an early sign of Carpenter's fascination with the visceral horror genre or simply the kind of thing that any little boy would relish, is a moot point.

Forbidden Planet (1956), widescreen and in colour, was a favourite too. Carpenter loves big screens, and Cinemascope in particular. MGM's *Forbidden Planet* has a place in the heart of all science fiction and horror fans. Loosely based on Shakespeare's *The Tempest*, it is the first science fiction film to be set entirely on another planet. The Robby the Robot character is the first robot with character. *Star Trek*'s creator Gene Roddenberry said it was the inspiration for the series.

It was reworked as a jukebox musical by Briton Bob Carlton and won an Olivier Award for the best musical of 1989/90. Forbidden Planet is also the name of the science fiction, horror and fantasy bookshop chain.

In 1968, after a couple of years at Western Kentucky University, Carpenter went to Los Angeles and enrolled in the prestigious film-making course at the University of Southern California, where he says, 'they taught us all the plumbing' and where he gained a deep technical background.

At that time, guest lecturers included Orson Welles, Howard Hawks, John Ford, Alfred Hitchcock and Roman Polanski. 'It was,' said Carpenter, 'a fascinating time to be there because we were in contact with the old Hollywood classic directors and even some of the new ones. And you got a real sense of being trained to go into Hollywood.'

Carpenter always says he became a director with the intention of making westerns. His first (and as it turns out only real western) was a short called *The Resurrection of Broncho Billy* (1970), which won an Academy Award for Best Live Action Short.

Carpenter wrote, directed and composed the music for the thriller *Assault on Precinct 13* (1976). He also edited it under the name of John T. Chance, which is the name of John Wayne's character in Howard Hawks' *Rio Bravo*.

His explained his admiration for Hawks this way:

> Howard Hawks to me personally was the greatest director because he made a great movie in every genre. He did musicals, he did gangster movies, he did westerns, he did comedies. He moved with ease through all these different genres. But what he brings to it is his own personal vision of the world, his own personal concerns with people, with actors. He's a very deeply personal film-maker who worked with genres. That's what inspires me about him.

Assault on Precinct 13 was one of the big hits at the London Film Festival of 1977. British audiences warmed to it more than American audiences had done. Though Vincent Canby of *The New York Times* would later write:

> [*Assault*] is a much more complex film than Mr. Carpenter's *Halloween* though it's not really about anything more complicated than a scare down the spine. A lot of its eerie power comes from the kind of unexplained, almost supernatural events one expects to find in a horror movie but not in a melodrama of this sort.

He's right. In one scene, the gang members attacking the police station are shot down as they try to climb through the windows. But when the shooting stops there are no bodies to be seen outside.

This is implacable, unstoppable evil, which – like the aliens in *It Came from Outer Space* – will always be back. How many times has Michael Myers, the bogeyman in the *Halloween* franchise been dispatched, only to rise again? If nothing else, it's a way of guaranteeing a sequel. Even when he is beheaded at the end of *Halloween H20* (1998) we suspect that this will only prove to be a minor and temporary inconvenience.

Even the most bread-and-butter Carpenter thrillers are coloured by a hint of the supernatural. Lauren Hutton starred in *Someone's Watching Over Me* (1978), written and directed by Carpenter. She plays a professional single woman who moves to LA and finds that she is being stalked. *Eyes of Laura Mars* (1978) is a thriller starring Faye Dunaway. She plays a fashion photographer whose work seems to fetishise violence, but is plagued by visions of the violent deaths of friends and colleagues. It was written by Carpenter and directed by Irvin Kershner.

Halloween (1978) was Carpenter's breakthrough movie, co-written with producer Debra Hill, starring Jamie Lee Curtis – daughter of Tony Curtis and *Psycho* star Janet Leigh – in her film debut.

In 1963, on Halloween night in suburban Haddonfield, Illinois, 6-year-old Michael Myers stabs his older sister to death.

Fifteen years later, he escapes from the sanitarium where he has been incarcerated ever since and returns to Haddonfield on Halloween night to terrorise a new generation of teenagers, chief among them Laurie Strode (Jamie Lee Curtis), who is babysitting that evening.

Donald Pleasence plays Myers's psychiatrist Dr Sam Loomis. In *Psycho*, Sam Loomis is the name of the boyfriend of the character played by Janet Leigh who meets her end in the shower.

Again, Myers is real but there is also a demonic, supernatural aspect. Why else would he, having been shot many times before tumbling from a window, simply … disappear?

The music – once heard, never forgotten, always recognisable – is written in a strangely disconcerting 5:4-time signature. Carpenter says he was inspired by the music in both Dario Argento's lurid thriller *Suspiria* (1977) and by Mike Oldfield's Tubular Bells in *The Exorcist* (1973).

Produced for $300,000, *Halloween* took $47 million at the US box office, making it the most successful independent movie ever (at the time) in relation to its cost.

Alfred Hitchcock's *Psycho* (1960) is sometimes called the first slasher movie, but *Halloween* (which owes a lot to Hitchcock too) really kickstarted the splatter movies of the 1980s.

Halloween was followed by *Halloween II* (1981), *Halloween III: Season of the Witch* (1983), *Halloween 4: The Return of Michael Myers* (1988), *Halloween 5: The Revenge of Michael Myers* (1989), *Halloween: The Curse of Michael Myers* (1995), *Halloween H20: 20 Years Later* (1998), *Halloween: Resurrection* (2002) and *Halloween* (2018) in which Jamie Lee Curtis returned to play Laurie Strode.

Sean Cunningham's *Friday the 13th* (1980) began the saga of Jason Voorhees, which meandered on for more than a decade. Wes Craven's *A Nightmare on Elm Street* (1984) – take a bow Freddy Krueger – gave rise to nine sequels. Wes Craven and Kevin Williamson's *Scream* franchise revived the slasher genre in 1996, and there were four films up until 2011.

The films generally involve a collection of promiscuous American teenagers taking drugs, having sex, then dying in novel and bloody ways. Many of the films had well-known calendar connotations: Mother's Day, April Fool's Day, Valentine's Day, the Fourth of July. For all the gore, they invite the audience to share a joke. For all the suspense, everyone knows what's coming. Even the titles are knowingly funny in their repetitiveness. *I Know What You Did Last Summer* (1997), directed by Jim Gillespie and written by Kevin Williamson, could only be followed by the slightly nagging *I Still Know What You Did Last Summer* (1998) and *I'll Always Know What You Did Last Summer* (2006).

The convention that the horror genre is mostly popular with young people seems borne out by this long list of teen movies. And there's something in the critic James Twitchell's contention that the function of horror films is to teach adolescents how to behave.

John Carpenter followed up *Halloween* with *The Fog* (1980) which starred Adrienne Barbeau, whom he met on the set of *Someone's Watching Me* and married in 1979. They had one son, Cody, and divorced in 1984. The film also starred Jamie Lee Curtis and her mother Janet Leigh.

Barbeau plays Stevie Wayne, a husky-voiced DJ who broadcasts her late-night radio show to the people of Antonio Bay, California from a lighthouse.

Celebrations to mark the 100th anniversary of the town are marred by a mysterious, glowing fog that sweeps in from the sea, bringing the vengeful ghosts from a clipper ship that was deliberately sunk by the town's founder. It's not much of a plot, but the moments of jeopardy as the revenants hammer on the townspeople's doors are agreeably scary. Like many of Carpenter's films (*Assault on Precinct 13* and *The Thing*), it has since been remade.

Escape From New York (1981) gave Kurt Russell the role of Snake Plissken in this high-voltage dystopian movie set in 1997 when Manhattan has been turned into a maximum-security prison. Inspired by the Watergate scandal, the horror monster in this film is American society itself.

'Fans hated it, critics hated it. They thought I showed them too much of the monster,' said Carpenter about *The Thing* (1982), which received damning reviews for its goriness and excessive violence. In *The New York Times*, Vincent Canby dismissed it as 'too phoney looking to be disgusting. It qualifies only as instant junk.' *The Thing* is a nihilistic, depressing film and it came out in the same summer as the sunny and sentimental *E. T. the Extra-Terrestrial*, which seems to indicate to some that America had rediscovered its sense of wonder after its post-Vietnam hangover. Ennio Morricone, ever one of Carpenter's favourite composers, wrote the music, capturing the tone that Carpenter wanted. 'This is an end-of-the-world movie, a movie almost without any hope,' he said.

Carpenter's next film, *Christine* (1983), was based on a Stephen King novel about a teenage nerd Arnie Cunningham (played by Keith Gordon), a Billy-no-mates whose life is transformed when he buys a

beat-up 1958 Plymouth Fury which develops a malevolent, possessive and very female will of its own – and, as it does, so regains its former tail-finned, chrome and scarlet beauty.

The London listings magazine *Time Out* said: 'Carpenter and novelist Stephen King share not merely a taste for genre horror but a love of '50s teenage culture; and although set in the present, *Christine* reflects the second taste far more effectively than the first.'

Starman (1984) is a touching science fiction romance with Jeff Bridges and Karen Allen. It was produced by Michael Douglas who specifically wanted Carpenter to direct. But an action comedy, *Big Trouble in Little China* (1986), was an artistic and financial flop.

Since then Carpenter has made a couple of horror films of interest. In *Prince of Darkness* (1987) a physicist and his top students are asked by an ancient order of monks, the Brotherhood of Sleep, to investigate a strange cylinder containing a green liquid, which turns out to be the essence of Satan. Donald Pleasence plays the chief priest and there's Alice Cooper as one of the homicidal zombies lurking outside the brotherhood's HQ.

Carpenter wrote the screenplay but is credited as Martin Quatermass, in honour of Nigel Kneale's *Quatermass* TV series and films. As with the *Quatermass* stories, and much of Kneale's work, the line between science and the supernatural is compellingly blurred with scientific investigation of the paranormal being a part of the narrative. The priest and the physicist speculate that Satan is merely an offshoot of an older force of evil, the Anti-God which is related to anti-matter.

This sort of spine-chilling hokum shows Carpenter's debt to the American Gothic writer H. P. Lovecraft who, in his stories, created a number of deities known as the 'Great Old Ones' from outside space-time who once ruled the Earth and are still worshipped by certain cults.

Far more fearsome than any common-or-garden ghosts or vampires these things predate humanity. Anyone unlucky enough to see one of these tentacled, blobby, spidery, flying, crawling, slimy abominations invariably dies or goes mad.

Howard Phillips Lovecraft (1890–1937) barely scraped a living as a writer during his lifetime – mostly contributing to pulp magazines – and he died in extreme poverty at the age of 47. He was much influenced by Edgar Allen Poe and his best-known story is *The Dunwich Horror*, written in 1929.

The power of his stories lies in the way he finds the horrific and demonic in the most mundane details. He compares himself to the writer Nathaniel Hawthorne in that they both see 'a dismal throng of vague spectres behind the common phenomena of life'.

Like many of Carpenter's films, *Prince of Darkness* had so-so reviews but went on to acquire a cult status. *In the Mouth of Madness* (1995) was the third in what he calls the 'Apocalypse Trilogy', the first two being *The Thing* and *Prince of Darkness*. Like *Prince of Darkness* it is highly Lovecraftian.

Sam Neill plays John Trent, an insurance investigator searching for a missing horror novelist called Sutter Crane (Jürgen Prochnow) and his final manuscript. The trail takes him to a New Hampshire town called Hobb's End (another nudge for *Quatermass* fans as the tube station in *Quatermass and the Pit* is called Hobbs End).

Cane, tracked down, reveals that his potent stories have reawakened the monstrous, prehistoric creatures who will reconquer Earth, and that Trent is merely a character in the novel.

What links the films in the Apocalypse Trilogy is a real end-of-days feel. These three films very much conform to the rules of the game as laid down by Lovecraft in his brilliant and highly wrought essay, *Supernatural Horror in Literature*:

> A certain atmosphere of breathless and unexplainable dread of outer, unknown forces must be present; and there must be a hint, expressed with a seriousness and portentousness becoming its subject, of that most terrible conception of the human brain – a malign and particular suspension or defeat of those laws of Nature which are our only safeguard against the assaults of chaos and the daemons of unplumbed space ... . Therefore we must judge a weird tale not by the author's intent, or by the mere mechanics of the plot; but by the emotional level which it attains at its least mundane point ... . The one test of the really weird is simply this – whether or not there be excited in the reader a profound sense of dread, and of contact with unknown spheres and powers; a subtle attitude of awed listening, as if for the beating of black wings or the scratching of outside shapes and entities on the known universe's utmost rim.

Carpenter returned to something somewhat less doom-laden with *Village of the Damned* (1995), a remake of the 1960 film which in turn was based on British author John Wyndham's 1957 novel *The Midwich Cuckoos*. A mysterious blackout in a small California town is followed by the discovery that ten women are inexplicably pregnant (one is a virgin and one has not had sex for a year). When the children are born they are all pale, blonde, with piercing blue eyes, high intelligence and unsettling psychic powers.

This would be Christopher Reeve's last film – he plays the town's doctor – before the riding accident which left him paralysed.

Said Carpenter: 'It was fun to do a drama like *Village*, as opposed to *In the Mouth of Madness*, which had a little edge to it. This is more straight. This is more a baby-boomer, middle-class kind of a movie. There's nothing wrong with that; I just hadn't done one of those in a long time.' If he sounds as though he's damning the project with faint praise, that's exactly how it comes across on screen.

John Carpenter always wanted to make a western and in *Vampires* (1998) he made a vampire western about a gang of mercenary vampire slayers with the pale and menacing James Woods as the leader of the pack. It's like *The Wild Bunch*, with fangs. 'Forget what you've seen in the movies,' warns Woods. 'They don't turn into bats, crosses don't work … you wanna kill one you drive a stake right through its fuckin' heart.'

The aim was to get away from the blighted, melancholy nobility of the classic Dracula figure. Said Carpenter: 'My vampires are savage creatures. There isn't a second of brooding loneliness in their existence. They're too busy ripping and tearing humans apart.'

Later in his career, Carpenter became more involved with the *Halloween* franchise and the video game end of horror fantasy. In an interview in 1980 he said: 'I fight against becoming self-conscious. It's the death of a film-maker when he starts parodying himself.'

Yet he does exactly that in the made-for-TV horror comedy trilogy *Body Bags* (1993) that he directed with Tobe Hooper and Larry Sulkis. In it Carpenter plays (very much for laughs) the ghoulish host and coroner who ends up zipping himself into a body bag.

The combination of terror and knowing humour was one of the main ingredients in horror in the 1980s and 1990s, and beyond. The jokes come from playing on the audience's knowledge of the genre's conventions and the recurring tropes and images.

Sam Raimi's *Evil Dead* franchise, which began in 1981, mines the gory humour relentlessly, as do all the teenage campus 'splatsticks', which have expanded into books, comics, video games and TV.

Carpenter has two types of fans. There are those who respond to his love of old Hollywood, of Howard Hawks, of 1950s sci-fi and the influence of American Gothic writers such as Edgar Allen Poe and H. P. Lovecraft. And there are those who love gaming and slasher movies.

As a director, he developed tricks which have become standard practice. Though his music is instantly recognisable, it's sparingly used. He knows the value of silence, of the power of holding a shot so long that the audience moves from boredom to unease. He developed those prowling, gliding camera shots. And his love of widescreen means that often the bogeyman does not jump into view but will gradually make an appearance at the side of the screen. And when it comes to the question of whether to show the monster or suggest its presence, he is firmly on the side of showing.

In an interview he gave in 2000 he said:

> We're frightened of forces of chaos, forces of evil, or of things happening; anything can happen. It's that knowledge that really things are beyond our control. We're afraid of all that, and to really scare people would be to open that little door and say life is really about chaos and it's not being directed. It's aimless, it's by chance. People don't want to hear that at all; no-one wants to hear it. That's the exact opposite of what people want. People want reassurance that love triumphs, the hero triumphs.

And that's all fine. Though no self-respecting horror film would be complete without that final edge of unease, the suspicion that – as Richard Carlson says in *It Came from Outer Space* – 'they'll be back'.

Afterword

Do You Actually Like Horror Films?

'But do you actually *like* horror films?' That was the reaction of quite a few people when I said I was writing this book, and generally these were people who didn't like horror films themselves. Stephen King, master of horror fiction, many of whose books have been adapted for cinema, says there is the feeling 'that the taste for horror is abnormal'.

So yes, I did get the sense that my enjoyment of the horror genre was a mark against me, and that those with more fastidious and refined sensibilities despair of my lowbrow taste. But horror fans are used to that. Horror films are traditionally low budget and knowingly exploitative. In the heyday of independent cinemas in the 1970s, they were scheduled in late-night double bills and tucked away around midnight by TV schedulers. Television had given new life to the horror genre because it allowed successive generations to rediscover them, and in the twenty-first century the availability of all sorts of old movies on the Talking Pictures TV channel and on YouTube is an added bonus.

Those of us who seek out scary films have a sense of proprietorship about them. We are in a club. Like all cult movies they are (as Andrew Sarris wrote in *The Village Voice* about *Halloween* in 1978) 'both admired and despised'. Sometimes they can be filed under 'so bad they're good'. If you're in the horror camp (and camp is very much the operative word here), you make a virtue of the fact that critics often rubbish the films.

Horror and cinema were made for each other. Most of us probably watch films at home on our flat-screen TVs but this is a matter of convenience and economy. The authentic experience of viewing a film must still take place in a darkened cinema.

It is an experience very unlike that of going to the theatre, which is a joint endeavour between the audience and the actors on stage.

184

The Russian literary critic Boris Eikhenbaum – feeling his way around the subject in the first half of the twentieth century – wrote that:

> we do not, in essence, feel ourselves to be members of a mass at all, or participants in a mass spectacle, when we are sitting in a cinema, on the contrary – conditions at a film-show induce the spectator to feel as if he were in total isolation, and this feeling is one of the particular psychological delights of watching films.

That's true, but when you watch a horror film you often find yourself flipping from that pleasurable sense of isolation to one of communal enjoyment. Cocooned in the darkness, which confers on us a sense of invisibility, we are at the same time vaguely aware that we are part of an ordered social situation where there are others present. Moments in a horror film of shock or release allow us to enjoy that brief sense of community and share an emotional response. And nowhere was that sense of community more acute than in those famous 1970s screenings of Richard O'Brien's *The Rocky Horror Show*, a tribute to Hollywood's horror and sci-fi films, where the audience acted out the parts with props and costumes.

Rock music is also an element in camp, comic horror films, signalling that they're for the cool and hip. Squares need not apply. One of my favourites is John Landis's comic horror *An American Werewolf in London* (1981), with a soundtrack that includes Van Morrison's *Moondance*, Credence Clearwater Revival's *Bad Moon Rising* and different versions of *Blue Moon* by Sam Cooke, Bobby Vinton and the doo-wop take by the Marcels, which accompanies the closing credits. It's a nod to the 1935 Universal film *A Werewolf in London*. But now, almost forty years since it was made, *American Werewolf* has a quaint charm of its own. There wouldn't be much chance today of the authorities allowing Piccadilly Circus to be used as a location for the denouement. And it makes the modern viewer nostalgic for a time when a nurse (Jenny Agutter is Nurse Alex Price) could afford a cosy flat in central London.

A Quiet Place (2018) is a clever science fiction horror starring Emily Blunt and John Krasinski as Evelyn and Lee Abbott, trying to keep themselves and their children alive in a world where they are the prey of blind extraterrestrials with acute hearing. Most of the film takes place in the silence that the family maintains in order to survive, and it was very noticeable how everyone in the audience responded to the sounds made by other viewers as we flinched and squeaked in the scary but always silent bits. We laughed at ourselves, experiencing a sense of connection that you seldom find in the cinema.

The presence of a friend or partner also adds to the enjoyment, especially when watching scary films. In one study in the 1980s, it was found that male viewers enjoyed a screening of *Friday the 13th Part III* (1982) when their female companion showed signs of distress. Female viewers reported higher levels of pleasure when their male companions showed no signs of being scared (so brave!) It also made them think the males were more attractive if they toughed it out.

At the time of writing, *A Quiet Place, Part 2* is about to be released.

The horror genre thrives, in part, because it is so well-suited to sequels and remakes. Just as children enjoy hearing the same stories over and over, we enjoyed being scared once and we like to find the same ingredients re-arranged and re-packaged so we can be scared again. And again. And again.

We know the stock characters and essential elements – the appeasing scientist ('we must preserve this creature for science'), the mad scientist with a God complex, the thing that refuses to die, the dark house, the reckless heroine who doesn't switch on the light when she goes in the room, the evil child, the wanton girl who will almost certainly be punished, the tragic monster who is misunderstood, the vampires, the zombies, the witches, the werewolves, the deadly contagion, the ancient curse, the secret door, and so on.

We know all the rules and conventions even when they are subverted and turned on their head. That's why we know that evil can flourish in safe suburbia and broad daylight and in the most prosaic situations. We know from the start of John Carpenter's *Halloween* that the pleasant streets of Haddonfield, Illinois are nothing of the sort. We know that the bright sunlit colours in Ari Aster's *Midsommar* (2019) – which owes a lot to *The Wicker Man* (1973) where pagan practices happen in the summer – are as terrifying as any cobwebbed Gothic horror dungeon. We know that the deceptively peaceful countryside is the setting for 'folk horror'.

Hammer's popularity dwindled in the early 1970s but at the same time Hollywood realised that horror could make the shift from low-budget exploitation films to big-budget features. *The Exorcist* (1973) changed the terms under which horror films were viewed. As the critic Harry Ringel wrote in *Cinefantastique* magazine: '*The Exorcist* has done for the horror film what *2001: A Space Odyssey* did for science fiction: legitimised it in the eyes of thousands who had previously considered horror movies nothing more than a giggle.'

Low-budget horror had once provided ageing Hollywood stars – pleased to get the work – with a new lease of life. Bette Davis and Joan Crawford played darkly comic versions of themselves in Robert Aldrich's *Whatever Happened to Baby Jane?* (1962) and Davis starred as a child killer in Hammer's *The Nanny* (1965). But in the 1970s, big budgets created a string of movies which turned the horror genre mainstream with big stars: *Don't Look Now* (1973); *Jaws* (1975); *Carrie* (1976); *The Omen* (1976); *Alien* (1979); *The Shining* (1980) and *Poltergeist* (1982).

I haven't included the American director George Romero (1940–2017) among those who established the horror genre because his skill was to take what was there and run with it. There had been zombie films before Romero's *Night of the Living Dead* (1968), but this low-budget movie starring Duane Jones and Judith O'Dea gave Romero cult status.

Romero was also inspired by Richard Matheson's book *I Am Legend*, published in 1954, in which the world is taken over by vampires. This had already been made into a film, *The Last Man on Earth* (1964), starring Vincent Price, and would subsequently be adapted as *The Omega Man* (1971) and *I Am Legend* (2007).

In an interview in 2008 Romero said:

> Richard starts his book with one man left; everybody in the world has become a vampire. I said we got to start at the beginning and tweak it up a little bit. I couldn't use vampires because he did, so I wanted something that would be an Earth-shaking change. Something that was forever, something that was really at the heart of it. I said, so what if the dead stop staying dead? ... And the stories are about how people respond or fail to respond to this. That's really all [the zombies] ever represented to me.

There would be three more 'Dead' films, *Dawn of the Dead* (1978), *Day of the Dead* (1985) and *Land of the Dead* (2005). He also made *Martin* (1978) about a disturbed youth who is convinced he is a vampire.

187

The Canadian director David Cronenberg gave us 'body horror'. His visceral and disturbing sci-fi films explore themes of disease and social breakdown in films such as *Shivers* (1975), *Rabid* (1977), *The Brood* (1979), *Scanners* (1981), the remake of *The Fly* (1986) starring Jeff Goldblum, *Dead Ringers* (1988) and *Crash* (1996), based on the J. G. Ballard novel in which people get sexual pleasure from car crashes. As with Romero I regard him as a director who gave a new twist to an old format.

The twenty-first century saw the sub-genre of 'found footage' – horror films which are presented as though we are watching real video material retrieved after some catastrophe. *The Blair Witch Project* (1999) introduced us to a hapless trio of student film-makers hiking in the Black Hills of Maryland and investigating the local legend of the 'Blair Witch'. Treading the same path were films such as *Paranormal Activity* (2007) and *Cloverfield* (2008).

It's not too much of a stretch to see the connection between these films and Bram Stoker's original novel *Dracula*, which is presented in an epistolary form as a sequence of letters and diary entries. Similarly, Tobe Hooper's *The Texas Chainsaw Massacre* (1974) was cleverly marketed as a 'true story' based on the crimes of the mass murderer Ed Gein.

The role of women actresses in horror films necessarily comes under scrutiny in the Me Too era, especially as sex and sexiness are important elements of spiced-up Gothic cinema. I talked to Jenny Hanley, daughter of Dinah Sheridan and Jimmy Hanley, who presented the children's ITV show *Magpie*. She appeared in the Hammer film *Scars of Dracula* (1970) and in *The Flesh and Blood Show* (1972), directed by Pete Walker, who mixed elements of exploitation and slasher films and was 'very cross indeed' when Jenny Hanley stripped off bra and pants to reveal another set of bra and pants underneath. It was, she admits, difficult for a young actress to say no in those days. 'Directors would say, "what make you think you're better than Glenda Jackson or Helen Mirren?"' Both serious actresses who in their youth had no apparent problem with doing nude scenes.

One of Jenny's godmothers was Dame Flora Robson, the other was Hazel Court (1926–2008) who trained at the Rank Organisation's charm school and appeared in *The Curse of Frankenstein* (1957). It was the first Hammer film she would do, followed by several of Roger Corman's Edgar Allen Poe movies. 'I always played with great conviction,' she said. 'When I did all these horror films, I did not camp around.'

Barbara Shelley (born in 1932) made her debut in *Cat Girl* (1957). The director Alfred Shaughnessy wrote: 'By using her, I fear we have condemned a very beautiful and talented actress to a long career in horror films.' He was right. Hammer loved her and she appeared in *Blood of the Vampire* (1958); *The Gorgon* (1964); *Dracula, Prince of Darkness* (1966); *Rasputin the Mad Monk* (1966) and *Quatermass and the Pit* (1967). She was also in *Village of the Damned* (1960). Now in her eighties, she gamely made an appearance in 2019 at London Film and Comic Con, an annual fan convention.

The eerily beautiful Barbara Steele, born in Birkenhead, Cheshire, worked in Italian horror in the 1960s. Her breakthrough role was in Mario Bava's *Black Sunday* (1960), in which she is transformed from the heroine Katia to the witch Asa who has been entombed for a couple of centuries. She also worked with Roger Corman and was in David Cronenberg's film *Shivers*.

The scream queen with a heaving bosom, while ever popular, began to be replaced by more resilient heroines such as the resourceful Laurie, played by Jamie Lee Curtis in Halloween; Sigourney Weaver as Ripley in *Alien* (1979); Sarah Michelle Gellar in TV's *Buffy the Vampire Slayer* (1997–2003), and Kristen Stewart in the *Twilight* films (2008–2012) who, though a vampiress, was also the heroine.

Women directors have moved into the horror genre, though women writers have always been attracted to Gothic themes from Mary Shelley's *Frankenstein* to Anne Rice's *Interview with the Vampire*. Kathryn Bigelow's first commercially successful film (she directed the Oscar-winning *The Hurt Locker* in 2010) was a vampire film *Near Dark* (1987). And, in 2016, *Rolling Stone* magazine hailed 'the rise of the modern female horror film-maker', arguing that a new wave of 'horror films helmed by women ... have helped elevate the genre by opening it up to stories that unsettle audiences in new and different ways.'

Another director to take the horror genre in new directions is Jordan Peele, whose films *Get Out* (2017) and *Us* (2019) have been box-office successes. These are polished, though still relatively low-budget, films which relate the horror genre to the experiences of black Americans. In *Get Out*, Daniel Kaluuya plays Chris Washington, a photographer invited to meet his white girlfriend's parents. In *Us*, a middle-class family of African Americans meet horrifying doubles of themselves.

189

Jason Blum, the CEO of Blumhouse Productions which made Peele's films, says that horror films must feel modern and relevant and that a tight budget give creative parameters which make the product better. 'It's got to have great scares,' he said in an interview. 'But key to making a film scary is what comes in between the scares. You could have the greatest scare in the world but if you're not involved in what's going on and the psychology of the character, it doesn't work.'

It is a given that horror films reflect the concerns of the society that produces them. Yet they also have a universality and a timelessness. While we watch Don Siegel's *Invasion of the Body Snatchers* (1956) knowing that it spoke to an America that was obsessed with the communist threat, it also carries a punch that transcends a political interpretation. It's about being taken over by an invisible, insidious evil and not knowing who is human and who isn't. That's why we can watch it now and find it a powerful film, and that's why these stories can be remade (as *Body Snatchers* was in 1978).

Horror films always appeal to the young, offering a rite of passage. How scared will you be? How much calculated grossness can you take? Some have argued that Frankenstein's monster is a sort of clumsy adolescent, endlessly blundering around the adult world and getting it wrong. Stephen King says in his book *Danse Macabre*: 'What the good horror film does above all else is to knock the adult props from under us and tumble us back down the slide to childhood.'

All countries that have a film industry make horror films. Whether we're watching a silent German Expressionist film from the 1920s, a sexed-up piece of Hammer Victoriana or a teen slasher film, they all press the same buttons. It's a genre that's been written off many times but as any horror fan knows, when something is dead it's bound come back to life.

And at the end as good triumphs and the monster is destroyed we are left thinking that we were lucky and we got away with it … this time. So not yet … not this time. But soon…

Bibliography

Atkins, Thomas, R., 'Hammer Horror: The World of Terence Fisher' in *Graphic Violence on the Screen* (Monarch Press, 1976)

Bell, James, (Ed.) *Gothic: The Dark Heart of Film* (British Film Institute, 2013)

Blake, Michael, F., *A Thousand Faces: Lon Chaney's Unique Artistry in Motion Pictures* (Vestal Press, 1995)

Boulenger, Gilles, *John Carpenter: The Prince of Darkness* (Silman-James Press, 2003)

Brosnan, John, *The Horror People* (The Book Service, 1976)

Clarens, Carlos, *An Illustrated History of the Horror Film* (Putnam 1967)

Collier, Kevin Scott, *Lon Chaney: In His Own Words* (CreateSpace, 2017)

Conrich, Ian; Woods David, (Eds.) *The Cinema of John Carpenter: The Techniques of Terror* (Wallflower Press, 2005)

Cumbow, Robert, C., *Order in the Universe: The Films of John Carpenter* (Scarecrow Press, 2000)

Curtis, James, *James Whale: A New World of Gods and Monsters* (University of Minnesota Press, 2003)

Del Vecchio, Deborah; Johnston, Tom, *Peter Cushing: The Gentle Man of Horror and His 91 Films* (McFarland and Co, 2009)

Dixon, Wheeler, W., *The Charm of Evil: The Life and Films of Terence Fisher* (Scarecrow Press, 1991)

Ellis, Reed, *A Journey into Darkness: The Art of James Whale's Horror Films* (Ayer Co, 1980)

Gatiss, Mark, *James Whale: A Biography* (Continuum, 1995)

Gullo, Christopher, *In All Sincerity: Peter Cushing* (Xlibris, 2004)

Hanich, Julian, *Cinematic Emotion in Horror Films and Thrillers: The Aesthetic Paradox of Pleasurable Fear* (Routledge, 2010)

Hanich, Julian, *The Audience Effect: On the Collective Cinema Experience* (Edinburgh University Press, 2017)

Hills, Matt, *The Pleasure of Horror* (Continuum, 2005)

Jacobs, Stephen, *Boris Karloff: More Than a Monster* (Tomahawk Press, 2010)

King, Stephen, *Danse Macabre* (Everest House, 1981)

Lanchester, Elsa, *Elsa Lanchester Herself* (St Martin's Press, 1983)

Leggett, Paul, *Terence Fisher: Horror, Myth and Religion* (McFarland and Co, 2002)

Lennig, Arthur, *The Immortal Count: The Life and Films of Bela Lugosi* (University Press of Kentucky, 2010)

Murray, John, B., *The Remarkable Michael Reeves* (Cinematics Publishing, 2002)

Ogilvy, Ian, *Once a Saint: An Actor's Memoir* (Constable, 2016)

Pirie, David, *A New Heritage of Horror: The English Gothic Cinema* (I. B. Taurus and Co, 2007)

Price, Victoria, *Vincent Price: A Daughter's Biography* (St Martin's Press, 1999)

Rigby, Jonathan, *English Gothic: A Century of Horror Cinema* (Reynolds & Hearn, 2000)

Sandford, Christopher, *Polanski: A Biography* (St Martin's Press, 2008)

Siegel, Joel, E., *Val Lewton: The Reality of Terror* (The Viking Press, 1973)

Skal, David, J.; Savada, Elias, *Dark Carnival: The Secret World of Tod Browning* (Bantam Doubleday Dell, 1995)

Underwood, Peter, *Karloff: The Life of Boris Karloff* (Drake Publishers, 1972)

Acknowledgements

Thanks to David Pirie, author of *A New Heritage of Horror*; Geoff Andrew of the BFI; and Donal W. Smith of @FilmsHammer.

Index

Index

V

Vampire ix, 7, 11, 12, 15-17, 19, 30,
46-50, 61, 83, 104, 107, 125, 128,
129, 148, 160, 161, 180, 182, 186,
187, 189
Vampire Lovers, The 104, 107, 160
Van Eyssen, John 80
Variety magazine 16, 32, 58, 96
Veidt, Conrad 14, 45, 46, 94
Victor, Henry 1
Viertel, Salsa 57
Vigil in the Night 101
Village of the Damned 182, 189
Village Voice, The 184
Virgin of Stamboul, The 5

W

Waggner, George 32
Walker, Pete 188
Walsh, Dermot 79
Ward Baker, Roy 96, 109, 118, 160
Warner Brothers 36, 58, 86, 88
Waxman, Franz 57
Weaver, Sigourney 154, 189
Webling, Peggy 54
Wegener, Paul 46, 48
Weigel, Helene 158
Welch, Raquel 168
Welles, Orson 71, 89, 159, 176
Wells, H.G. 56, 64, 111, 159
Werewolf ix, 32, 83, 108, 142, 185
Werewolf in London, A 185
West of Zanzibar 8, 31
Whale, James v, vii, 8, 17, 28, 36,
38, 40, 51, 53-59, 64-67, 90, 100,
138, 191
Whatever Happened to Baby Jane? 187

Wheatley, Dennis 84, 130, 132
Where Eagles Dare 155, 159
Who Dares Wins 163
Wicked Darling, The 4
Wicker Man, The 132, 161, 162,
172, 186
Wiene, Robert 46
Wild Angels, The 141
Wild Geese 2 163
Williamson, Kevin 178
Wine of India 119
Wise, Robert 74
Witches, The 118
Witchfinder General 95, 97, 164, 165,
167, 169, 172
Wogan, Terry vii
Wolf Man, The ix, 32, 33,
Wong, Anna May 5, 89
Wood, Ed 19, 20
Woods, James 182
Woodward, Edward 132, 162
Worsley, Wallace 25, 26
Wray, Ardel 75
Wray, Fay vii
Wymark, Jane 120
Wyndham, John 182

Y

Year of the Sex Olympics, The 119
York, Michael 119
You Must Listen 113
Young, Terence 125, 130, 131

Z

Zinkeisen, Doris 52, 55
Zombies 9, 72, 74, 75, 107, 180,
186, 187